Battle Lines

Battle Lines

Poetry and Mass Media
in the U.S. Civil War

Eliza Richards

PENN

UNIVERSITY OF PENNSYLVANIA PRESS

PHILADELPHIA

Published by
University of Pennsylvania Press
Philadelphia, Pennsylvania 19104-4112
www.upenn.edu/pennpress

Printed in the United States of America on acid-free paper
1 3 5 7 9 10 8 6 4 2

A Cataloging-in-Publication record is available
from the Library of Congress
ISBN 978-0-8122-5069-5

For Kathleen

Contents

Introduction

"How News Must Feel When Traveling"

How News must feel when traveling,
If News have any Heart.
Alighting at the Dwelling
Twill enter like a Dart!

In these lines, Emily Dickinson implies that though news may not have "any Heart," poems do, and it is their duty to imagine the emotions that the news generates in people while it circulates, even if they are excruciating. The autonomy and anonymity of Dickinson's news, along with its travels and seemingly random, violent visits to homes, emphasize mass circulation networks over more intimate circulatory modes, like gossip, or epistolary exchange. Alternative lines for the first stanza, noted at the end of the manuscript, affiliate the poem more closely with wartime violence: "Advancing on the Transport / 'Twill riddle like a Shot." The riddling of the mind, aligned with a body riddled with bullets, are so perfectly analogized they present as one experience in the poem. These terse lines begin to lay out the process I will explore in this book.

Battle Lines charts transformations of American poetry during the U.S. Civil War, which, I argue, are fueled by a symbiotic relationship between the development of mass media networks and modern warfare. A syncretic conjunction of new technologies and catastrophic events stimulated the development of news into a central cultural force. Reacting to the ascendance of the news, poets articulated an urgent need to make their work not only relevant, but immediately responsive to current happenings. Poetry's compressed forms traveled more easily than stories, novels, or essays through ephemeral print media, allowing it to move alongside and rapidly respond to news reports. Civil War–era poets took on the task of imagining what correspondent mental states arose for readers upon receiving news from the war front: how to think and what to feel about the mass violence of modern warfare happening elsewhere, but brought close with new intensity via mass media networks. Newspaper and magazine poetry had of course long editorialized on political happenings: Indian wars, slavery and abolition, prison reform, women's rights. But the unprecedented scope of what has been called the first modern war, and the centrality of the issues involved for national futures, generated a powerful sense of single-minded collectivity among readers and writers, which altered the terms of poetic expression.[1]

Writers of the time thought about the ways that new communication technologies affected individual and collective states. In an essay entitled "Bread and the Newspaper," published in the September 1861 issue of the *Atlantic Monthly*, Oliver Wendell Holmes Sr. dubs the Civil War communications network "our national nervous system." Dr. Holmes speculates that the "iron nerve pathways" of the newspaper and telegraph and the "iron muscles" of the railroad, along with the animating force of the war, have created a superhuman national body. These "new conditions of existence": "make war as it is with us very different from war as it has been. The first and obvious difference consists of the fact that the whole nation is now penetrated by the ramifications of a network of iron nerves which flash sensation and volition backward and forward to and from towns and provinces as if they were organs and limbs of a single living body. The second is the vast system of iron muscles which, as it were, move the limbs of the mighty organism one upon another." The nervous network binds the nation (which is specifically the Union, for Holmes) into a living, responsive entity that acts on impulses: a central aggressive force with a single aim coordinates the massive technological body to enact state violence. Once the iron nerves send their messages, the iron muscles respond, resulting in a mass mobilization that Holmes hopes will win the war. He offers an example of perfect military coordination: "What was the railroad-force which put the Sixth Regiment in Baltimore on the 19th of April but a contraction and extension of the arm of Massachusetts with a clenched fist full of bayonets at the end of it?"[2]

The nervous network that powers troop movements extends to civilians, who are kept in a constant state of excitement by what Holmes calls "perpetual intercommunication."[3] Being wired into a force so much larger and more powerful than individuals takes a toll. For Holmes, the impact of news circulation upon noncombatants results in a version of the "war fever" contracted by soldiers. Associating the absorption of shocking events with troop movements, he tells readers that thinking about news ages the brain prematurely: "When any startling piece of war news comes, it keeps repeating itself in our minds in spite of all we can do. The same trains of thought go tramping round in a circle through the brain like the supernumeraries that make up the grand Army of the stage show. Now, if a thought goes round the brain a thousand times in a day, it will have worn as deep a track as one which has passed through it once a week for 20 years. This accounts for the ages we seem to have lived since the 12th of April last."[4] Because people can't stop reading and thinking about the news, their brains register the physical stress of war. In defining and diagnosing this mental condition, Dr. Holmes forges correspondences between external and internal events via trope. Just as soldiers tramp in line for a stage show, so those who read about the spectacle of war will find that their thoughts leave deep grooves in their brains. Though he uses metaphor and analogy, Holmes goes beyond loosely associating the massive intake of information with troop movements, instead asserting a direct, causal impact. He imagines that, in thinking about the calamity, the brain receives shocks—or "impressions"— that are as physical as wounds to other parts of the body.[5] Trains of thought are as inexorable and potentially lethal as the trains that carry troops bristling with bayonets. Holmes's idea of the national nervous system blurs the distinction between figure and ground, vicarious and direct experience of events. Because violent shocks are transmitted directly from the war front to the home front, readers of the news become casualties of war.

Though Holmes's particular theory may seem idiosyncratic, he addresses a central concern of his time: the effect on perception of mass media warfare. The conglomeration of new communication and transportation technologies, combined with a large literate population, created the conditions for the flow of information to influence the struggle, and the war in turn to stimulate the development of news into a central cultural force.[6] By the late 1850s, technological developments had transformed American newspapers into "truly mass media, with the power that term now implies": the steam press allowed for rapid reproduction of newspaper copies; railways supported broad dissemination of the news; and a network of telegraph lines could almost instantaneously transmit information across large distances.[7] Journalism became a profession in this period; an early generation of war correspondents traveled with army regiments in order to convey eye-witness accounts back to the home front.[8] Illustrated newspapers established a popular audience during the war years (they were already popular in England); sketch artists conveyed renditions of battle scenes that appeared alongside verbal reports.[9]

The consolidation of mass media networks in wartime informed what Holmes called a profound "change in our manner of existence." Because "reading habits changed dramatically with the onset of the war," the literary landscape transformed. Booksellers complained that the public was entirely absorbed by current events and was no longer buying books. Alice Fahs asserts that during the Civil War, "newspapers suddenly became an urgent necessity of life, with readers eagerly gathering at bulletin boards outside newspaper offices in order to read the news as soon as it was printed."[10] A poem in *Harper's Weekly* portrays this scene:

> The "Extras" fall like rain upon a drought,
> And startled people crowd around the board
> Whereon the nation's sum of loss or gain
> In rude and hurried characters is scored.[11]

Stimulated by bulletins traveling over the nervous network, "startled people" experience collectivity, becoming part of a national body. Crowding around the board, they receive the news together; its characters, the poem suggests, are "scored" into the people as well as on the bulletin: the news is imprinted upon them. The news itself has become news as people contemplate this "new necessity": sketch artists capture groups of people reading newspapers and telegraph bulletins in various locations, from New York City to the army camps (figs. 1–2).

Walt Whitman recalls a similar scene in New York City when the news of Sumter was transmitted: "I bought an extra and crossed to the Metropolitan Hotel, where the great lamps were still brightly blazing, and, with a small crowd of others who gather'd impromptu, read the news, which was evidently authentic. For the benefit of some who had no papers, one of us read the telegram aloud, while all listen'd silently and intently. No remark was made by any of the crowd, which had increas'd to thirty or forty, but all stood a moment or two, I remember, before they dispers'd. I can almost see them there now, under the lamps of midnight again."[12] Whitman marks a moment of collective introspection. The same thought travels not only through the mind of one individual, "tramping around in a circle through the brain." It circulates through all the people present, causing them to fall silent because no words are needed. That the news is "evidently authentic" draws attention to a general understanding that the news was frequently wrong, incomplete, and subject to change. That knowledge intensifies the immediate moment of common understanding. If coherence cannot be found in the unfolding narrative of

Figure 1. "News from the War.—Drawn by our Special Artist, Mr. Winslow Homer,"
Harper's Weekly, June 14, 1862, 376–377. This is a close-up of the lower right-hand section
of the illustration, which presents a collection of news scenes. Courtesy of HarpWeek.

events, it can be found collectively in a moment of common understanding.
The moment haunts Whitman in its perfect sense of union.

With the news, poetry thrived, published alongside and often working
together with the reports on the conflict in Northern papers. Hundreds of
poems tracked, responded to, and shaped the reception of multiple aspects of
the war. Poems urged men to enlist, fight, and die for the sake of the Union;
they urged civilians to support the soldiers and to accept the sacrifice of loved
ones; they insisted that soldiers' deaths would sanction and promote the
growth of a stronger democratic nation purged of the sin of slavery. A number
of critics have recently shown that a central rhetorical task during wartime
is to invest death with meaning, so that the weight of human sacrifice gives
national ideology force and persuasive power.[13] The poems published during
the Civil War repeatedly proclaimed that this was a just war for a moral purpose, and that the thousands who were losing their lives were not doing so in
vain. "The Volunteer," for example, published anonymously in May 1862 in
the highly influential, widely circulated, strongly pro-Union genteel magazine
the *Atlantic Monthly*, concludes that "To fight in Freedom's cause is something
gained— / And nothing lost, to fall."[14] The poems about wartime sacrifices
circulated widely during the Civil War, binding together communities of readers and forging relations between civilians and combatants. Via mass media

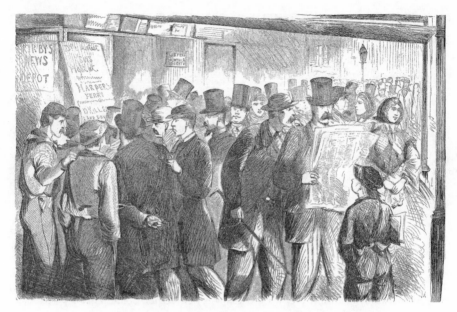

Figure 2. "Reading the War Bulletins in Broadway, New York,"
Harper's Weekly, July 20,1861, 458. Courtesy of HarpWeek.

circulation, poetry served a crucial role in negotiating new necessities of representation, both political and poetic, instigated by the war.

Some of the poems responding to the emotional and political necessities of wartime were closely tied to news reports in all their immediacy and particularity. As soon as news of a battle appeared, so did poems that responded to events: the hanging of John Brown; the unexpected retreat of Union troops at the Battle of Bull Run; the massive death tolls at Antietam, Shiloh, and Gettysburg; the heroism of the Massachusetts 54th at the Battle of Fort Wagner; the Siege of Charleston; the Battle of Mobile Bay. These and hundreds of other "aspects of the war," to use Herman Melville's phrase, were documented and circulated not only through journalistic reports but through poetry. When Confederates fired on Fort Sumter on April 12, 1861, and Union troops surrendered, Union poets were forced to admit an embarrassing defeat. In *Harper's Weekly*, a poem entitled "The War" muses on the event:

> *Fort Sumter* taken! and its siege will fill
> No bloody chronicles in after-time.
> It was a tame bombardment, if you will,

But in its consequences how sublime!
The first boom of the cannon sent a thrill
Not through the North alone, for every clime
Where liberty is prized, struck with deep sorrow,
Mourns for to-day, and fears the dread to-morrow.[15]

Notable in the poem is the lack of heroicization of the event. It would be difficult to turn such an anticlimactic defeat into stirring legend, and the speaker
says as much. With an obligation—newly felt—to adhere to the facts, the
speaker turns to the moment's implications for "liberty" rather than commemorating an unlikely battle. With mixed feelings, the poem combines the
political promotion of Union ideals with an adherence to journalistic facts in
order to supplement news reports. This journalistic fidelity combined with
an editorial function grounds much of the poetry of the period. Journalism's
influence on poetry is evident in a new fascination with facticity; poetry of
the Civil War explores the incantatory, gripping power of facts in aesthetic
configurations (fig. 3).

But the very conditions that bring together poetry and events also foreground the difference between them. The intense relations between poetry
and the news in a mass media war register in a range of formal and topical
ways that this study will explore. Alongside Holmes, poets insist that wartime
"impressions" literally imprint themselves on the minds of readers, generating
new mental states. The necessity of figuration in the translation of the physical
event to verbal sign becomes the subject of inquiry, as writers seek to articulate
the ways that lines of communication convey the shocks of war to readers.
Civil War poetry tests figurative language's capacity to forge correspondences
between writing and fighting. Because "perpetual intercommunication" generates a direct line between distance and presence, violence and inscription
become exchangeable. At its most extreme, the equation makes writing lethal
and war articulate in the print culture of the period. Mass media networks
destabilize the relation between figure and ground, and poetry explores the
consequences of this instability. Socially constructive rather than purely "literary," poems articulate correspondences among different parts of the informational system, generating an interface to the war for readers at home via
trope. Tropic practices are unsettled and reconfigured as a result. Figurative
language is not the privileged realm of poetry, of course, as Holmes's essay
shows, but poetry offers a crucial vehicle to explore transformations in figuration and their implications. Poems formulate a transitive relation between

IRON ON IRON—A MONITOR SONG.

SIXTY dread minutes of iron hail,
Point of steel against riveted mail,
Rocks from the mightiest catapult flung
To these were but pebbles, that lightly sail
From the sling round an urchin's finger strung:
     Those were ripe minutes to quail!

Quail? They smiled in their turrets strong,
The iron crash was their battle song;
Bolt, and rivet, and bar, and screw,
Splinter of iron a cloth-yard long,
Like quarry from loosened crossbow flew
     Deadly amid the grim throng.

Cannon, whose smoky mouths laid bare
Caverns might serve for a lion's lair;
Salvos, whose thunder the tranced could hear;
Vast globes of iron, that spun through air
Like meteors flung from a whirling sphere,
     Welcomed our Monitors there.

Thirty guns on the mail-clad nine,
Fifteen score in the rebel line;
What was the tale when the work was done?
Of iron on iron full many a sign,
But every iron-clad staunch, save one—
     A craft of another design.

Nile fight, Gibraltar, Trafalgar,
Battles of history, near and far,
What were all that ever were waged
To that one hour over Charleston bar?
The record to come must be bright paged
     That tells what Monitors are.

Honor to those who have battled for right—
Tears for the brave who fell in the fight.
What if the traitors' walls still stand?
Patience! A day shall the strife renew,
That will leave but a ruin upon the sand
     To mark where rebellion grew.

Figure 3. Anon., "Iron on Iron—A Monitor Song," *Frank Leslie's Illustrated Newspaper*, May 23, 1863, 133. The song tells the story of the First Battle of Charleston Harbor, which took place on April 7, 1863. In spite of high hopes for the U.S. fleet of ironclads, the nine ships were unable to penetrate the harbor's line of defenses. Like many other poems of the Civil War period, "Iron on Iron" was published soon after the battle and offers an interpretation of the conflict in historical and nationalist terms. Courtesy of HarpWeek.

language and event to quite various ends; those formulations are a heritage of the period, even if much of the poetry has been forgotten.

Receiving news bears a troubled relation to making news in U.S. Civil War poems. The conjunction of a new mass media network with the mass death that resulted from a full-scale war foregrounded the gap between vicarious and direct experiences of the conflict. For strangers and loved ones alike, reading the news may have been analogous to receiving a battle wound—Dickinson warned that "'twill riddle like a shot"—but it certainly wasn't the same.[16] Even so, reading the news was an experience in itself, and many Civil War poems mark the difference.[17] Poems enforce a difference between direct and indirect forms of experience while nevertheless positing relations between them. In doing so they mark productive distinctions between the distant suffering on the battlefield, reports of that suffering, and readers' reception of those reports.

Meditating on these lines of connection, popular Civil War poet George Boker envisions newsprint as a circulatory system, or a system of recirculation, for the blood of the dead. War news animates, nourishes, and brings together readers over a common, luridly fascinating topic. He connects lines of print to arteries opened on the battlefield:

> Blood, blood! The lines of every printed sheet
> Through their dark arteries reek with running gore;
> At hearth, the board, before the household door,
> 'Tis the sole subject with which neighbors meet.
> Girls at the feast, and children in the street,
> Prattle of horrors; flash their little store
> Of simple jests against the cannon's roar,
> As if mere slaughter kept existence sweet.[18]

Like Holmes, Boker imagines a national body connected through lines of mass communication. Stressing the continuity between the physical conflict and the talk about it, between the "cannon's roar" and the "flash" of "jests," large-scale killing and the "prattle of horrors," he is critical of the vicarious pleasure that derives from the remote reception of violence. He also acknowledges that such a dynamic is unavoidable, for he cannot possibly exclude his own poetic lines from his condemnation; the "dark arteries" of his "printed sheet" also "reek with running gore." Or not—his metaphor shows that people on the home front are feeding on bloody impressions, not blood; their vicarious pleasure depends upon print's removal from physical violence. The horror that Boker seeks to convey is one of abstraction. There seems to be no way around it; a compulsive circulation of violent figures animates the public, who forge community from the dead without understanding the cost. When battle lines become headlines or lines of poetry—and they must because the conflict is on everyone's mind—animating force is transferred from the dead to the living at the cost of understanding. The transitive relation between physical violence and verbal expression means that people on the home front appropriate soldiers' sacrifice while overlooking it.

While poets adapted their skills in order to render themselves useful during the national crisis, their participation was by no means uniform. Foregrounding the difference between the bloody conflict and its verbal representations raised questions about how properly to write about wartime experience. Poets had the complex task of discovering or creating the purpose of art in wartime. Not everyone was as assuredly evenhanded as Thomas Wentworth Higginson, who, in his "Letter to a Young Contributor" in the *Atlantic Monthly* of April 1862, insists that "It is not needful here to decide which is intrinsically the better thing, a column of a newspaper or a column of attack, Wordsworth's 'Lines on Immortality' or Wellington's Lines of Torres Vedras; each is noble, if nobly done, though posterity seems to remember literature the longest."[19] An officer in the war who was wounded, a man of action as well as words, Higginson balances literary and military pursuits against each other, using the words "column" and "line" for orders of both type and people, emphasizing the difference between them but valorizing both. Higginson suggests that while poets may in earlier times have been considered "pleasant triflers," at the present moment, the "pursuits of peace are recognized as the real, and war as the accidental."

Another *Atlantic Monthly* poet, Julia Ward Howe, would certainly disagree with Higginson's valorization of the peaceful pursuit of literary ideals untouched by war. In a poem entitled "Our Orders," published in July 1861, she calls on poets to sharpen their words into swords, or to accept their total irrelevance:

And ye that wage the war of words
With mystic fame and subtle power,
Go, chatter to the idle birds,
Or teach the lesson of the hour![20]

If the war of words is to help the Northern cause, poets must purge themselves of personal ambition and purely aesthetic aspirations and enlist their services in the cause of wartime propaganda. And indeed, Howe was highly successful in lending her verbal power to the physical struggle. Her poem "The Battle Hymn of the Republic," first published in the *Atlantic Monthly* in February of 1862, became an unofficial Union anthem set to the melody of "John Brown's Body," one that Howe enjoyed imagining the soldiers singing in unison: "I knew, and was content to know, that the poem soon found its way to the camps, as I heard from time to time of its being sung in chorus by the soldiers."[21]

Other poets were less certain than Howe that words could make a difference when the physical sacrifices of war were so overwhelming in their scope. Negotiating their relation to the news of the day, many poets expressed guilt that they were writing rather than fighting for their country, yet nevertheless sought a purpose for their work. Some of the poems in the *Atlantic Monthly* articulate and seek to negotiate this dilemma. In the August 1862 issue, in a poem entitled "In Wartime," Quaker abolitionist poet John Greenleaf Whittier laments the impotence of poets, who

> . . . doomed to watch a strife we may not share
> With other weapons than the patriot's prayer,
> Yet owning, with full hearts and moistened eyes,
> The awful beauty of self-sacrifice,
> And wrung by keenest sympathy for all
> Who give their loved ones for the living wall
> Twixt law and treason,—in this evil day
> May haply find, through automatic play
> Of pen and pencil, solace to our pain,
> And hearten others with the strength we gain.[22]

The war has caused Whittier to think that, for better or worse, the sword outweighs the pen: writing cannot provide the necessary solace for the suffering of wartime. The speaker offers the "automatic play / Of pen and pencil" as his insufficient contribution. Whittier suggests that solace might be found by submitting to the play of a medium unconscious of its message, and by sharing that message with those who need it most. Though he went on to write such patriotic classics as "Barbara Frietchie" (published in the *Atlantic*

Monthly in October 1863), at the outset of the war Whittier could not imagine an effective way to make writing an agentive force. The resigned solipsism of poetic self-comfort, extended to others to "hearten them," is especially striking because Whittier had already spent years as a public poet speaking out against the evils of slavery. The war has presented a challenge that requires a realignment of poetry's functions and forms.

While Howe and Whittier offer more or less practical meditations on the question of how to adapt poetry writing to wartime, Ralph Waldo Emerson's poem on the subject presents a mystical riddle. In "The Test, Musa Loquitur," published anonymously in the *Atlantic Monthly* in January 1861, when the war was imminent, Emerson displays the kind of "mystic fame and subtle power" ridiculed by Howe:

> I hung my verses in the wind;
> Time and tide their faults may find.
> All were winnowed through and through;
> Five lines lasted sound and true;
> Five were smelted in a pot
> Than the South more fierce and hot.
> These the Siroc could not melt.
> Fire their fiercer flaming felt,
> And their meaning was more white
> Than July's meridian light.
> Sunshine cannot bleach the snow,
> Nor Time unmake what poets know.
> Have you eyes to find the five
> Which five thousand could survive?[23]

Emerson—or the muse, who speaks—casts the change wrought by war as primarily stylistic. Like enlisted men, the poet's lines must stand the test of intense violence; they survive only if they pass trial by Southern fire. Like weapons and ammunition, the lines are smelted and forged to stand up to the tests of warfare. Always condensed and runic, Emerson's poetry, he suggests, must become—is becoming in this poem—even more so to stand the tests of the current moment and still "survive" across time. The last lines of the poem tell us only five of the lines on the page before us will pass the test; like men in battle, it is impossible for the reader to predict which lines will continue to live on. War is metaphoric in this poem. The figuration suggests that language production should undergo harsh conditions analogous to the equipment and men used in fighting the war.

These three poems call for very different poetic responses to war: engaging directly with the fight, providing emotional support for suffering, and adapting stylistically in order to create something cryptic, but able to carry the weight of contemporary knowledge into the future. As even three poems from the same magazine suggest, the sense of poetic vocation varied widely, and this study will range over the breadth of response. But however different their approaches, Howe, Whittier, and Emerson divorce poetic utterance from personal expression and attribute the necessity of this shift to the vicissitudes of war.[24] Howe serves the collective voice of Northern wrath, Whittier abnegates personal expression in favor of the automatic play of the pen, and Emerson lets the muse speak without interference; it speaks the truth of war's necessities (Emerson's impersonality is of course a trait that precedes the war). That general turn to what might be called the affective, impersonal, collective mode is a feature of the poetry in the Northern newspapers and magazines of the period with a national circulation.

But while I explore the changes wrought on poetic tradition by the war, I emphatically do not claim that a certain kind of poetry originated out of these cataclysmic events.[25] In fact, the more catastrophic the events, seemingly the more important literary inheritance becomes. The writers in this study work within traditions and modify them thoughtfully and with great effort to render current circumstances affectively legible. It is precisely the familiarity of the tropes, forms, and rhetorics—the materials the poets inherit—that enable them to craft differences for readers to recognize, allowing them to process wartime events and place them within broader historical contexts. I will explore a range of these transformations by focusing on specific events and the revisions of convention they demand.

In analyzing these shifts in figural, formal, thematic, and perspectival emphases, I contend that it is no accident that experimental poetic practices emerged from what is often called the first "modern" war. I further argue that this shift, while marked in Dickinson, Whitman, and Melville, is culture-wide, and that we undervalue the variety and historical and aesthetic significance of much of the poetry of the time by continuing to focus on a small number of "major," largely Northern, literary figures.[26] Poetry of the nineteenth century has been critically separated between popular and experimental, and the two are often figured in opposition. This study finds these terms inadequate for the subtle differentiations and overlapping practices between writers like Henry Howard Brownell, for example, a tremendously innovative poet who was one of the most popular writers of the war, and Herman Melville, who reached a narrow audience but shares many of the same concerns and aesthetic practices, and indeed was influenced by Brownell. I show that poets of all orientations responded to wartime events in order to forge a new understanding of the ways language can communicate under the conditions of mass media. What distinguishes writers like Dickinson, Whitman, and Melville from many poets of the period is a largely remote, often retrospective perspective that shifts attention away from war's immediacies and toward its linguistic effects. Other poets seek to engage the conflict more directly, responding to events as they unfold. While I sometimes distinguish between popular and experimental poetry, in reality they form a continuum. Studying the poems of Dickinson, Whitman, and Melville alongside the work of other poets, many of them well known at the time but less so, if at all, today—Brownell, Elizabeth Akers Allen, Frances Ellen Watkins Harper, George Boker, Amanda Jones, and many others—I explore what holds these kinds of poetry together, as well as what differentiates them.

By tracing networks of poetic practice, the study challenges the ways that critics have delineated starkly polarized, monumental forces in studies of Civil War literature: the North and the South. The treatment of the poetry surrounding the Battle of Fort Wagner, for example, shows both internal divisions and allegiances among African American soldiers and white civilians in the North. I raise questions about the difference that gender makes in poetic responses to the war, though the emphasis here is on how poets of both genders join in communal reactions to current events. The poetic networks I trace, moreover, sometimes cross sectional boundaries, even though there are significant differences between print circulation in the two sections that pose problems for extending this study to Southern poetry of the war period. While Northern readers witnessed an unprecedented expansion of mass media networks, Southerners experienced the war years as a struggle to compensate for the loss of the national information system they had depended upon before the war. There were twice as many newspapers in the North as in the South during the period, with four times the circulation.[27] With few resources, and while their territory was under siege, the Confederacy sought to develop an independent communication system that could promote the ideals of a newly declared nation. I treat Southern Civil War poetry, then, when it marks a point of direct engagement with Northern poetry: in the first chapter, where images of Northern and Southern weather enter into dialogue, and especially in Chapter 4, which treats the strange parallelism between Northern and Southern expressions of violence against one another in the Siege of Charleston.

In order to map out networks of response, I organize the project, loosely chronologically, by specific events and the poetry that responds to them. A series of case studies, the chapters each treat a significant battle along with the tropes and formal practices that mediate them for readers. Remediating events via literary traditions, poets work through what to think and how to feel about current happenings. The responses accrue within a print network that quickly generates a tropic repertoire within a recognizable poetic field. Collectively and with a sometimes remarkable consistency, given the newness of the news, poems draw out key features and draw on common tropic practices to mythologize, commemorate, and consider the consequences of events. The lines of communication reach outward through newspapers and magazines to the poems of writers like Dickinson, Whitman, and Melville, who drew their inspiration from their peers' practices and reconfigured them in ways that bear the traces of their engagements.

Chapter 1 examines the physical power of snow to disrupt, freeze, erase, and bury, as well as the power of the tropes that derive from these traits. A bombardment that can seem malevolent but is also just simply a part of an impersonal, ineffable system, snowstorms and battles bear strong resemblances that have been treated in a long poetic tradition, stretching at least back to the *Iliad*, that deploys snowstorms as a figure of war. Poets—Emily Dickinson and Elizabeth Akers Allen among them—capitalize on this resemblance in order to figure war in a mass media age as a circulatory system that envelops both home and battle fronts. The chapter closes with a focused analysis of the Battle of Fort Donelson (February 11–16, 1862), during which a blizzard in Tennessee was as lethal for Union troops as Confederate fire. I read Melville's poem "Donelson" to show that this poem and the others I discuss absorb material events and use them as a kind of necessary substrata for complex poetic transformations. The conclusion of the chapter addresses the way Confederate poet Henry Timrod adapts Northern climatic figures to offer an alternative grounded in the "SNOW OF SOUTHERN SUMMERS": cotton.

Like snow, autumn has a long poetic tradition of associations with death and dying. Chapter 2 charts the ways this figure is adapted to address the issue of mass death after the Battle of Antietam, in which thousands of men died in a Maryland cornfield before Confederate troops retreated. The extreme irony of the enormous number of dead men destroying the corn at harvest time gave rise almost immediately, in the journalism as well as the poetry of the time, to the image of the ghastly harvest. I explore the ways romantic harvest imagery is transformed into gruesome, often surreal figurations of environmental devastation that open up the possibility of atheism and the annihilation of natural cycles. This chapter traces the circulation of the image of the ghastly harvest through eyewitness coverage of the event and numerous poetic treatments, from anonymous newspaper poets to Emily Dickinson and Walt Whitman.

Chapter 3 takes up figurative practices of commemoration associated with the sonnet and the ode and places them in relation to popular traditions of song in order to make sense of the response to the unprecedented events of the Battle of Fort Wagner (July 18, 1863), one of the first times African American men fought in the war, proving their courage under fire. The battle gave rise to numerous poems seeking to commemorate the event in a way that would capture the democratic promise of racial equality. This chapter traces two conflicting traditions arising from that event. The first is affiliated with African American soldier songs, which celebrate collective agency and a new image of black military manhood. The second tradition focuses on white commander Robert Gould Shaw, whose memory is carried forward in odes and sonnets that elide black agency. Analyzing the powers of commemoration to carry events, selectively, through history, the chapter traces these two traditions through the end of the century's unveiling of the Robert Gould Shaw monument on the Boston Common. A comparative study of the traditions and their interactions shows the commemorative capabilities and limitations of specific poetic forms. It also indicates the ways memorial traditions can come at the cost of historical knowledge. A diverse range of writers including Anna Quincy Waterston, Frances Ellen Watkins Harper, Private Frank Myers, Henry Howard Brownell, Marian Bigelow, James Russell Lowell, and Paul Laurence Dunbar help forge these commemorative traditions.

Chapter 4 explores the journalism and poetry surrounding the prolonged siege of Charleston, paying particular attention to the figure of the talking gun. As the center of Confederate intellectual culture and the first state to secede from the Union, Charleston was the focus of particular Union animus for symbolic even more than strategic reasons. The erection of the Parrott Gun, nicknamed the Swamp Angel, off the coast of Charleston made possible one of the first incendiary bombings of civilians in wartime. As communicators of state violence after verbal negotiations have halted, guns, cannons, and ammunition were frequently figured as engaging in a perverse form of speech. This chapter traces dialogues between the talking weapons in Northern and Southern poetry during the escalating violence of the siege. The excess of verbal violence in these poems conveys a sense of the limits of poetic expression when it comes up against the desire to become a weapon of lethal force. The chapter's concluding section examines poetry by two writers—Henry Timrod and Herman Melville—who seek a way out of this tragic end game.

The final chapter addresses the adaptation of ballads to the conditions of modern naval warfare. Wooden sailing ships have long been a central figure in sea ballads. The invention of the ironclad muddled those terms of representation while radically changing the conditions of naval warfare. Clashes between wooden sloops and ironclads served as occasions for reconfiguring ideas about what constitutes heroism. The highly visible and vulnerable captains and crew of sailing ships were long figured as iconic images of heroic bravery; in the new ironclads, in contrast, the crew was completely hidden from view, operating within protective shells of steel. The confrontations between these two kinds of ships staged dramas between the traditional and the modern, the past and the future, the legendary and the immediate. This chapter takes up two noteworthy naval engagements—the Battle of Hampton Roads and the Battle of Mobile Bay—in order to explore the ways that poets negotiate the symbolic disruptions and new figurative and formal possibilities opened up by the fights. Poets identify the limitations of inherited ballad forms and adapt them through an acute attention to the new forms of naval warfare. The chapter includes an extensive comparison of Henry Howard Brownell's eyewitness poem about the Battle of Mobile Bay, written while an officer aboard the *Hartford*, and Melville's "Battle for the Bay," which, I argue, engages intensively with Brownell's poem.

The epilogue turns to the end of the nineteenth century to explore the question of Civil War poetry's legacy by taking up the work of Stephen Crane. Though Crane is often positioned as a future-oriented poet, I argue that his work is permeated by a sense of loss of the collective poetic practices enabled by the conditions of the Civil War. Whereas poetry held a central place in the war, circulating to a national readership and sharing a common sense of mission, Crane expresses a sense of isolation predicated on the absence of such conditions for the turn-of-the-century poet. Writing at the time of other, less culturally central wars, publishing in magazines that reached a highly selective readership, Crane searches for ways to speak to and for the people even while acknowledging that they may not be listening. This crisis of social belonging, commonly understood as an anticipation of modernism—has strong roots in an awareness of poetry's earlier central role in the Civil War.

Chapter 1

"Strange Analogies"

Weathering the War

Walt Whitman entitles a passage he wrote during the last year of the war, and then included in *Specimen Days*, with a question: "The Weather—Does it Sympathize with These Times?"

> Whether the rains, the heat and cold, and what underlies them all, are affected with what affects man in masses, and follow his play of passionate actions, strain'd stronger than usual, and on a larger scale than usual—whether this, or not;—it is certain that there is now, and has been for twenty months or more, on this American continent north, many a remarkable, many an unprecedented expression of the subtile world of air above us and around us. There, since this war, and the wide and deep national agitation, strange analogies, different combinations, a different sunlight, or absence of it; different products even out of the ground. After every great battle, a great storm. Even civic events the same.[1]

M. Wynn Thomas tells us that this passage "brings us back to the semi-science of meteorology in Whitman's day, a 'science' uneasily (but fruitfully for a poet) suspended between a new materialist and an old spiritual-animist view of the world."[2] That uneasy suspension between two conceptions inspires Whitman's speculation about the meaning of weather in wartime: do storms in the sky sympathetically correspond to the passionate actions of "man in masses"? Are wars on earth generating storms in the air? Is the sky trying to tell us something, or are we reading something into it? The "unprecedented expression of the subtile world of air above us, around us" may reflect our own inchoate feelings projected outward, or it may be a message from an animate world that feels with us. At any rate, the Civil War, according to Whitman, has affected the ways people understand the weather; it has inspired "strange analogies, different combinations, a different sunlight, or absences of it." Indeed, it seems to have generated a certain confusion about what is the figure and what is the ground, what is literal and what is metaphoric, what is sunlight and what is its analogue. Something is in the air during the Civil War, and it causes poets to look up and try to read its message in the sky.

Whitman is by no means alone in turning to the weather to try to make sense of war. In Civil War poems, the coincident, interpenetrating, and transitive circulation of weather, troops, and news generates instabilities in the metaphoric and symbolic properties of language; poetry's task is to reconfigure expression so that even at a distance, war can make an impression. Mary Favret has traced such a tradition in English poetry of the eighteenth and early nineteenth centuries, demonstrating that poets such as William Cowper, Anna Barbauld, and Samuel Taylor Coleridge think through the question of "war at a distance" via the weather. England's empire building, Favret argues, inspires poets to read the weather—in particular harsh, winter weather—as a way of thinking through what it means to be a citizen of a nation perpetually at war abroad. Remote wars pressure English poets to find a way of relating distant events to present experiences, especially in sensory terms; the weather provides a medium for such meditations.[3] With some key differences—the American conflict is staged within the boundaries of a nation that has become two—Favret's insights hold true for U.S. Civil War poetry, which recognizes and refers to an English tradition. More particularly, Civil War poetry of all kinds—Northern and Southern, popular and experimental, broadly or narrowly circulated—draws sustained parallels between weather and the circulation and reception of news in wartime. The consistent association over time of the lethal capacities of winter storms with war suggests that in one way, war resists history by annihilating force (that is one of Favret's central points).[4] But the change in these figurations also shows that the interdependent development of technologies of communication and of killing transform the way that writers think about weather, war, and the functions and possibilities of poetry.

By the second year of the conflict, when it became clear that the South would not easily give up its fight to establish a new nation, and when the death tolls mounted to unprecedented highs, poetry was used increasingly as a way of thinking through the aesthetics and ethics of distant violence. For it was a paradoxical effect of the rapid transmission of information from the battlefronts made possible by telegraph and railway networks that people on the home front became acutely aware that others were fighting and dying for them elsewhere. On a daily basis, the lists of the dead published in local newspapers, along with images and reports of battles in a range of local and national periodicals, confronted civilians with their own relative safety, gained at the cost of the lives of others. What to make of this situation—how to feel when strangers die for you, how to imagine mass death at a distance, how to visualize invisible suffering—these are some of the pressing topics in much Civil War poetry.

The weather mattered on both literal and figurative levels of significa- tion, and those levels were inextricably linked in Civil War journalism and the poetry inspired by it. Weather was first of all an important condition of battle. As a writer remarked in an essay entitled "Weather in War," published in the *Atlantic Monthly* in 1862, "It is not very flattering to that glory-loving, battle- seeking creature, Man, that his best-arranged schemes for the destruction of his fellows should often be made to fail by the condition of the weather."[5] In a war fought primarily in southern climates that differ starkly from those of the North, unpredictable weather more than once contributed to the Union army's difficulties in unknown terrain: heavy rains, mud, extreme heat, and sudden shifts from hot to freezing temperatures caused problems with over- exposure, implementing strategic initiatives, and recovering the wounded from battlefields (fig. 4).[6] The differences in weather between the North and South were ripe for interpretation in terms of the incompatible political and cultural character of two peoples, especially when scientific theories of the time attributed a people's character to the climate they lived in: southerners were supposedly more hot-blooded and emotional, northerners more tem- perate and rational.[7] As much as climate separates and differentiates, how- ever, observing the weather allows those differences to be physically imagined at a distance, at least according to Civil War poets: watching snowflakes fall in Massachusetts, for example, summons the thought of soldiers falling on Southern battlefields in uncountable numbers. The U.S. Civil War was exter- nal and internal simultaneously, because one nation threatened to become two. What was far away for Northern civilians could be in the backyard of their Southern counterparts, so that proximity and distance are held in a com- plex, ever-shifting relation, and the weather reports in newspapers and poetry of the period tried to chart and make sense of these dynamics.

Figure 4. "March of the Army of the Potomac towards Richard's Ford,
Rappahannock River, under General Burnside, interrupted by the storm of
Wednesday, January 21.—From a Sketch by our Special Artist," *Frank Leslie's
Illustrated Newspaper*, February 14, 1863, 328–329. Courtesy of HarpWeek.

In "The Snow at Fredericksburg," for example, published on January 31,
1863, the anonymous author uses the snowfall to draw together the enormous
number of dead Union soldiers and their mourners over the distance between
the Battle of Fredericksburg (December 11–15, 1862) and the Northern home
front. The speaker addresses the snow:

> And here, where lieth the high of heart,
> Drift—white as the bridal veil—
> That will never be worn by the drooping girl
> Who sitteth afar, so pale.
> Fall, fast as the tears of the suffering wife,
> Who stretcheth despairing hands

Out to the blood-rich battle-fields
That crimson the Eastern sands!

Fall in thy virgin tenderness,
Oh delicate snow, and cover
The graves of our heroes, sanctified
Husband and son and lover!
Drift tenderly over those yellow slopes,
And mellow our deep distress,
And put us in mind of the shriven souls
And their mantles of righteousness![8]

Versatile in its amorphous whiteness, the snow offers myriad "strange analogies": a ghostly version of the bridal veil the girl will not wear, of the widow's tears, of the sanctification the buried soldiers lack. It whitens the crimson blood, it reaches where the widow can't, it softens sadness and stands for the heroism and virtue of the fallen soldiers. Snow didn't fall during the Battle of Fredericksburg—a Confederate victory with huge death tolls—though the poem suggests that it fell afterward both at home and on the battlefield.[9] The poem's snow imaginatively counters the stark images of the dead in the illustrated newspapers, serving as an active response to the coverage of the war. The poet calls on the snow to soften the news of the unidentified dead far from home, to reach backward toward the news' emergence in a gesture of mourning and patriotism (fig. 5).

This chapter examines a cluster of poems that adapt a meteorological poetic tradition to the particular circumstances of a civil war with enormous death tolls in a mass media age. Science of the period had recently come to understand weather as a global system, which meant that what goes around comes around: what is elsewhere will eventually arrive here, perhaps in altered form.[10] The figure of snow set alongside its physical reality enables a poetic contemplation of war as a massive circulatory system that involves civilians and soldiers alike. The first section, "An Even Face," follows the ways snow's capacity for erasure summons the death tolls of Southern battlefields for Northern civilians, as well as their own insularity from immediate physical harm. The second section traces figures of weather in Confederate poet Henry Timrod's work in order to demonstrate that poetry itself works like a circulatory system across sectional lines during the war; Timrod offers a response to

Figure 5. "The dead around the regimental flag of the 8th Ohio, in front of the 'Stonewall' at the Battle of Fredericksburg. Sketched by Our Special Artist, Arthur Lumley," *New York Illustrated News*, January 10, 1863, 145. Courtesy of HarpWeek.

a primarily northern tradition of snow poems, figuring the South as a nation well-fortified in preparation for the North's fierce storms. The final section brings together North and South, home front and battlefront, snow and its tropes via an analysis of Herman Melville's "Donelson," a nuanced meditation on weather and war focused on a battle that took place in a deadly snowstorm. Unlike the other poems in the chapter, Melville's demands of his reader a complete immersion in the details of the event as well as their widespread, multiply mediated circulation in order to begin understanding the complexities of media reception of war at a distance. The poem offers an occasion to think about the massive challenges confronting soldiers in the field as well as the conditions that necessarily impede civilian understanding. By stressing the immersion of soldiers and civilians in particular conditions at specific locations, Melville shows the way that war, weather, and media draw people together within overlapping circulatory systems in ways that are only partially knowable.

"An Even Face"

In 1726, James Thomson was already thinking about the problem of how to feel about suffering from a comfortable distance. In "Winter," the first of the poems later collected in *The Seasons*, Thomson's central concern is whether anyone cares for those who suffer elsewhere. The speaker imagines someone less fortunate than himself floundering and dying in a blizzard, then extrapolates from that scenario to wonder

> How many feel, this very moment, death,
> And all the sad variety of pain.
> How many sink in the devouring flood,
> Or more devouring flame. How many bleed,
> By shameful variance betwixt man and man.[11]

Thomson's multiplication of "how manys" makes the point that neither he nor anyone else can "feel, this very moment" with multitudes suffering elsewhere. Their plights are so abstracted in his list that the poem charges common expressions of sympathy with failing to summon more than a general idea of a problem. His poetic solution to generality is to evoke an individual, sentimental scenario, "One scene of toil, of suffering, and of fate," in the hopes that it will summon "the social tear . . . the social sigh," which, in turn will make "the social passions work."[12] Thomson raises the question of whether that scenario succeeds in making a reader feel.

Responding to "Winter" almost sixty years later, William Cowper's "Winter's Evening," in *The Task* (1785), expresses skepticism about the ability of poetry to summon the social tear or the social sigh for distant suffering.[13] He identifies the newspaper as the source of an enhanced indifference; his summary "argument of the fourth book" portrays a newly remote reader: "The post comes in. The newspaper is read. The world contemplated at a distance. Address to Winter."[14] The relation between the contemplation of the world and the address to winter is itself disjunct. Whereas Thomson summoned a swain who wallowed and died in the snow while others were warm and safe at home, Cowper's suffering populations are only vaguely imagined; the subject of the poem is rather the newspaper reader's lack of feeling, or even his pleasure in the remote suffering of others. The news messenger is the first to convey this "cold and yet cheerful" attitude: "Messenger of grief / Perhaps to thousands, and of joy to some, / To him indifferent whether grief or joy."[15]

For the recipient of the newspaper, the primary emotion is pleasurable curiosity. He looks forward to "wheel[ing] the sofa round" in front of the fire, "clos[ing] the shutters fast," and vicariously experiencing the world's news: "Is India free? And does she wear her plumed / And jeweled turban with a smile of peace, / Or do we grind her still?"[16] Rather than contemplating the suffering of others, the speaker makes his subject his own vicarious emotions, strangely removed from the terrors he contemplates: "I behold the tumult and am still. / The sound of war / Has lost its terrors ere it reaches me. Grieves but alarms me not."[17]

However "pleasant" it is "through the loop-holes of retreat to peep at such a world," the pleasure is accompanied by a sense of dislocated dread that emerges in the speaker's depiction of the snow.[18] After meditating on the news extensively, the speaker shifts his attention to the weather outside his window. There a transformation takes place that echoes the numbing of emotion that a mediated depiction of current events brings the newspaper reader:

> Tomorrow brings a change, a total change!
> Which even now, though silently perform'd
> And slowly, and by most unfelt, the face
> Of universal nature undergoes.[19]

"The face of universal nature undergoes" a smoothing of expression, an erasure of feeling, a transformation into blankness and indifference that marks and mirrors the unconscious horror of the comfortable reader in his unfeeling reception of the pain of others. However unconscious one is of current events, a change occurs that surpasses understanding and awareness; via the figure of snow, Cowper comments on the strangeness of this new world where war can lose its terrors in transmission.

Cowper's "Winter Evening" left its mark on the American snow poems that followed in its wake. Before the Civil War, New England writers in particular took up the figure of snow in order to define an aesthetic indigenous to the region and the new nation. To do so, they implicitly contrasted Cowper's comfortable fireside scene of contemplation with American poets who walk outside into the storm and experience the weather more directly. Emerson's 1835 "The Snow-Storm" is a touchstone in this collective endeavor. Echoing Cowper's poem in order to counter it, Emerson casts the north wind as a barbaric artist that, through the medium of snow, transforms the world into a whimsical architectural wonderland while people huddle together inside a farmhouse. His poem, like Cowper's, starts with heraldic imagery of sound-ing horns; but whereas Cowper's horns signal the arrival of a news carrier, Emerson's trumpets are "of the sky." The storm itself is the news rather than the impediment to the transmission of information, and it announces its own arrival:

> Announced by all the trumpets of the sky,
> Arrives the snow, and, driving o'er the fields,
> Seems nowhere to alight: the whited air
> Hides hill and woods, the river, and the heaven,
> And veils the farmhouse at the garden's end.
> The sled and traveller stopped, the courier's feet
> Delayed, all friends shut out, the housemates sit
> Around the radiant fireplace, enclosed
> In a tumultuous privacy of storm.
>
> Come see the north wind's masonry.
> Out of an unseen quarry evermore
> Furnished with tile, the fierce artificer
> Curves his white bastions with projected roof
> Round every windward stake, or tree, or door.
> Speeding, the myriad-handed, his wild work
> So fanciful, so savage, nought cares he
> For number or proportion. Mockingly,
> On coop or kennel he hangs Parian wreaths;
> A swan-like form invests the hidden thorn;
> Fills up the farmer's lane from wall to wall,
> Maugre the farmer's sighs; and at the gate
> A tapering turret overtops the work.
> And when his hours are numbered, and the world
> Is all his own, retiring, as he were not,
> Leaves, when the sun appears, astonished Art
> To mimic in slow structures, stone by stone,
> Built in an age, the mad wind's night-work,
> The frolic architecture of the snow.[20]

Emerson briskly condenses Cowper's elaborate fireside scenario into three lines. "Enclosed / In a tumultuous privacy of storm," the "housemates" are extraneous rather than central to the poem's drama. The "mad night wind" replaces the contemplative patriarch in Cowper's poem as the central agent. Enough traces of the distant wars underpinning Cowper's meditation remain in Emerson's poem to signal their active erasure. The wind's transformation of the landscape is cast in militaristic terms: "trumpets of the sky" herald its arrival, and it quickly wrests the land from its human inhabitants, imprisons them indoors, and lays waste, albeit temporarily and playfully, to the competitors' territory. Emerson has imported war's energies into the metaphorical realm of art, purging them of tragic, literal associations so that they may serve to renovate and liberate the imagination.

The intense political discord that culminated in the U.S. Civil War rendered this liberation of the imagination from material circumstances and political exigencies obsolete almost as soon as it was formulated. Many writers of the '50s and '60s—including Emerson, eventually—returned to the question of poetry's social responsibility, particularly to address the question of slavery and the possibility, and then reality, of civil war. This is Elizabeth Akers Allen's starting point in "Snow," published in the *Atlantic Monthly*, one of the leading pro-Union periodicals, in February 1864, after the battles of Shiloh, Antietam, Gettysburg, Chickamauga, and others had claimed tens of thousands of lives.[21] A prolific and popular poet who was perhaps better known under her pen name Florence Percy, Allen published poems in periodicals throughout the war; her "Rock Me to Sleep" was one of the most popular poems to emerge from the war years.[22] She marked the climate of the conflict through the changing seasons in poems such as "Spring at the Capital," in which the speaker imagines seeing blood on white flowers after looking at a "white encampment" in the distance, outside of Washington DC.[23] Explicitly working from formally experimental predecessors, both Emerson's "Snow-Storm" and Henry Wadsworth Longfellow's "Snow-Flakes" of 1858, in "Snow" Allen smooths, tames, and shapes their work into tetrameter lines, balanced between iambs and trochees, with an unbroken abaab rhyme scheme. She revises Emerson's depicted scenario as well, by putting things in their place:

> Lo, what wonders the day hath brought,
> Born of the soft and slumberous snow!
> Gradual, silent, slowly wrought;—
> Even as an artist, thought by thought,
> Writes expression on lip and brow.

> Hanging garlands the eaves o'erbrim,
> Deep drifts smother the paths below;
> The elms are shrouded, trunk and limb,
> And all the air is dizzy and dim
> With a whirl of dancing, dazzling snow.

So much for Emerson's mad wind's unruly disruption; we seem to have a highly conservative poet here, one who seeks to make her own poem a proper counterpoint to Emerson's by offering a tidied version of the farm scene that his night wind messed up. Allen's "soft and slumberous" snow hangs "garlands," not on chicken coops and dog kennels, but appropriately, on the eaves of a house. Her snow etches an analogous double of the human gradually, silently, and slowly, "Even as an artist, thought by thought / Writes expression on lip and brow." Less wildly ambivalent and unsettling than Emerson's poem, Allen's first stanzas personify nature so fully that he only knows how to sculpt a form as a human artist would. Harnessing and stabilizing Emerson's night wind's myriad-handed work, Allen's poem gives the impression of reaching a conclusion by the end of the second stanza of a six-stanza poem.

A first hint of the return of war from its banishment to metaphor in Emerson's earlier poem is the comparison of the snow to an artist who "writes expression on lip and brow"; the snow portrait recalls Cowper's "universal face" from a "Winter's Evening," registering a displaced awareness of the numbness inflicted by the remote reception of violence. Upon consideration, the second stanza does not seem so cheery after all: the "dancing, dazzling snow" recedes, and Allen sketches a much starker picture. The "deep drifts smother the paths," "the elms are shrouded, trunk and limb," and even the air, "dizzy and dim," seems unable to breathe. The poem takes a dark turn from there, beyond stasis to death and even killing. Allen's poem, which at first dramatized the evasion of current events, becomes gripped by them; the whimsical scene of exterior decoration, fully evocative of Emerson's earlier poem, warps into a nightmare vision in the next three stanzas:

> Dimly out of the baffled sight
> Houses and church-spires stretch away;
> The trees, all spectral and still and white,
> Stand up like ghosts in the failing light,
> And fade and faint with the blinded day.

Down from the roofs in gusts are hurled
The eddying drifts to the waste below;
And still is the banner of storm unfurled,
Till all the drowned and desolate world
Lies dumb and white in a trance of snow.

Slowly the shadows gather and fall,
Still the whispering snow-flakes beat;
Night and darkness are over all:
Rest, pale city, beneath their pall!
Sleep, white world, in thy winding-sheet!

The violence continues "Till all the drowned and desolate world / Lies dumb and white in a trance of snow." Rather than covering to re-create, like Emerson's night wind, this windless snow smothers to kill, "hurls downward" to make and join "waste." Allen depicts a total annihilation that wraps the entire world in a winding sheet. Her apocalyptic, depopulated poetic landscape supplants Emerson's animating personifications.

The Civil War is the not-so-hidden subtext, disrupting the Emersonian aesthetic in which the imagination is free to remake the world in its own image without damage or cost. If we need more evidence, beyond the snow "hurled" down like missiles and laying "waste," we might notice the corpse-like description of the elms whose articulated parts, "trunk and limb," summon the amputation and dismemberment so ubiquitous during the war. The "banner of storm," stridently patriotic in its unrelenting demands, insists on continuing its siege until the entire "pale city" is buried in a single "winding-sheet" (the Civil War dead, especially regular infantry, were frequently buried in mass graves or left to the elements).[24]

The speaker can still talk after the whole world has been destroyed, because, like Emerson's "housemates," she has sought shelter out of the storm in a room. Instead of Cowper's comforting fire, Allen's speaker stares at a picture of Rome and a wreath on her wall. Here the war surfaces fully as the subject of the poem, and the weather metaphor recedes:

Clouds may thicken, and storm-winds breathe:
On my wall is a glimpse of Rome;—
Land of my longing!—and underneath
Swings and trembles my olive-wreath;
Peace and I are at home, at home!

Shut in, a lone survivor, the speaker turns away from the present toward the ancient history of civilization in order to imagine a place "at home, at home" with peace. Even that dislocation from the natural world and the present moment, however, does not keep the threat of destruction at bay, for the very place she looks to reassure herself of the rise of civilization has fallen, as a result of war. The late eighteenth-century English historian Edward Gibbon famously attributed the "decline and fall of the Roman Empire" to barbarian invasions that were possible due to the loss of civic virtue.[25] Allen's snow actively recalls Emerson's frolic savagery in order to obliterate it, suggesting that poets, or at least her poem, can no longer use the natural world as a playground where the imagination is free to roam. The snow imposes a vision of mass death upon the speaker in spite of herself, one she seeks to escape. Bunkered in her home, she assembles pieces into a collage-like figure of a shrine—a picture of Rome in place of the world outside her window, an olive-wreath beneath—shoring up fragments in a vain attempt to look elsewhere and see differently. The weather brought the news home to the speaker, who invokes peace as a desperate plea in response.

To distill a difference between the antebellum aesthetics of Emerson and the "bellum" aesthetics of Allen, we might say that the work of a creative imagination transforming the world has been replaced by the grimmer task of picking up the pieces and trying to construct something out of what seems like nothing. Emily Dickinson's Poem #291B both validates and develops this distinction, echoing many of the images discussed thus far.

> It sifts from Leaden Sieves –
> It powders all the Field –
> It fills with Alabaster Wool
> The Wrinkles of the Road –
>
> It makes an even face
> Of Mountain – and of Plain –
> Unbroken Forehead from the East
> Unto the East – again –
>
> It reaches to the Fence –
> It wraps it, Rail by Rail,
> Till it is lost in Fleeces –
> It flings a Crystal Vail

On Stump – and Stack – and Stem –
The Summer's empty Room –
Acres of Joints, where Harvests were –
Recordless – but for them –

It Ruffles Wrists of Posts –
As Ancles of a Queen –
Then stills it's Artisans – like Swans –
Denying they have been – [26]

Rather than remaking the world in a fantastic jumble (Emerson), or burying it in a winding sheet (Allen), Dickinson's "It"—at first the snow, then something more mysterious—gives the world a sinister facelift, covering up signs of devastation. Like a cosmetician, it "powders all the Wood" and "fills with Alabaster Wool / The Wrinkles of the Road." Fixing up the landscape might not seem so bad, until we hear that "It makes an Even Face" and an "Unbroken Forehead" of the entire world, "from the East, / Unto the East, again." That leaves us to wonder, if the globe is a head, where the rest of the body is. It also suggests that a face is made up for posthumous viewing. In *This Republic of Suffering*, Drew Gilpin Faust discusses the advances in embalming during the Civil War. Families who could afford it hired embalmers near the front to prepare bodies for shipment home—often a long way by train for Union soldiers—so that loved ones could be seen one last time and given a proper burial.[27] Embalmers and other middlemen in this process quickly realized that there was money to be made identifying and preserving the dead for distant burial. Dickinson's image of filling wrinkles with wool on a bodiless face begins to suggest the detached, clinical gaze that would accompany such engagements with the Civil War dead.

Dickinson's "even face" updates the "universal face[s]" of both Thomson and Cowper. Thomson's snowy visage shows nature's indifference to human suffering:

Earth's universal face, deep hid, and chill,
Is one wild dazzling waste, that buries wide
The works of man.

In Thomson's poem, winter is a murderer, but the focus is on individual casualties, like that of the "swain" who "sinks / Beneath the shelter of a shapeless drift" while his family waits for him to come home. Dickinson's snow buries countless bodies—a world of bodies—beneath a shapeless drift of global proportions. She emphasizes the enormity of the burial by nodding to and magnifying Thomson's depiction; a snowstorm that can "make [ ] an even face / Of Mountain – and of Plain –" leveling peaks and valleys, would have precipitation levels of hundreds or thousands of feet. Snow would have to be that deep, Dickinson implies, to cover the massive number of casualties. The unimaginable proportions death takes in modern warfare summons a hallucinatory depiction. Dickinson has given up on crafting an appropriate affective response; in the "even face" response has been overwhelmed, the onlooker numbed in a mimic facsimile of the distant masses of dead soldiers she cannot summon to the mind's eye. Death has become so remote and so vast that registering and absorbing the fact of it is inconceivable; the poem asks us simply to think about the blankness of shock that would accompany such an encounter. Dickinson's "even face" exaggerates the transformation "by most unfelt" of "the face of universal nature" that in Cowper signified a kind of numbness.[28] She elevates that numbness to shock.

The poem foregrounds the fragmentation not only of poetic understanding and worldview, as Allen's "Snow" does, but also of the human body. "It sifts" through images of body parts, vainly trying to reassemble the human, an aesthetic task, Dickinson indicates, that inevitably accompanies modern warfare. Countless Civil War reports of battlefields (Dickinson replaces the first version's "Wood" with "Field" in this second version, strengthening the military association) covered with wounded and dead soldiers used metaphors of autumn harvest (discussed in Chapter 2), underscoring the gruesome yield of war. Dickinson also aligns the botanical world with human anatomy; "stump" can refer to both botanical and human portions (the hospital where Silas Weir Mitchell worked was known as the "Stump Hospital"). Once that association is established, we can read "Stem" as shorthand for human decapitation, and "stack" for human corpses piled like so much hay. The next phrase, "Acres of Joints," fully inverts the metaphoric valence, so that now human dismemberment signifies agricultural harvest; we do not commonly refer to mowed fields as full of "Joints." If "Acres of Joints" are "where Harvests were," then we can understand that, rather than metaphoric equivalence, Dickinson has moved to a literal description of substitution: where grain was harvested now lie human bodies and their dismembered parts. Simultaneously closing and opening the distance between Southern battlefields and Northern home fronts, the snow of winter covers the summer's field, where the remains of harvest evoke amputation.

Out of supposedly "recordless" carnage, a new body of poetry arises, albeit in parts, parts that recall those just-buried pieces. The harvest of the dead may be "recordless" (Faust notes that many bodies were buried without record during the war), or their records may be resurrected in altered and denied form.[29] As if covering wounds that have no possibility of healing, "it flings a Crystal Vail," doling out forgetfulness or numbness to the condition. Buried in the snow of amnesia, the stumps, stacks, stems, and joints are left to memorialize themselves. Yet the poem does register the ramifications of remote violence in its shattered language and logic. The ruffling of the posts' wrists suggests that the speaker has difficulty distinguishing body parts from other things, so that her simile is oddly doubled and broken: ruffling the posts' wrists is like ruffling the Queen's "Ancles." Corporeal disaggregation haunts the poem, disrupts a more conventional form of troping, and records the ramifications of the recordless dead that the poem on the face of it—the artificially composed face—denies.

While Dickinson makes plain her poetic debt to Emerson, Cowper, Thomson, and perhaps Allen, she also reaches back to Greek literary associations of winter and war. The variant for "Artisans" is "Myrmidons," the warlike people that Achilles led to battle against Troy. This single word summons the story of the Trojan War, as depicted in Homer's *Iliad*, in the language of Alexander Pope's translation (that translation was in her family library, as were volumes by Thomson and Cowper).[30] An extended passage in the *Iliad* compares in detail a warlike snowstorm with the Greeks' blizzard-like bombardment of Troy with stones:

> And now the Stones descend in heavier Show'rs.
> As when high Jove his sharp Artill'ry forms,
> And opes his cloudy Magazine of Storms.[31]

This excerpt suggests that Dickinson's poem is infused with the metaphoric logic of the *Iliad*: the heaviness and minerality, for lack of a better word, of her snow metaphors—lead, alabaster—summon the storm of rocks in the epic. Her sifting and powdering "It" suggests Jove's godly impersonality; both deliver lethal, aerial messages to humans without concern for the consequences, but Dickinson's "It" is so far removed that it doesn't have a name or a place in a belief system as Jove does. Even so, in one way "It" is more intimate, for it is engaged in domestic activities that are suitable for a war at home. The poems also share "fleeces" as an evocation of snow:

> The circling seas, alone absorbing all,
> Drink the dissolving fleeces as they fall:
> So from each side increased the stony rain,
> And the white ruin rises o'er the plain.

Dickinson's synonym for fleeces, "alabaster wool," further underscores the connection: Alabaster is a word derived from Greek for a fine white stone from which ornamental vessels and sculptures were carved.[32] Dickinson inverts the earlier metaphoric valence: if in the *Iliad*, battle is described as a snowstorm, in Dickinson's poem, a snowstorm is described as a battle . . . or is it? By the end of the poem, "It" is also "lost in fleeces," and it is unclear which is the tenor and which is the vehicle. Dickinson underscores the remoteness of present violence by referring to even more elusive and remote past violence, historical, but also mythical and beautiful, inspiration for an enduring poetic tradition that, she suggests, must both resonate and be renovated in order to make sense of the present violence.

Though many critics and historians have found nature poetry of the period to work in the service of naturalizing and rationalizing state-sanctioned violence, both Dickinson and Allen offer a thoughtful meditation on mass violence via the language of natural phenomena. They forge connections between remote scenes of suffering, largely in the South, and the Union home front.[33] The weather is not only a metaphor for war; it is also a metaphor for news. The "simple news that nature told," as Faith Barrett has suggested, is not that simple once the war begins, and not just for Dickinson.[34]

"The Snow of Southern Summers"

Though Confederate and Union poetry are usually characterized as discrete, opposed wartime forms of expression that do not enter into communication with one another, Confederate Henry Timrod's poems are clearly engaged with a tradition of English and New England snow poems as a way of infusing climactic differences between North and South with contrasting symbolic valences. "Ethnogenesis" inaugurated the birth of a new nation on the occasion of "the meeting of the Southern Congress, at Montgomery, February, 1861," as the extended title tells us.[35] Published in the *Charleston Daily Courier* on February 23, 1861, it was reprinted not only in Southern papers, but also in *Littell's Living Age*, a weekly Boston publication.[36] Timrod's nature poetry had been popular enough in the North before the war that he published a volume of poems in the prestigious Ticknor and Fields series in 1860.[37] Northern readers of "Ethnogenesis," curious how secession changed the poet's outlook, would see that Timrod is quite familiar with poetic traditions that associate winter with war even if, as a lifelong resident of South Carolina, he did not have the substantial experience with blizzards that residents of Massachusetts could claim. Working both within and against that tradition, Timrod broadcasts a new kind of snow that he promotes as superior to the northern sort. This kinder, gentler snow, along with the rest of a more amenable, milder climate, will help the South win the war:

> Beneath so kind a sky—the very sun
> Takes part with us; and on our errands run
> All breezes of the ocean; dew and rain
> Do noiseless battle for us; and the Year,
> And all the gentle daughters in her train,
> March in our ranks, and in our service wield
> Long spears of golden grain!
> A yellow blossom as her fairy shield,
> June flings her azure banner to the wind,
> While in the order of their birth
> Her sisters pass, and many an ample field
> Grows white beneath their steps, till now, behold,
> Its endless sheets unfold
> THE SNOW OF SOUTHERN SUMMERS! Let the earth
> Rejoice! beneath those fleeces soft and warm
> Our happy land shall sleep
> In a repose as deep
> As if we lay intrenched behind
> Whole leagues of Russian ice and Arctic storm![38]

Rather than, like the winter snow, competing against those living in its atmosphere—alienating, isolating, and confusing the human population—Timrod's summer weather "takes part with us." Personification is far less ambiguous and more persistent in "Ethnogenesis" than in the poems of Emerson, Allen, and Dickinson: the sky, the sun, the breezes, the year, the months ("all the gentle daughters"), all take human shapes so they can take up arms—fanciful arms—a "fairy shield," a "spear" of grain—in the name of cotton.[39] Cotton, the thing not named, and one of the few things not personified in the passage, behaves atmospherically, like southern snow, rather than like a plant. It blankets the earth in "fleeces," like Dickinson's and the *Iliad's* snow, only hospitably, nurturing the earth and keeping it warm. Its whiteness becomes the very atmosphere of moral purity that Timrod hopes will inspire the new Southern nation. At the same time, he associates the color of cotton with racial superiority. Timrod thus posits an alternative to northern snow that appeals to the slaveholding South; this snow is far more ideologically saturated, and unlike the Northern poems, it is directly tied to nation building.

There is one strange ambivalence about the Confederate project worth noting, however. The cotton stretches out in "sheets" like clouds, or like Allen's "winding sheets," but rather than wrapping the dead, it cultivates an opiate "sleep" that Timrod casts positively. He suggests that cotton inures white Southern populations from Northern criticism as effectively as Russian ice and Arctic storm would deter travel; yet to "lay intrenched" conflicts defensively with the "deep" "repose" of a sleeping "happy land," suggesting that the white Southern conscience that Timrod constructs and bolsters here might require anesthesia in order for its dream of perfect whiteness to operate properly. "Ethnogenesis" self-consciously works within a Northern tradition in order to oppose it, but in responding to Northern criticisms of Southern slavocracy, Timrod's poem betrays influences of the positions he opposes.

Timrod clearly hopes his readership will extend beyond his region and sway foreign readers to a Confederate viewpoint of the conflict. While Dickinson's "even face" stretches grimly around the world from "east to east," Timrod imagines that markets for cotton, like the Gulf Stream, will transport the warmth of Southern hospitality far and wide, convincing the world that there is a kinder, gentler alternative to the capitalism of the North:

> The hour perchance is not yet wholly ripe
> When all shall own it, but the type
> Whereby we shall be known in every land
> Is that vast gulf which lips our Southern strand,
> And through the cold, untempered ocean pours
> Its genial streams, that far off Arctic shores
> May sometimes catch upon the softened breeze
> Strange tropic warmth and hints of summer seas![40]

The Gulf Stream travels from Florida north along the East Coast of the United States to Newfoundland before crossing the Atlantic to warm the western shore of Europe (Timrod is significantly silent about the southern branch of the stream, which circulates off the coast of West Africa). Ocean currents, like news, weather, and desirable commodities, circulate widely; Timrod's snowy cotton evokes all these currents in its appeal for global acceptance for the new nation, which he promises will be superior to the former United States and its remnant, the Northern states.

A companion piece to "Ethnogenesis," "The Cotton Boll" (published in the *Charleston Mercury* on September 3, 1861) underscores the inevitability that Southern cotton trump Northern snow. Its infinitude rivals its competitor's only as blessed land rivals a wasteland:

> To the remotest point of sight,
> Although I gaze upon no waste of snow,
> The endless field is white;
> And the whole landscape glows,
> For many a shining league away,
> With such accumulated light
> As Polar lands would flash beneath a tropic day![41]

The "waste of snow" is countered by an "endless" white field that glows with holy light. Timrod could not be more adamant about the righteousness of the Southern cause, which he articulates by turning an inherited tradition of winter war poetry back against itself. In order to accomplish this rhetorical feat, however, he must turn cotton into weather, vaporize its materiality so that it may become a medium of illumination, a means of communication, rather than a substance imbricated in material forms of exploitative labor.

In "The Cotton Boll," even more than in "Ethnogenesis," Timrod registers awareness of his evaporation of materiality that renders his poetic logic suspect. The poem begins by drawing attention to the very figure he almost erases: the slave.

> While I recline
> At ease beneath
> This immemorial pine,
> Small sphere!

(By dusky fingers brought this morning here
And shown with boastful smiles),[42]

The poem presents a rhetorical problem from the outset: the white speaker's "ease" depends upon the labor of the "dusky" other. The cotton he casts as a pure, ethereal symbol—of global interconnectedness ("small sphere!"), of white superiority, of mystical climatic harmony—only underscores the presence of a slave system that removes the speaker from the very thing he claims fully to possess. If leisured white superiority and black servitude were so natural, the slave would either be more fully present—an entire body rather than fingers and smiles—or totally absent, as he is in "Ethnogenesis," where the sister "months" plant, cultivate, and grow the cotton without visible help or effort. Here the slave leans into the frame of the poem, partially materialized and partially dematerialized. In a poem where white signifies holy illumination, it is not surprising that the slave is the absence of light, but he is not fully turned to night; his "dusky fingers" and "boastful smiles" linger, as a reminder that the dream of the South hinges on a mythology of "the little boll," "a spell" like that "in the ocean shell."[43] Timrod draws attention to the fantastic element of his reverie even as he seeks to naturalize it, suggesting that the material conditions of slavery are more present and contrary to the vision than he or his readers might longingly wish. The "dusky fingers" hold and support the small, white globe, after all, in much the same way as a divine creator secures the earth. In choosing cotton as his ideal mode of disseminating the good news of the South, Timrod acknowledges that his "trembling line[s]" form a "tangled skein" that he fails to unravel.[44]

By 1863, snowy cotton has disappeared from Timrod's poetry. "Spring," published in the *Southern Illustrated News* on April 4, tries to celebrate the beauty of the South in springtime, but, as in the Northern poetry of this time, thoughts of the dead and the wounded seep into the images, until the war finally takes over the poem. As in Allen's "Snow," the process is gradual; it seems unconscious or accidental at first, and then gains momentum. At the outset, only "pathos" indicates the darker, advancing vision:

Spring, with that nameless pathos in the air
Which dwells with all things fair,
Spring, with her golden suns and silver rain,
Is with us once again.[45]

Soon, blood appears, at first only as part of a playful personification—"In the deep heart of every forest tree / The blood is all aglee."[46] The tree's blood rises to the surface in a "flush" it shares with the sky: "the maple reddens on the lawn, / Flushed by the season's dawn." The seeds working their way toward the sun, figures of rebirth, unsettlingly recall the myriad war dead:

> As yet the turf is dark, although you know
> That, not a span below,
> A thousand germs are groping through the gloom,
> And soon will burst their tomb.

The thousand groping germs are suggestive of future flowers, but also of dead men, who strive uncertainly for resurrection—to "burst their tomb." Just before facing the submerged topic of violence directly, the viewer sees a flood of purple in anticipation of the imminent profusion of blossoms:

> Still there's a sense of blossoms yet unborn
> In the sweet airs of morn;
> One almost looks to see the very street
> Grow purple at his feet.

Drawing attention to the sense of unbirth summons the possibility of abortion. The purple pool on the street extends that line of thought: though the speaker may be anticipating the blossoming of hyacinths or violets, the figure of the undifferentiated, spreading mass is just as readily associated with blood.

The undertones of morbidity are confirmed retroactively when the poem turns directly to the topic of "war and crime" and "the call of Death" in "the west-wind's aromatic breath."[47] Unthinkably, Spring may awaken the sap in trees and the song of birds, but she will also "rouse, for all her tranquil charms, / A million men to arms." Then, the fields will run with real blood rather than the flushed hues of dawn, the purple flowers, and the dark red of just-unfolded maple leaves. Metaphors will become material truths:

> There shall be deeper hues upon her plains
> Than all her sunlit rains,
> And every gladdening influence around,
> Can summon from the ground.

Oh! standing on this desecrated mould,
Methinks that I behold,
Lifting her bloody daisies up to God,
Spring kneeling on the sod,

And calling, with the voice of all her rills,
Upon the ancient hills
To fall and crush the tyrants and the slaves
Who turn her meads to graves.

Spattered with actual blood, the daisies carry spring's plea for relief and a return to the pastoral ideal they used to inhabit; the personifications of nature that so blithely populated Timrod's earlier poems that celebrated the new Confederacy pray for an end to slaughter.

Only in the final stanza does Timrod address the politics of the conflict, and he does so in a cryptic way that suggests, as in "The Cotton Boll," doubts about the Southern cause. Spring calls for the landscape to "crush the tyrants and the slaves," but leaves the reader to determine their identity. The slippage leaves the phrase open to overlapping interpretations. Conventionally the Civil War–era rhetoric of the South depicts Northerners as tyrants and white Southerners as slaves; a Georgia secessionist, for example, proclaimed "we are either slaves in the Union or freemen out of it."[48] If Timrod is deploying that conventional rhetoric, then he is suggesting that the Northern "tyrants" and the white Southerners they "enslave" are equally responsible for turning the earth into a repository of death, destroying the animating cycle of life. If Timrod means to suggest that Northerners, along with actual Southern slaves, are responsible for the carnage, he has mixed that conventional metaphoric use of "slave" with its literal meaning. In that case, he is explicitly admitting the fact of slavery in his tribute to Southern purity when he very clearly avoided the topic in "Ethnogenesis" and "The Cotton Boll" because it disrupted the pastoral ideal of the peaceful and effortlessly bountiful South. And if the slaves are literal slaves, then the fact that their graves are overwhelming Spring's meads and staining the daisies suggests that white Southerners, again, have blood on their hands. Death and injustice have infiltrated Timrod's vision of Southern righteousness. He cannot make the South as pure as the driven snow, or as the cultivated cotton. He doesn't need to explicitly acknowledge the failure on that score for it to be evident in the logic of the poem.

The beginning of a complex pattern emerges that offers insight into the aesthetics and ethics of violence in U.S. Civil War poetry, North and South. When confronted with the fact of violent, divisive conflict, Allen, Dickinson, and Timrod all look to the sky for explanation. Early in the war, Timrod, like Emerson before him, asserts the transformative power of the imagination; Emerson's night wind and Timrod's seasons both create a fleecy substance that covers the existing world and remakes it into an idealized wonderland. For Emerson, writing more than two decades before the war, that wonderland is created by a force described in militaristic terms that are clearly whimsical; Timrod, in 1861, also whimsically, enlists nature to fight for the Confederacy. Emerson aestheticizes the weather in order to give shape to an abstract idea, while Timrod summons aesthetic power to vaporize commodities—cotton and slaves—and turn them into ethereal symbols. Cotton becomes a mode of communication analogous to the North's mass media networks; Timrod imagines cotton traveling far and wide, like tropical winds, touching people in foreign lands and converting them to the Southern cause. In 1861, Timrod in South Carolina, surrounded by the unspoken, perhaps unspeakable, violence of slavery, which he seeks to justify without mentioning, turns slave labor into twilight in order to make present violence remote. He fails; dusky fingers and boastful smiles, however idealized, return us to the material subjects he begins to erase. Dickinson and Allen, at a distance from the war, conversely draw upon the weather to materialize the news of the battlefront at home; winter's freezing temperatures and frozen precipitation brings the war home, in all its remoteness. By 1863, Timrod comes closer to their understanding of the ethical relation between materiality and metaphor. All three wartime poets, as distinguished from Emerson's earlier practice, show the ways that events shape perception as much as perception shapes events. Involuntarily, perhaps, the Civil War poets must leave themselves open to the elements—including an elemental media environment—and whatever they carry with them through the air. The next section shows Melville working within this tradition, but binding it tightly to the historical details of weather in wartime and its devastating impact on physical bodies; his insistence on explicitly articulating the physical ground for the proliferation of figural practices allows us to explore the media underpinnings of this circulation of literary meditations on wartime violence.

"The storms behind the storms we feel" in "Donelson"

Melville locates his 1866 collection *Battle-Pieces, or Aspects of the War*, and particularly "Donelson," within this tradition of contemplating the question of remote suffering via figures of the weather (indeed, he prepared to write his first book of poems by reading Thomson's poems, among others).[49] Melville identifies the abstraction of violence into figures of weather as a problem as well as a necessity for thinking about war at a distance; the abstraction is an inevitable result of the mediated immediacy of the Civil War's reception. The difficulty of apprehending mass suffering that both Thomson and Cowper identify is made newly specific and urgent in Melville's poem, for the masses are Confederate and Union soldiers, killing each other at a distance from the Northern home front, but, at least for Unionists, within the boundaries of the same nation. Near and far are therefore juxtaposed with extreme compression that, in turn, pressures the poet to generate "strange analogies" and new "combinations" in response.

Melville stages this scenario in all its complexity in "Donelson." The poem juxtaposes reportage of the Tennessee battle on the banks of the Cumberland River, which took place in stormy weather February 11–16, 1862, with reception of the news via telegraph, also in stormy weather, at a city bulletin board in the North. Day after day, people surround the board, eagerly awaiting each additional posting, responding changefully and fitfully as the story unfolds. Rather than stressing the miraculous quality of the rapid transmission of the news, as do many of his contemporaries, Melville makes the highly mediated and imperfect transmission of information the subject of the poem. He foregrounds the impressionism of the reporter, the remarks of an editor, the weather's disruptions of telegraphic transmission, errors in the reportage, the further intermediary steps of the man who posts the bulletins, and of another man who reads them to the crowd. He emphasizes his own layers of poetic mediation as well. Doubling the figure of the journalist reporting on the battle, the poet is *"our own reporter,"* who *"a dispatch compiles, / As best he may, from varied sources."*[50] Melville presents his poem as a theatrical staging or script, in which different tenses and fonts are used for those on the home front reading and listening to the news and those who compose and disseminate the news.[51]

Melville meticulously follows the reportage of the event, as if it were crucial in accessing whatever comprehension of the war might be possible.

Indeed, "Donelson" is partially constituted of newspaper reports; it is not simply a poetic rendition of them. In writing the poem, Melville pored over newspapers; as Frank Day has demonstrated, "Donelson" is saturated in quotations and paraphrases from the coverage more than any other poem in the collection, many of which foreground their intensive debt to journalistic sources.[52] Those sources, in turn, are steeped in linguistic conventions derived from a romantic poetic tradition, so that it is impossible to stipulate where the poem leaves off and its newspaper sources begin: paraphrasing blurs the difference. In offering this hybrid form, Melville presents his reader with a range of entangled questions: What is the difference, if any, in the information derived from newspaper reportage and poetry? How can poems make us feel the news, and vice versa? What is the relation between media and genre? These questions cloud and complicate the relation among suffering, its representations, and their reception. This endless complication is the subject of inquiry, and the weather is Melville's mode. Melville takes the battle's circumstances—a cold snap in Tennessee kills primarily Northern soldiers supposedly more accustomed to cold weather—as an occasion to meditate on the rhetorical and psychological functions of weather in wartime in their unsettled and unsettling configurations. The poem ricochets back and forth between the home front and the war front, mimicking media circuitry, and I will follow the form in my analysis of the deliberately overwhelming complexity of the poem.

Melville follows the minutely detailed temporal unfolding of ongoing, unsynthesized reports on the ground to convey a sense of the radical shifts in subjectivity that accompany unpredictable shifts of both weather and war. Strange analogies are formed between Melville's crowd around the bulletin board and the soldiers on the distant battlefield, and it is up to the poem's reader to discern their significance. Meteorological thinking is ubiquitous in the poem—it is its atmosphere—and it works in every which way. At first, there is a difference between the weather on the home front and the battlefront. A crowd gathers around the board even though they are "pelted by sleet in the icy street"; they go home at night, frustrated that the story is unfinished, and return again in the daytime.[53]

The listeners hear news of balmy weather in the South—recited by a "tall" man, who reads the reports aloud—and the troops, as well as the reporter, are in high spirits. Melville's lyrical reporter of events seems inappropriately stuck in romantic modes of describing the weather:

The welcome weather
Is clear and mild; 'tis much like May.
The ancient boughs that lace together
Along the stream, and hang far forth,
Strange with green mistletoe, betray
A dreamy contrast to the North.[54]

The reporter could be setting the stage for an encounter between lovers, rather than armies; the "dreamy contrast" suggests that Southern weather seduces the Northern soldiers, who perceive a beautiful, possibly deceptive, wonderland. While the passage is in the Wordsworthian tradition of nature poetry, it nevertheless also enhances the *New York Times*' own enamored report of Tennessee's weather: "The scene here was magnificent beyond description—the night was as warm as an evening in August, in our more northern latitudes, a full moon looked down from an unclouded sky, and glanced off the bayonets, plumes, and sword-hilts without number."[55] The soldiers glittering in the moonlight offer a romantic vision of military engagement that later reportage on the conflict will make a mockery of. The deeply harmonious relation between the poem and the *Times* report suggests that Melville's poem resonates with the news rather than, or in addition to, simply critiquing it, as some readers have suggested.[56] Perhaps because of its inconsequentiality, this first report, transmitted on Wednesday the twelfth in the poem's meticulous timeline, has no readers on the home front; the bad weather is enough to discourage reading so that the bulletin was simply "Washed by the storm till the paper grew / Every shade of streaky blue."[57]

Melville suggests not simply that the reporter is unreliable, but that it would be impossible to generate a truthful and coherent account of such rapidly shifting conditions and events; the analogies the poem draws between Union troops and shifting weather cannot be stabilized into a patriotic narrative of destined victory. As the poem unfolds alongside the battle, the conditions shift radically, as does the reporter's viewpoint. On Thursday the weather turned severely cold, making the skirmishes in the woods around the fort physically painful as well as deadly. The reporter blends the fighting men with the weather: "*we stormed them on their left / A chilly change in the afternoon.*"[58] The "chilly change" is a drop in temperature, but it is also a turn for the worse in the soldiers' circumstances. "*The cold incites / To swinging of arms with brisk rebound.*" Melville makes no distinction between human limbs and their military extensions; the need for warmth causes men to move their "arms," which in turn causes them to fight more fiercely. Men's actions are fueled by their natural surroundings, no longer through a romantic reverie, but in a metonymic fusion of deadly forces. Imagining, as Whitman does, that the weather sympathizes with human events, the reporter persistently suggests that the weather is on the Union's side: he tells us "*The sky is dun / Fordooming the fall of Donelson*," and urges the Union soldiers to victory. The *Times* report that was one of Melville's primary sources for "Donelson" is equally saturated with this logic: "Thursday morning dawned beautifully, and seemed to smile upon the efforts of the national troops. The men cheerfully accepted the omen."[59] The poem's reporter further states that the people of Tennessee have never seen such cold weather and believe the Northern soldiers brought it: "*Yea the earnest North / Has elementally issued forth / To storm this Donelson.*" This insistence on the weather's Union sympathies is particularly incongruous in this case, however, because in fact, the weather turned vicious, and the Northerners suffered severely from it. Experiencing a balmy day on the march to Donelson, the Union soldiers discarded their coats and blankets. Two days later, many of them froze to death in the sleet and snow, dying of exposure.[60] The reader of "Donelson" might note at this point that the reporter's initial report must then be incorrect—residents of Tennessee understand that the weather can change suddenly from balmy to cold, so they weren't imagining it as an accompaniment to righteous Northern wrath, and it is the Northerners who project an ill-fitting tropical ideal onto the region, at great cost. But the correspondent doesn't revise, or even seemingly remember, his own previous figuration. It is left to the "listeners" at the bulletin board within the poem and the readers of the poem to note, or to overlook, the dramatic irony.

The reporter's meticulous, elaborately crafted description of the first day of battle is wasted on the people reading and listening to those reports. When Melville shifts to the reception on the home front, we see that, jarringly, no one notes the suffering of the soldiers. They use the occasion not to think about what has happened at Donelson, but to express their simplistic, overly general opinions about the fight. The first man to speak is merely irritated at the tedious length of the conflict: "'Twill drag along—drag along,' / Growled a cross patriot."[61] Another offers a cheer for Grant that "urchins" and some adults mindlessly repeat. A "Copperhead" reminds the crowd that the Confederates are giving the Union a good fight.[62] The disconnection between home front and war front is complete; the civilians use the report as an occasion to editorialize without a thought to the suffering of those who are fighting the war.

As Friday's report grows more gruesome it is clear that the reporter himself is at a loss, having shifted rhetorical modes rapidly in ways that don't properly accommodate the suffering he is trying to convey. The prospects seem dimmer for the Union; the weather turns worse, so that *"hapless wounded men were frozen."* Again the reporter finds an inappropriately romantic simile—*"Our heedless boys / Were nipped like blossoms"*—but this is not because he is callous. As if unsure of how to convey such an event—the boys dying not only by bullets but also by frost— just a few lines later he offers a completely different metaphor that conflicts with the first: the Union soldiers are now *"ice-glazed corpses, each a stone / A sacrifice to Donelson."*[63] Now he has turned to the language of patriotic sacrifice to recuperate the losses, but the odd juxtaposition of the two unrelated registers of diction suggest that he doesn't know how to give meaning to the happenstance of Northern soldiers freezing to death during a battle in Tennessee.[64]

Timothy Sweet has suggested that in deploying these verbal clichés Melville critiques the ways patriotic rhetoric dehumanizes soldiers and defaces their suffering. He argues that the poem exposes how wartime poetic discourse and journalistic reportage "aestheticize the war," thus contributing to the ideological work of converting casualties into symbols of patriotic sacrifice: "ideological discourse displaces the body" "once the body has served its purpose in war."[65] This claim overlooks both the struggle to find adequate language on the part of the reporter as well as Melville's own immersion in the heterogeneous rhetorical conventions he "compiles." The reporter is searching for ways, however ineptly, to convey, rather than erase, the plight of the Northern soldiers. His observations exceed the pro-Union narrative he places upon them: this complicates Sweet's thesis of an ironclad, inescapable ideology. Rather, projecting simplified, sense-making narratives on chaotic events is a tendency that no one in the poem is immune to, even though those stories coexist with all kinds of information that refutes them. The poem's journalist reports that the soldiers who witness their comrades freezing tell themselves *"it is a sacrifice to Donelson"*: *"They swear it, and swerve not, gazing on / A flag, deemed black, flying from Donelson."*[66] Thinking about the slaughter in this way, Melville suggests, is a survival strategy, and the soldiers themselves may well know that if they don't keep swearing to themselves, they could give up and freeze even sooner. Their awareness of the pragmatic quality of their belief is suggested by the word "deem," as if they know that imagining the enemy as an evil empire with a black flag will help them survive. Their practical self-deceit is further underscored by the immediately subsequent observation that the Confederate soldiers do what they can to help their freezing foes even though they too are "in shivering plight":

> *Some of the wounded in the wood*
> *Were cared for by the foe last night,*
> *Though he could do them little needed good,*
> *Himself being all in shivering plight.*[67]

The *Times* notes this interlude as well, which is completely inconsistent with the reporter's tendency to elevate the Union soldiers at the expense of the Confederate soldiers.

Observation, it seems, exceeds the ideological power to contain it, but ideology is useful and necessary, not only for political reasons. The reporter's romantically saturated simile—"*our heedless boys / Were nipped like blossoms*"— as well as his language of monumental sacrifice—"each one a stone / A sacrifice for Donelson"—are poignantly inadequate as well as ideologically motivated. Attempts at rationalizing the carnage in terms of the natural cruelty of frost, or of a higher moral power, reveal themselves to be fragile attempts at holding onto meaning in a circumstance that threatens to annihilate it. Romantic similes and patriotic rhetoric can't account for the Northerners freezing to death in Tennessee, but nothing arrives to take its place. Melville thus foregrounds an urgent need for what Whitman calls "strange analogies" and "different combinations" and suggests in the process that all this talk about the weather might be an attempt to forge relations and correspondences that take the place of romantic modes of troping, which at that point are functioning as little more than dead metaphors that further dehumanize the soldiers rather than bring their suffering closer to home.

Before the Northern listeners can feel something for distant strangers, they must feel for abstract representations in new media forms. The catastrophic situation as well as the sheer length of the battle finally allows the people on the home front to think about the plight of the Union soldiers. The fact that the Union experiences setbacks and momentarily appears to be losing allows room for meditation rather than formulaic expressions of patriotic support. Donelson was a river battle as well as a land battle; Union ironclads shelled the fort from the Cumberland River while land soldiers tried to breech the walls (fig. 6). The fervent belief in the inviolability of the ironclads led to premature reports of victory. But that report is quickly reversed as news arrives that one of the ships was actually disabled by Confederate fire. This setback, on top of the descriptions of the soldiers' severe suffering, causes the listeners on the home front to meditate on the situation. They may not achieve total fusion with the suffering soldiers, but they do begin to think about how little they know. The listening throng turns inward, to "silent thought." This brooding in the brooding storm—"whose black flag showed in heaven" over their heads, corresponds inscrutably with the flag deemed black at Donelson:

> Many an earnest heart was won,
> As broodingly he plodded on,
> To find in himself some bitter thing,
> Some hardness in his lot as harrowing
> As Donelson.[68]

Rather than expressing their own feelings about the war, the brooders try to make correspondences between private and public campaigns, finding in themselves something as bitter as the soldiers are experiencing. In this they are forging new kinds of relations, infusing technological innovation with human desires for connection with others:

> Flitting faces took the hue
> Of that washed bulletin board in view,
> And seemed to bear the public grief
> As private, and uncertain of relief.

Their faces "every shade of streaky blue" the color of ink washed away by rain, the listeners have to feel with and through a sheet that has been transcribed from a telegraphic report that was submitted by an onlooker (or someone who poses as such; no one can be sure) far away in Tennessee. This isn't easy. It requires different combinations, as Whitman said, "strange analogies," new modes of verbal relation. For, Melville suggests, in order to find relation, we reach out beyond our bodies into our surroundings, and we relate to what we find.

As soon as news of Northern victory arrives, the quest for understanding ends and is immediately forgotten. The uneven process Melville has arduously charted becomes abstracted into lines that resemble a drinking toast, which summons no pain or cost:

Figure 6. "Storming of Fort Donelson—decisive bayonet charge of the Iowa
Second Regiment on the Rebel entrenchments at Fort Donelson, Saturday evening,
February 15, resulting in the capture of the works on the following morning—
From a Sketch by our Special Artist, H. Lovie," *Frank Leslie's Illustrated Newspaper*,
March 15, 1862, 264–265. The snow reported in the journalistic coverage is not visible
in the sketch—the men themselves are the "storm." Courtesy of HarpWeek.

> . . . . . . *all is right: the fight is won,*
> *The winter-fight for Donelson.*
> *Hurrah!*[69]

Victory dispels all musings and broodings; "eyes grew wet" but only with
"happy triumph." The erasure of the event is sealed with the drunken reverie
that ensues and the warm houselights that block out the weather:

> O, to the punches brewed that night
> Went little water. Windows bright
> Beamed rosy on the sleet without.

The last residues of the crowd's memory are lodged in those with a personal loss, who, forgotten by the revelers, retain some knowledge at a painful cost. The poem's final scene is of the dissolution of boundaries between person and environment required for partial understanding:

> But others who were wakeful laid
> In midnight beds, and early rose,
> And, feverish in the foggy snows
> Snatched the damp paper—wife and maid
> The death-list like a river flows
> Down the pale sheet
> And there the whelming waters meet.

Tears, the rain, and the names of the dead dissolve into a single body of water that summons the specter of the Cumberland River, which still flows by the gutted Fort Donelson. What remains is a new figure, one that signifies the challenges to come in representing mass suffering in an age of mass media: the blank sheet of paper, like a bluish gray sky, like an expressionless face. Melville has returned us to Cowper's earlier figure of the frozen, snowy universal face, transposed now onto the telegraphic bulletin.

Critics have divided in their interpretations of the elaborate staging of Civil War news in "Donelson." Hennig Cohen and Stanton Garner emphasize the pains Melville took to forge correspondences between soldiers and civilians, especially via the weather: while the Union soldiers freeze to death in an unanticipated cold snap and storm, the listeners also endure "rain and sleet," which "takes them in spirit to the weather and the storm of battle that the soldiers at Donelson experience." Cohen goes so far as to say that this results in a "total fusion" between the listeners and the soldiers, perfect solidarity in "universal suffering."[70] On the other hand, Franny Nudelman and Faith Barrett stress the shortcomings and failures of these correspondences, arguing that Melville posits these relations only to expose their inadequacy. For Nudelman, "Melville emphasizes the unreliability of communication, and, by extension, the unbridgeable distance between battle and home fronts." For Barrett, Melville shows that "poetry and journalism equally fail at the task of representing the horrors of war."[71]

Melville indeed meticulously forges correspondences between home front and war front via figures of weather and the news, and he shows these correspondences to be faulty, insufficient, partial, ideologically saturated, and even delusional. Like the soldiers, the listeners may be rain soaked and shivering while waiting for the latest bulletins to be posted, as Cohen and Garner point out, but that does not so easily indicate "their essential similarity of situation" and the "universal prevalence of suffering." The listeners have coats, and one even has an umbrella that Melville rather extravagantly likens to "an ambulance-cover / Riddled with bullet-holes, spattered all over."[72] The simile shows the distance and difference more than the sameness of the listeners' experiences; the hail that damaged the umbrella may be related to, but is only a soft echo of, the bullet-perforated, mud-spattered ambulance. He and the other listeners can and do go home each night of the three-day battle, returning in the morning; many of the soldiers contract frostbite and die of exposure while they sleep.

Melville stages this difference, but he does not wholly condemn it; he himself is immersed in it, and it is this unavoidable immersion that he most strongly indicates. It is a circumstance to be confronted, not overcome. The gap, both produced and made visible by the journalistic reportage intermixed with Melville's poem, can be measured and perhaps diminished as a result. Melville, like Thomson and Cowper before him, takes as a starting point that apprehending remote suffering is a difficult if not impossible task. Milette Shamir notes that in "Donelson" particularly, Melville performs "a dynamic back and forth investigation of the civilian author, whose distance allows a broad vision of the war even as it undermines that vision's access to truth and ethical viability."[73] At the same time that ethical viability is undermined, it is ethically necessary for the civilian to seek and recognize truth's limits. The difficulty multiplies when those suffering are strangers who are dying en masse out of sight and sound in circumstances that bear no relation to those of the bystanders, who learn of their circumstances in highly mediated, if relatively immediate, ways. The poem is less concerned with portraying the perfection or fallibility of remote apprehension of Civil War suffering than with posing it as a problem to be articulated, considered, and analyzed, if not solved. New communication technologies, Melville suggests, require new ways of processing the information that is transmitted, because the medium and its particular forms of mediation change the message. Whereas Thomson perhaps believed he had found a solution to the problem by summoning a perfect sympathy in readers through the image of a suffering individual, and Cowper showed the inadequacy of Thomson's solution for newspaper readers in the age of empire, Melville tenaciously explores both the impulse to understand another's suffering and the obstacles that impede that understanding in the hopes of finding a way to some partial insight. He does not so much critique human limitation as try to work within it, since the rhetoric of war that people share—poetic traditions and current poetic practices, the proliferation of journalistic reportage in all its heterogeneity—is the only available medium of communication.

Though U.S. Civil War poetry acknowledges and draws from a British poetic tradition of imagining war at a distance via figures of the weather, coterminous and cooperative developments in technologies of killing and communication demand new figurations of the climates of war. If reading the newspaper generates dislocated feelings on the part of readers remote from their nation's conflicts, the increasingly rapid and continuous transmission of information—what Oliver Wendell Holmes Sr. calls "perpetual intercommunication" via national "nervous networks"—intensifies the strangeness; Holmes tells us that readers of the news experience a version of the "war fever" that soldiers experience in battle.[74] If soldiers are overwhelmed by the proximity of massive violence, readers at home are overwhelmed by a continuous bombardment of information about bombardments. The problem of remoteness is complicated by the fact that the Civil War was both far and near, internal and external, at home and abroad, depending on one's geographical location, Union or Confederate perspective, and personal investments. Receiving news of war at a distance prevented readers from fully distinguishing between internal and external states of mind and country.

While all the poets discussed express skepticism over the possibility of perfect understanding between onlookers and sufferers, they nevertheless foreground a universal tendency—of poetry, journalism, reporters, poets, soldiers, and listeners—to create meaning in events by forging imaginative relations. The trope of choice is metaphor. Metaphor, after all, has its root in the idea of transport; it is suited to reconfiguring significance within circulatory networks. To establish relations between inner and outer states, all the poems, and all the players in the poem "Donelson," metaphorize their surroundings. They do this in particular via the weather. A single line serves as an example: "The lancing sleet cut him who stared into the storm."[75] After an immersion in the atmospheric approach of "Donelson" to linguistic representation, it is clear that metaphor is at work here, but it is unclear what is the tenor and what is the vehicle: Does a soldier stare into an actual storm, weaponizing it in his reverie? Does a listener stare into the storm of war? Are we readers staring at a stormy poem that throws "a shower of broken ice and snow, / In lieu of words"?[76] Interior and exterior states, states of mind and states of weather, battlefield attacks and storms, all run together, the "way a river flows / And there the whelming waters meet."[77] In Civil War poetry, the coincident, interpenetrating, and transitive circulation of weather, troops, and news generates instabilities in the metaphoric and symbolic properties of language; poetry's task is to reconfigure expression so that even at a distance, war can make an impression.

The "Ghastly Harvest"

The pastoral tradition is well suited to explore war's environmental devastation, but only if poets strain the tradition to accommodate the sorts of scenarios it consistently denies; otherwise, the poems themselves offer a form of denial. Imagery of harvest time was ubiquitous in Civil War poetry. Autumnal poetic traditions offered a vocabulary with which to compare mass death in wartime—the "ghastly harvest"—with natural cycles signifying perpetual renewal.[1] This chapter explores the ways that writers adapt the conventions of autumn poetry to the conditions of war. Claiming "that the pastoral and picturesque aesthetics were important in the constitution of nationalist ideology in the antebellum period," Timothy Sweet stresses the ways that Walt Whitman and others "mobilize the idealized representation of the Union encoded in these aesthetics to heal the wounds of war and to envision the restoration of the nation" at the cost of acknowledging the physical reality of mass death.[2] Interpretations of Emily Dickinson's "The name – of it – is 'Autumn' – " offer a counterpoint to this formulation. Tyler Hoffman, David Cody, Faith Barrett, and others have read the poem as a critique of war, one that so strongly associates the red leaves of autumn with the bloodshed of Antietam (whose name echoes the season) that it is impossible to imagine the poem as an innocent meditation on New England fall: the tenor overrides the vehicle.[3] But as is often the case with her poetry, Dickinson's "The name – of it – is 'Autumn' – " is understood as an exception to a more general practice. According to Barrett, for example, "what separates Dickinson's poem from its popular counterparts . . . is Dickinson's refusal to read battlefield bloodshed as a cycle of redemptive suffering for the nation that is endorsed by God."[4] This chapter demonstrates that the evocation of the pastoral in poems of the period doesn't necessarily support national ideology, nor must it serve as a means of creating escapist fantasies that evade the acknowledgement of war's human or environmental tolls. On the other hand, the poems examined in this chapter do not uniformly critique war's carnage. Instead, I identify a broad range of ways this aesthetic is used. Through figures of autumn, some poets affirm the righteousness of the Northern cause, while others raise questions about nature's regenerative powers, the possibility of human extinction, God's existence, and whether poetry has lost its relevance in the face of total destruction. The pastoral tradition offers not a set ideological viewpoint, but a vocabulary with which to address the complex issues accompanying environmental and human devastation, issues that necessarily evoke mixed, confused, and unsettled responses that extend beyond political binaries. Writers, ranging from popular newspaper poets to Dickinson and Whitman, draw upon seasonal tropes to grapple with the costs of total war, offering meditations on wartime violence as well as the capacities of poetic language to accommodate it. The first part of the chapter traces the prominence of the figure of the ghastly harvest in response to the Battle of Antietam, which epitomizes a more widespread treatment of environmental devastation and untimely death via autumnal figures. The second section shows the way some poets explicitly acknowledge and contemplate the effect war has had on these autumnal figures; these writers are as interested in the aesthetics of violence as in articulating their response to unfolding events.

Antietam's Autumn

The Battle of Antietam (September 17, 1862), in which Union soldiers turned Confederate troops back from Maryland, across the Potomac River into Virginia, resulted in the largest casualty count of the war for a single day: twenty-three thousand dead and wounded.[5] The engagement was also, according to a number of reports, the most visually stunning. For George Smalley, a reporter for the *New York Tribune*, the battle was a "magnificent, unequalled scene"; no one "could be insensible of its grandeur."[6] Edwin Forbes, a sketch artist for *Frank Leslie's Illustrated Newspaper*, recalled that "the Battle of Antietam was probably the most picturesque battle of the war, as it took place on a corn field and could be fully viewed from any point north of Antietam Creek, where our reserve batteries were posted. The engagement with the spectacle was not surpassed during the whole war, as the hills were black with spectators."[7]

Noncombatants watched the spectacle from a position close enough to feel awe but far enough away to totalize and aestheticize the battlefield; newspaper readers at home were encouraged to assume a similar perspective through sketches, such as Alexander Waud's, of unfolding events (fig. 7).

The coverage was laden with a central irony that was immediately noted by the reporters and crystallized in the poetry that emerged after the battle. Many of the dead had fallen in a field ready for harvest, bloodying and destroying the corn. The substitution of young men killed in their prime for the corn that would normally nourish their growth gave rise to the image of the "ghastly harvest." Smalley's report coins the term and offers the first delineation of the figure: "The field and its ghastly harvest which the reaper had gathered in those fatal hours remained finally with us. Four times it had been lost and won. The dead are strewn so thickly that as you ride over it you cannot guide your horse's steps too carefully. Pale and bloody faces are everywhere upturned. They are sad and terrible, but there is nothing which makes one's heart beat so quickly as the imploring look of sorely wounded men who beckon wearily for help which you cannot stay to give."[8] Shifting to the present tense and zooming in to a far more intimate frame than the panoramic descriptions of the battlefield at a distance, Smalley transmits his immediate, downward gaze to readers, encouraging them to associate reading the page with looking upon the faces of the dead.[9] His description tightly links the materiality of the dead to the materiality of the page that contains his inscription. In doing so he brings the metaphor of the ghastly harvest before the reader in vivid, stark detail.

General Joseph Hooker's description provides the details informing Smalley's concise figuration, bringing out the doubled image of harvest: "In the time that I am writing every stalk of corn in the northern and greater part of the field was cut as closely as could have been done with a knife, and the slain lay in rows precisely as they had stood in their ranks a few moments before. It was never my fortune to witness a more bloody, dismal battle field."[10] Heavy fighting neatly cut the corn, and the men fell just as "precisely," as if both had been carefully mown. The men's death in harvest time substituted bodies for grain, killing for sustenance. The figuration is repeated in news reports, memoirs, and poems about the battle with remarkable regularity. Overdetermined by the facts on the ground as they were first reported, the figure of the ghastly harvest was indelibly inked in the public imagination in a way that mirrored the shock of participants and onlookers. A sketch by F. Schell from *Frank Leslie's Illustrated Newspaper* on October 8, 1862, conveys a sense of linearity of the

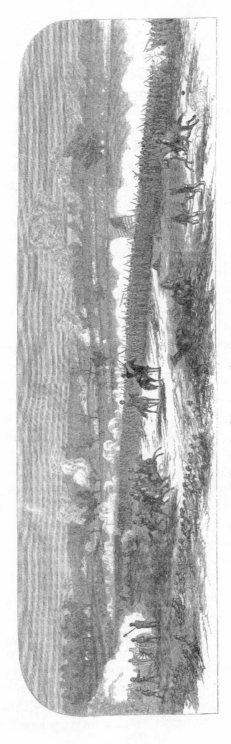

Figure 7. "The Battle of Antietam, fought September 17, 1862—General Mansfield's Corps in position in the centre—Sketched by Mr. A. W. Waud," *Harper's Weekly*, October 11, 1862, 648–649. Courtesy of HarpWeek.

scene that General Hooker evokes: the battle trenches, the fallen lines of the dead, and the long graves being dug to accommodate them (fig. 8). One row, stretching to the horizon, suggests the seemingly limitless number of dead, which in turn recalls the rows of corn no longer standing. On the right, spectators, surrogates for the viewers at home, and perhaps representatives of the farmers of the region, watch the scene closely; they summon a recent, peaceful past that lent itself more to unreconstructed—or deconstructed—pastoral poetry. The image suggests military order as well as carnage, foregrounding the Union's control over the scene.

Another illustration in *Frank Leslie's Illustrated Newspaper* also shows the way that viewers at home are encouraged to take on the position of onlookers at the scene, exemplifying the kind of mediated immediacy that characterized the experience of reading Civil War periodicals (fig. 9). Visually staging the juxtaposition between an antebellum agrarian ideal and the ghastly harvest of war, the sketch depicts farmers—identified in the title—including a woman and a child, looking at the men's bodies piled where crops would normally be growing. The background, where a pair of men carry away the dead and wounded and piles of bodies fade away into shapeless forms, is lightly sketched, as if the horror of the immediate scene has riveted the farmers' attention and prevented them from seeing anything beyond the pile of dead in front of them. Readers are encouraged to compare the gruesome scene with the indications of nature's continued presence: the line of birds draw the eye to the horizon and toward the trees in the distance that remain unharmed.

The newspaper poems about Antietam draw on such visual depictions, expressing verbally the emotions that the images evoke, making use of literary tropes and traditions in attempts to translate eyewitness reportage into intelligible verbal patterns. One of the most extreme responses to the event, an unsigned ballad entitled "After the Battle of Antietam," published in the July 4, 1863, issue of *Harper's Weekly*, elaborates on the image of a cornfield overlaid with a more perverse harvest:

> The harvest-moon o'er the battle-plain
> Shines dim in the filmy eyes of the dead,
> And the yellow wealth of the later grain,
> Ground by the millstones of death and pain,
> And wet with the life-blood of the slain,
> Is kneaded to horrible bread.[11]

Figure 8. "Battle of Antietam—The 130th Pennsylvania regiment of volunteers burying the Rebel dead Friday, Sept. 19 . . . From a Sketch by our Special Artist, Mr. F. H. Schell," *Frank Leslie's Illustrated Newspaper*, October 18, 1862, 52. Courtesy of HarpWeek.

Figure 9. "Maryland and Pennsylvania farmers visiting the battle-field of
Antietam while the national troops were burying the dead and carrying off the
wounded, Friday, Sept. 19. From a sketch by our special artist Mr. H. F. Schell,"
Frank Leslie's Illustrated Newspaper, October 18, 1862, 49. The juxtaposition
of the farmers with the devastation evokes the destruction of the pastoral
lamented in many of the poems of the period. Courtesy of HarpWeek.

In these shocking lines, the dead and dying soldiers grind the "later grain"
beneath them, mixing it with their blood. The metaphorics of communion—
bread and wine as the body and blood of Christ—are conflated. Here blood
instead of water is mixed with grain to make a "horrible bread" that figures the
impossibility of transubstantiation. An inedible substance takes the place of
resurrection's sign, indicating the possibility of God's nonexistence. Alice Fahs
and other critics and historians have noted the ways that the deaths of Civil
War soldiers are figured in terms of Christian martyrdom, justifying state violence: "sentimentalism provided a way of making sense of the bodily sacrifices
of soldiers within an explicitly Christian framework."[12] In many poems of the
period that certainly is the case. Here and elsewhere, however, the invocation
of Christ's resurrection challenges rather than reinforces the rhetoric of patriotic sacrifice. As Drew Gilpin Faust notes, religious doubt was not new to the

war; new forms of biblical criticism, geological discoveries about the earth's vast age, and theories that biologized consciousness raised questions about religious faith: "into this environment of cultural ferment, the Civil War introduced mass death."[13] This caustic passage, which refuses affirmation of the soldier's martyrdom, was made possible by these combined circumstances.

"After the Battle of Antietam" responds to horrifying events by adapting inherited traditions of autumnal poetry, while also engaging with the news. Two transformations are particularly notable across the field of wartime autumnal poems: attention to recalcitrant external conditions that often disrupt the tropic play of the imagination within the poem; and a movement away from the expression of individual emotional states toward expressions of shared feeling. In Keats's earlier ode "To Autumn" (1820), for example, the speaker expresses personal feelings rather than a general condition of existence. He descends into an increasingly depressive state, first reveling in the sensuality of harvest-time, when the season conspires "to bend with apples the moss'd cottage trees, / And fill all fruit with ripeness to the core."[14] Taking a counterintuitive pleasure in violence, the speaker and autumn together watch the crushing of ripe apples into cider until "the last oozings" of their juice is gone. Here, juice is metaphorized into blood, as the apples bear a curiously luxurious meditation on death. On this point, "To Autumn" contrasts neatly with "After the Battle of Antietam," where blood is not a metaphor but a physical substance that has displaced its tenor. The speaker of "To Autumn" projects blood onto cider, while the speaker of "After the Battle" fails to turn blood into wine. The difference suggests that the imagination or "fancy" in the later poem is compelled not only by a despairing mood, but also by the exigencies of external, untransformable conditions.

Another notable difference between the two poems lies in the relation of the speakers to their readers. Keats's speaker doesn't stop at self-indulgence, but descends further into a despair in which he can no longer imagine spring's return and is left to mourn winter's death among nature's inhabitants—with gnats as well as "full-grown lambs." Though he still finds companionship in the natural world, he is isolated in mood from his readers, and from people more generally. In "After the Battle," the speaker doesn't speak only for himself: he declares the current conditions of existence for all those who inhabit the landscape of the war. Men's violence has created a universal theological and environmental crisis. This commonality bears a troubled, even hostile relation to the Union; the poem implicitly asks whether this collective experience of pained displacement can carry ideological significance.

"After the Battle of Antietam" also draws on specifically American strains of autumnal poetry in which writers struggle, as David Cody notes, "to convey . . . something of the stunning visual impact of the extraordinary intensity of color that one encountered in the autumnal landscape in the northeastern United States."[15] In the antebellum period, writing in the service of establishing a specifically American national identity embedded in the natural environment, poets like William Cullen Bryant, Lydia Sigourney, and Henry Wadsworth Longfellow wrote odes to New England autumn that stressed a rich palette of colors in which red is most prominent. As Cody notes, before the war, "sanguinary imagery had long been present in American descriptions of the autumnal landscape."[16] Martial imagery too had long been a feature of this poetry, though before the war it assumed other forms. In Lydia Sigourney's "Vision of a Birthplace," for example, collected in *Pocahontas and Other Poems* (1842), autumn is "speaking of decay":

> Yon lofty elms, the glory of our land
> So lately drooping 'neath their weight of leaves
> With proud, yet graceful elegance, to earth
> Stand half in nakedness, and half in show
> Of gaudy colors. Hath some secret shaft
> Wounded the maple's breast, that thus it bends
> Like bleeding warrior, tinging all its groves
> With crimson?[17]

It is no coincidence that the martial figure is a bow and arrow; many of Sigourney's poems mourn the passing of Native Americans from the landscape, associating them with the fleeting quality of "The Indian Summer," explicitly so in a poem by that name.[18] The dying crimson of the fall leaves, "like bleeding warrior," marks the displacement of Indians from the New England landscape. Sigourney's figure is more whimsical than topical in "Vision"; the poem is not "about" the decline of Indian presence, but about Sigourney's own meditations on aging during a visit to her birthplace. It is a passing trope rather than a sustained figure integral to the central meditation of the poem. The difference in the use of martial imagery in "After the Battle" is clear; in the latter poem, the martial trope overwhelms the vehicle so that the fall landscape runs with blood rather than sporting blood-colored leaves.

John Greenleaf Whittier's "The Battle Autumn of 1862" extends the treatment of natural and human devastation in "After the Battle," meditating in a

sustained way on the issues the other poem raises with immediate fury. One of
the most popular poems to emerge from the conflict, Whittier's poem relies on
the recent events at Antietam for its power: it was published just weeks after
the battle in the *Atlantic Monthly* and reprinted widely in places as diverse as
the *Country Gentleman*, the *Liberator*, the *Advocate of Peace*, and the *Saturday
Evening Post*. The poem questions whether nature can absorb the quantity
of suffering it has witnessed and still remain a divine force that withstands
human violations. The poem strangely juggles expressions of unequivocal certainty about nature's stolidity and doubt about her capacity for endurance:

> The flags of war like storm-birds fly,
> The charging trumpets blow;
> Yet rolls no thunder in the sky,
> No earthquake strives below.
>
> And, calm and patient, Nature keeps
> Her ancient promise well,
> Though o'er her bloom and greenness sweeps
> The battle's breath of hell.
>
> And still she walks in golden hours
> Through harvest-happy farms,
> And still she wears her fruits and flowers
> Like jewels on her arms.[19]

"Calm and patient," Nature neither sympathizes with the Union nor punishes
bellicose aggression by sending earthquakes or thunder: she simply watches.
Whittier's depiction of her equanimity is strained, however, by the third
stanza. Walking with "jewels upon her arms" through a pastoral landscape
where Antietam is not, while "the battle's breath of hell" destroys "her bloom
and greenness," Nature's indifference comes to resemble vanity, and she starts
to seem uncaring rather than stalwart.

Certainly the poem wishes to cast her as transcendent and resilient, but
the extremity of conditions increasingly strains the figuration until the speaker
acknowledges the oddity:

> What mean the gladness of the plain,
> This joy of eve and morn,

> The mirth that shakes the beard of grain
> And yellow locks of corn?
>
> Ah! eyes may well be full of tears,
> And hearts with hate are hot;
> But even-paced come round the years,
> And Nature changes not.
>
> She meets with smiles our bitter grief,
> With songs our groans of pain;
> She mocks with tint of flower and leaf
> The war-field's crimson stain.

Unchanging in the face of the most tragic and potentially evil human behavior ("crimson stain" suggests sin), Nature displays hints of cruelty, mocking war with the beauty of autumn leaves that assume the color of blood, countering groans with bird songs. Whittier insists that her indifference arises from being "too near to God for doubt or fear," but he dwells on the point so long that his affirmation opens the possibility of doubt:

> She knows the seed lies safe below
> The fires that blast and burn;
> For all the tears of blood we sow
> She waits the rich return.
>
> She sees with clearer eye than ours
> The good of suffering born,—
> The hearts that blossom like her flowers
> And ripen like her corn.

Whittier turns from doubt to reaffirmation, which is common in the tradition of autumn poems, but the horrifying possibilities he seeks to negate persist in spectral form. The image of total devastation, where not even seeds can survive the blasting fires of war is more vivid than the insistence on a future regeneration that can't be proven in the present. The hearts like ripened corn counter the bloodied corn of Antietam, but also summon the painful counter image. So too, the blossoming hearts evoke the "tears of blood" that fertilize them. The context of war brings the physical referent too near and prevents the hearts, like corn and flowers, from standing alone as emblems of future peace.

The speaker's final plea suggests that he does not feel comforted:

> Oh, give to us, in times like these,
> The vision of her eyes;
> And make her fields and fruited trees
> Our golden prophecies!
>
> Oh, give to us her finer ear!
> Above this stormy din,
> We, too, would hear the bells of cheer
> Ring peace and freedom in!

He asks for nature's discerning eyes and "finer ear," but like a genteel woman preoccupied with the finer things in life, Nature doesn't note or attend to more pressing human need; she leaves the speaker to plead to an unknown figure—perhaps it is a prayer to God—and readers to wonder whether the battle autumns have scorched the earth beyond repair. While the fields and fruit trees long served the role of prophesying perpetual well being in autumnal poetry before the war, now they stand mute, unresponsive to the poet's call. They need to be made into "golden prophecies," and it is unclear to the speaker whether that will happen.

Many autumn poems after Antietam, then, trouble the relation between the literal and the metaphorical; they insist on the external event and subordinate personal interiority to a collective consciousness that can range from lyrical to epic, and from specifically allusive to generalized and abstract. What they do not share is any particular ideological position on the war. In "Antietam," Charles Morris provides a dramatic counterpoint to "After the Battle" and "Battle Autumn," offering an epic narrative of the battle that is faithful to the news coverage of the event while elevating it to Iliadic proportions. In direct opposition to the previous poems, Morris depicts the massive violence as sublimely just and necessary: the "red dawn" gleams

> On two embattled hosts that line the banks
> Of swift Antietam; while the leaping beams
> Fall with a sullen light on bayonets

Drawn in array, and on the edge of swords
Kindle new stars.[20]

The speaker witnesses the battle from a panoramic perspective, participating in the rhetoric of sublimity that permeated the reportage and memoirs of the scene. Again the martial imagery is not the tenor, as in Sigourney's poem, but the vehicle. Autumn is both the literal atmosphere in which the battle takes place and a metaphor for the dead, presided over by the Grim Reaper:

It is the reaper, Death, who hither comes
To gather in his sheaves and gain his seat
At this red harvest-home. From his left hand
Drop pain and agony upon the field.
Destruction from his right; for never leaves
By the chill lips of autumn from the trees
In sad profusion blown, so thickly fell
As men this fiercer autumn. Everywhere
The ruinous bullets through their close-knit ranks
Rush in dense volleys, deadly-freighted shells
Burst in their midst, and valor-breathing men,
In life's full gush are hurled to bleeding death.
Red Ruin sits upon the crimson plain
And all the ether groans in agony.[21]

There is autumn, with its falling leaves, and there is the "fiercer autumn" of men falling more thickly. Rather than absorbing and justifying violence through a pastoral palliative, Morris heightens the violence and celebrates the bloody loss of life, which lends weight to Union claims for a higher moral ground. The "surgeon war" tears "rudely out" "the rank sores that fester the world's heart" in order to heal the nation. Morris echoes Oliver Wendell Holmes Sr., who, when speaking of Antietam's dead, declares that "war is the surgery of crime."[22] Morris expresses certainty that "Truth and Justice" will win out even if massive slaughter must be their means. "After the Battle of Antietam," "Battle Autumn of 1862," and "Antietam" suggest the diversity of ways poets draw on figurations of autumn to question or justify mass death after the catastrophic battle, from evoking the death of god, to questioning nature's solace and capacity for regeneration, to asserting the necessary cost of justice.

Because it was one of the first battles with an enormous casualty count, and because events enabled such uncannily appropriate figurative possibilities, Antietam emerged as a symbol of mass death in the popular culture of the period. James McPherson notes that "many cornfields were the scene of fighting during the Civil War, but this one was ever after known as *the* Cornfield."[23] Poets needed only to sound the word "Antietam" to conjure for readers, in a compressed form, the extensive media coverage of the costly Northern victory with its shocking level of loss. Poets made use of this shorthand for a range of reasons: to commemorate bravery, commend patriotic sacrifice, mourn the loss of life, or lament the staggering costs of war. In a poem by Lucy Larcom, published in the May 1864 *Atlantic Monthly*, a mother celebrates her son's reenlistment and encourages other mothers to do the same by evoking his courage through this national shorthand:

> Through blood and storm he's held out firm, nor fretted once,
>   my Sam,
> At swamps of Chickahominy, or fields of Antietam.[24]

It is sufficient to gesture toward the "fields of Antietam" to bring up the constellation of associations broadly disseminated in the press. Larcom's invocation of a staunch, fearless mother mirrors on the home front the son's heroism on the battlefield. In "The Return of the Regiment," frequent *Atlantic Monthly* contributor Elizabeth Akers Allen contrasts the "unbroken rank and file" that went off to battle with the "handful of haggard men" returning. The few men who survived are:

> Men who have stepped in crimson stains
> Warmly flowing from traitorous veins,—
> Soldiers from red Antietam's plains,
> Heroes of battles ten.[25]

Confederate blood flows so amply there is no way for Union survivors to remain unstained, and Antietam is entirely "red" with blood. In a poem entitled "At Gettysburg," another soldier-speaker recalls the men at Antietam during his charge at the later battle. One might anticipate that the soldier would find thoughts of Antietam's carnage unnerving; instead they spur the men to commit the same scale of violence in the same way:

> A mist in our rear lay Antietam's dark plain,
> And thoughts of its carnage came o'er us;
> But smiling before us surged fields of ripe grain,
> And we swore none should reap it before us.[26]

Here the Confederate soldiers are conflated with Antietam's fields of grain, and the soldiers imagine harvesting them as a way of spurring themselves to the kill. Antietam's ghastly harvest structures the Battle of Gettysburg, past violence promoting future violence.

While the single word "Antietam" served as shorthand for large-scale slaughter in a range of poetry, the word "autumn" also came to signify battle deaths as much as it signified a season. The constellation of associations were consolidated in the Battle of Antietam, but they were certainly strengthened every time a bloody battle took place in a rural setting in autumn. Countless poems played on the metaphorics of autumn in a way that swung free from the particulars. A poem entitled "Roll-Call," for example, published in *Harper's Monthly* in December of 1862, may very well refer to the Battle of Antietam, but never mentions it. The drama of the poem relies on the number of times no one responds during roll call, because he is either missing in battle or dead. That scenario was certainly duplicated countless times throughout the war on both sides:

> "Cyrus Drew!"—Then the silence fell—
> This time no answer followed the call;
> Only his rear-man had seen him fall,
> Killed or wounded he could not tell.[27]

The missing men were scattered on a formerly idyllic, now blood-saturated landscape;

> The fern on the hill-sides was splashed with blood,
> And down in the corn, where the poppies grew
> Were redder stains than the poppies knew
> And crimson-dyed was the river's flood
> For the foe had crossed from the other side
> That day in the face of a murderous fire
> That swept them down in this terrible ire;
> And their life-blood went to color the tide.[28]

The location of Antietam is suggested by the hillsides (from which spectators watched the battle), the corn, and the river (the Confederates crossed the Potomac from Virginia into Maryland and then back again in their retreat). But while the poem may cue the reader to remember Antietam, the memory is not necessary to respond to the poem, which could be set in many places. Important is the figure of a stained, innocent place and the violation of an extant conception of pastoral beauty by a physical event that inhabits and strains against that poetic tradition.

Autumn Strains

Poets recognized and grappled with this strain, even when treating the war more obliquely. Poems by John James Piatt, Whitman, and Dickinson offer meditations on how to adapt autumnal traditions to account for mass death; all arrive at different conclusions, none of them fully satisfying. The poets mark dissatisfaction and a sense of tragic discontinuity between pastoral traditions and present conditions, peace and wartime, civilian tranquility and battlefield calamity. None of the poems fully accept the limitations of poetic traditions in addressing critical aspects of the war. None of them offer the pastoral as a kind of solace or refuge. Noting the stark difference between the autumn tranquility surrounding Northern civilians and the bloody autumn of war, these poets challenge themselves and their readers to make war at a distance real enough to disrupt comfort and safety at home. They conclude that reading about the war in newspapers and meditating on the experience of war from a remote position can't overcome the gap.

This state of mind is remarkably expressed in a poem by Piatt, who worked as a clerk in Washington, DC, during the war. A contributor to the *Atlantic Monthly*, Piatt published, with his wife, Sarah Morgan Bryan Piatt, a collection of poems entitled *The Nests at Washington* (1864).[29] Starting from the title, the book confronts the vexed issue of living a life of comfort even while communications about the war permeate one's surroundings: Washington was within earshot of some of the Civil War battles. Judging from the collection of pointedly autobiographical poems, the writers were newly married and had small children. Many of their poems are not about the war at all, but about the pleasures of familial companionship. Others, however, interspersed throughout the volume, attend to the sense of guilty displacement from the violence the couple registers but cannot feel in more than a spectral way. "First Fire" celebrates the family's hearth, but the title also alludes to the first battles of the war, a topic Sarah Piatt also attends to in "Hearing the Battle," included in the same volume. John Piatt celebrates the first autumn fire as part of a family tradition:

> Dearest, to-night upon our Hearth
> See the first fire of Autumn leap:
> Oh, first that we with festal Mirth
> For loving Memory keep!
> Sweet Fairy of the Fireside, come
> And guard our altar-flame of Home![30]

The poem celebrates a cult of domesticity in an exaggeration of its familiar aspects: from the affectionate address to the beloved wife, to the description of the fire as the "altar-flame" in a pagan ritual celebrating the home, to the playful but nevertheless serious summoning of a magical sprite to protect the family's peace and happiness. The chill of autumn serves as a way to bring the family together within the warm protection of the home.

The first sign that this scenario is not sealed off completely from external events comes in a vivid and startling image. A spark flies near the speaker's eyes:

> Ha! the lithe flame leaps red, and tries
> With bursting sparks to shell my eyes![31]

The motiveless violence of a flying spark, tiny in comparison to an exploding shell, brings to mind bombardment on the battlefield and its debilitating injuries. There are two versions of this poem; the first, published in the *Saturday Evening Post*, uses the word "blind" instead of "shell." Both variants evoke a sudden invasion of the speaker's reverie by thoughts of the war; considering them together makes the violence of the fantasy all the more vivid.[32] The image is out of character with the speaker's line of thought. "Flights of fancy," a recognizable poetic mode in the early nineteenth century associated with domestic settings, are emphatically whimsical. The speaker then notes that the metaphor is out of place, summoning the not-so-distant referent of what he inappropriately calls a "gay conceit":

Ill-timed the gay conceit, I know:
On the dark hills that near us lie
(The Shadow will not, need not, go)
Beneath the Autumnal sky
Stand battle-tents, that, everywhere,
Keep ghostly white the moonless air.

The sentinel walks his lonely beat,
The soldier slumbers on the ground:
To one hearth-glimmers far are sweet,
One dreams of fireside sound!
From unforgotten doors they reach,
Dear sympathies, as dear as speech.

I think of all the homeless woe,
The battle-winter long;
Alas, the world—the hearth's aglow!
And, hark! the cricket's song
Within!—the Fairy's minstrel sings
Away the ghosts of saddest things![33]

Autumn for the soldiers is not a chilly idea that heightens the pleasures of sitting beside a warm fire, but a real atmosphere that surrounds and penetrates them. The speaker stresses not just his inability, but his unwillingness to entertain thoughts of the soldiers' camps not far from Washington and the soldiers missing their homes and the comfort of their families—though of course he thinks about them while he insists he won't. He holds the thought at a distance even as he articulates it: the tents are "ghostly" because he refuses to fully substantiate them, and he notes that fact guiltily in a parenthetical: "(The Shadow will not, need not, go)." There is a big difference between refusing to and not needing to follow a thought, and both are true in this case. The first version of the poem substitutes "The Real" for "The Shadow," suggesting that the speaker is called to realism but resists because of a willful desire to linger in the domestic idyll he has constructed. He calls attention to his willed selfishness at the end of the passage: "Alas the world! The hearth's aglow!" The abrupt dismissal of the weighty fact of human suffering implicates the speaker: he betrays, or perhaps confesses, his shallowness. Because the speaker is not a soldier, he can choose not to think about their discomfort, but he cannot keep himself from acknowledging his callousness.

The question of what to write about in wartime, how to write about it, and the integrity of those choices permeates the rest of the poem and troubles the speaker's desire to continue to dwell on personal pleasures even as he keeps trying to do so:

> The firelight strikes our walls to bloom—
> Home's tender warmth in flower, I deem;
> And look, the pictures in the room
> Shine in the restless gleam—
> Dear, humble fancies of the heart
> When Art was Love in love with Art:

Even as he writes, Piatt expresses a sense that his formulations are out of step with the times. His home may be full of "tender warmth," or at least he "deems" it so in his poetry, but the form of expression has become estranged enough that he can also condescend to it as a naïve, outdated time "when Art was Love in love with Art." He places the present moment of writing in the past to archive a set of feelings that have little place in the midst of "general sorrow," to paraphrase Dickinson.[34] The chiasmic formulation of Art suggests an insular solipsism, a self-indulgent pleasure in artistic representation at the cost of looking outward at difficult things.

In spite of the recognition, the speaker insists on continuing to enjoy the beauty of his surroundings and their reflection in poetic expression. He nevertheless registers an awareness of what he is not writing about:

> Without, the funeral of the year
> Is preach'd by every mournful tree;
> The tree in blossom here
> Knows no lost leaves, no vanish'd wing—
> In vain will Autumn preach to Spring![35]

The speaker has set the poem during autumn's "first fire," so it is strange that he insists it is springtime in his home. That is because Autumn is now tainted with a set of associations he would rather avoid—the red of the trees is now "mournful," the season now funereal. The speaker's insistence on having "spring" in his home out of season foregrounds the willfully illusory quality of his reverie, which persists until the conclusion of the poem:

> Sing, cricket, sing of these to-night—
> The First Fire of our Home is bright!
>   Georgetown, D.C., October, 1861.[36]

The author locates the poem in Washington, DC, the logistical and political center of the Union, during the war's first autumn. It would be difficult to read the date and location and not think about the incongruity between the peaceful domestic setting of the "first fire of our Home" and the recent Battle of Bull Run just outside of Washington that had "enlightened by the vollied glare," in Melville's phrase.[37] In "First Fire," Piatt dramatizes a poetic problem brought on by the war: continuing to write about the same things in the same way nevertheless signifies differently in a new environment. Piatt portrays a scenario in which sentimental sincerity inadvertently becomes self-mockery, and the loving husband now seems insular and self-involved. The pleasures of home life are indulgent luxuries when set in relation to the strain of suffering that Piatt allows into his poem to challenge his stylistic and thematic choices.

Whitman dramatizes a similar problem with domestic autumnal figurations in *Drum-Taps*, both within certain poems and in the volume as a whole. Whitman insists on simplicity and innocence in short sentimental poems such as "A child's amaze," "Mother and babe," and "A farm picture"; the poems serve as a radical contrast to the explicitly themed war poems, raising questions about their inclusion (these poems are removed from the war cluster in later editions).[38] "A farm picture," for example offers two lines of sunny tranquility just after the darker, war-torn poem "A sight in camp in the day-break grey and dim":

> Through the ample open door of the peaceful country barn,
> A sun-lit pasture field, with cattle and horses feeding.[39]

Though the poem itself is so simple it defies commentary, its placement is jarring, coming after a meditation on three corpses covered in "grey and heavy" blankets.[40] Because the relation is one of juxtaposition with no explanation, the reader must posit reasons for the sequence: it may be that Whitman is showing the discontinuity between home front and battlefront; it may be that he is offering solace in the idea that nature, "the mother of all," remains unchanged in wartime; or it may be he is providing a counterpoint to heighten the sense of horror in the earlier poem.[41] This perplexing ambiguity is replicated on a macro scale in the popular magazines and newspapers of the period; alongside poems that insist on the absolute irrelevance of pastoral settings for wartime tragedy are poems that perpetuate antebellum configurations of the natural world. The latter poems offer a comforting continuity with prewar sensibilities, but they are also jarring, as Piatt makes us aware, because they seem out of place in the present circumstances. In *Drum-Taps*, Whitman seems to be mimicking the heterogeneity of the poetic print culture of the war years, practicing inclusivity without passing judgment, suggesting that there is a place, however inscrutable, for all these responses to the war.

At the same time, Whitman also challenges this inclusivity. Like many other poets, he remarks more than once, in *Drum-Taps*, on the need to change his poetic focus and practice in wartime. He explicitly repudiates the perpetuation of practices like John James Piatt's in "1861," where he declares:

Arm'd year! Year of the struggle!
No dainty rhymes or sentimental love verses for you, terrible year!
Not you as some pale poetling, seated at a desk, lisping cadenzas
     piano;
But as a strong man, erect, clothed in blue clothes, advancing, carrying a rifle on your shoulder,[42]

In *Drum-Taps*, the poet conspicuously assumes the soldier persona, never "advancing" in the present moment, but remembering battle (in "The veteran's vision" and "The dresser") and observing its aftermath (in "A march in the ranks hard-prest, and the road unknown" and "Vigil strange"). In this passage the poet's personal identity is so unimportant that it is not he, but the "terrible year" he addresses that must be a "strong man, erect," with "a masculine voice." Whitman only "repeats" the year's song of enlistment, marching, and killing. In "1861," Whitman repudiates the amplitude of "Walt Whitman, an American, one of the roughs, a kosmos" from prewar *Leaves of Grass*, and commits himself wholly, without individual will, to the war cause.[43]

Part of this commitment means subordinating the natural world in *Drum-Taps*, though he still includes it. Whereas grass is ubiquitous in the 1855 *Leaves of Grass*, it is mentioned only three times in *Drum-Taps*: once it is "reddened" by soldiers' blood (in "The dresser"), once it finally absorbs the dead "many a year hence" (in "Pensive on her dead gazing I heard the mother of all").[44] The third time, in "Give me the splendid silent sun," grass is untainted by the war, but the image is framed as a fantastical wish on the part of the speaker, not a present reality:

> Give me the splendid silent sun, with all his beams full-dazzling;
> Give me juicy autumnal fruit, ripe and red from the orchard;
> Give me a field where the unmow'd grass grows;
> Give me an arbor, give me the trellis'd grape;
> Give me fresh corn and wheat—give me serene-moving animals, teaching content;
> Give me nights perfectly quiet, as on high plateaus west of the Mississippi, and I looking up at the stars;
> Give me odorous at sunrise a garden of beautiful flowers, where I can walk undisturb'd;
> Give me for marriage a sweet-breath'd woman, of whom I should never tire;
> Give me a perfect child—give me, away, aside from the noise of the world, a rural domestic life;
> Give me to warble spontaneous songs, reliev'd, recluse by myself, for my own ears only;
> Give me solitude—give me Nature—give me again, O Nature, your primal sanities![45]

While grass is plentiful in antebellum versions of *Leaves of Grass*, the phrase "give me" is not. It appears only three times in the 1855 edition, and never in an anaphoric structure. That is because *Leaves of Grass* is about having what the speaker of "Give me the splendid silent sun" does not; the possibility of singing about nature no longer exists in the same way during the war. In calling for what he cannot have, Whitman demonstrates the distance between 1855 and the war years; what recently seemed a civic duty—celebrating nature's "primal sanities"—now seems perverse.

Timothy Sweet claims that Whitman tries to "keep" the earlier image in an act of denial of the violence surrounding him: "The rural field as he represents it in 'Give me the splendid silent sun' is the site of nostalgia rather than action and of a wholeness of life rather than any consciousness of violence or death. Preserved pure and intact, the pastoral scene is a repository of a fictional antebellum harmony. The language of renunciation—'Keep your fields of clover and timothy'—encodes the pastoral nostalgia: keep it because now the poet cannot want it but also keep it in the sense of preserve and maintain it."[46] In Sweet's reading, Whitman acknowledges that his earlier, pastoral formulations are useless in the present moment, but he seeks to "preserve" them in the face of the violence of war as an escape. Faced with mass death, he similarly naturalizes the dead soldier by "drawing a pastoral frame around the corpse." In this way Whitman preserves a fiction of "democratic adhesiveness" at the expense of acknowledging the "politics" of war.[47] In her study of ecopoetics in Whitman, M. Jimmie Killingsworth also finds that Whitman summons a desirable figure of nature in the poem. Whitman is torn between, on the one hand, "the active principle of emotional intensity, human control over natural processes, and even aggression that characterizes the experience of total war and the building of big cities, . . . and on the other hand, the more passive and contemplative openness that characterizes a meditative approach to life on earth."[48] In contradistinction to both arguments, I suggest that Whitman makes nature unreal in "Give me the splendid silent sun" in a way it never was in the earlier *Leaves of Grass*. Whitman summons the memory of the antebellum poem, but only through a pointedly artificial simulation of its rhetoric. The first section of "Give me the splendid silent sun" is not in the style of the organicist celebration of *Leaves of Grass*. Nature here is idealized to the point of irreality. This poem invokes what the earlier poem pushed against: the abstraction of pastoral figures that lift free of physical particulars. The "trellis'd grape," "juicy autumnal fruit," "beautiful flowers," "serene-moving animals," "a sweet-breath'd woman," "a perfect child": the idealized, clichéd quality of the description conveys the tragic inaccessibility of an earlier visionary practice that was previously available to the poet. The portrayal of nature has become mechanical and rote in "Give me the splendid silent sun," as if Whitman has forgotten or now finds irretrievable his earlier, overflowing exuberance.

Compare the displaced, abstract images with the spatial and temporal particularity of this passage in the 1855 *Leaves of Grass*, to which Whitman directly alludes in "Give me the splendid silent sun":

> The big doors of the country-barn stand open and ready
> The dried grass of the harvest-time loads the slow-drawn wagon,
> The clear light plays on the brown gray and green intertinged,
> The armfuls are packed to the sagging mow:
> I am there . . . . I help . . . . I came stretched atop of the load,
> I felt its soft jolts . . . . one leg reclined on the other,

I jump from the crossbeams, and seize the clover and timothy,
And roll head over heels, and tangle my hair full of wisps.[49]

Here everything is particularized in its specific beauty. Light plays over the multicolored grass, which is also heavy, plentiful, soft, and entangled in the speaker's hair. This speaker would never describe grass simply as "unmow'd"; here, it is mowed, harvested, packed, loaded, cushioning, wispy, and still just as beautiful as it was when it was growing. Whitman alludes to this passage in the second part of "Give me the splendid silent sun" when he tells an unknown figure, perhaps his earlier self, to "Keep your fields of clover and timothy, and your corn-fields and orchards": instead of "seizing" the clover and timothy, somersaulting in it, and tangling it in his hair, he pushes it away. They are no longer relevant or accessible in their poetic life in Whitman's language. Similarly in "A farm picture," the door of the country barn also stands "open," but in that short *Drum-Taps* poem there is no more to say. Whitman doesn't interject himself into the "picture," which is framed and set apart in the title; the cattle and horses are left to graze without the odd interjection of a frolicking poet. It is set apart, inaccessible, remote, flattened. In "Give me the splendid silent sun," it is not a question of trying to "preserve the pastoral" out of a regressive sense of nostalgia. Whitman repudiates something that no longer exists, underscoring its absence through the jeweled, artificial quality of the perfect images. The inaccessibility of an abundant, multifaceted, infinitely inspiring natural world is reinforced by the speaker's strident and obsessive demands that intimate its nonexistence, that verify that it can no longer be given.

The speaker himself admits his frenzied state of mind even before he turns to his celebration of the nerve-wracked city:

—These, demanding to have them, (tired with ceaseless excitement,
    and rack'd by the war-strife;)
These to procure, incessantly asking, rising in cries from my heart,
While yet incessantly asking, still I adhere to my city;[50]

Overstimulated, with no place that is not saturated with the frenetic energies of war, he ineffectively tries to summon the possibility of rest. Rather than seeking escape, however, he admits the desire to evade the nervous energy that grips him, thereby demonstrating the emotional costs of living in the "rack'd" moment. With Whitman's "march in the ranks" in another *Drum-Taps* poem, or his mourning for the dead and wounded, this is one more response to war, a longing for an earlier time fused with a knowledge that it is no longer accessible. Whitman's "autumn," like Piatt's, is kept separate from the blood of Antietam and other battles that permeates the figure in other poems, but neither poet is ignorant of the deadly associations that now adhere. Both show the obsolescence of their figurations, as if they were at a loss of how to reconfigure autumn to encompass the current conditions of war.

Death's Surprise, Stamp'd Visible

Whereas Whitman deems the autumnal poetic tradition irrelevant, except perhaps as a point of contrast, Dickinson draws upon it both to mark the difference between the home front and the battlefront and to bring them together in complex relations. Acknowledging the disconnection between the two that Piatt so astutely delineates, Dickinson works on forging relations via explicitly imagined states of mind. A number of critics have examined the ways that Dickinson turns autumn leaves into a figure of ghastly harvest in "The name – of it – is 'Autumn' – ," one of her most widely interpreted "war poems."[51] Tyler Hoffman stresses that the poem "is specifically about the inability of the civilian to identify fully with the experience of war, to be wholly integrated into its frame of violence."[52] Dickinson characterizes her own civilian position as "shut out, abandoned, left behind as the fighting carries on," and yet she ironically claims a position of authority in "her passive station" in order to "refuse[] totalizing fictions of the war."[53] I build on Hoffman's perspicacious insights, but I differ in some important aspects: rather than stressing the way the civilian is "left behind," I find that Dickinson insists on the imbrication of civilians in warfare, whether they acknowledge it or not. Dickinson's autumn poems are not, moreover, expressing a personal relation to the war. Rather they explore the immediate effects of mediacy more generally, suggesting that the experience of learning about battle remotely is analogous to battlefield death.[54] Those who live while others die for them, or in their place, may or may not realize that they acquire a deadened aspect by proxy. Dickinson posits these specific relations in part through a consideration of the complex dynamic between viewer and viewed that the photographs of the period, remediated through print, generate.[55]

The photograph, according to Roland Barthes, is an "image which produces death while trying to preserve life" because it records what was there and is there no longer.[56] But if arresting life is the basis of photographic power, what is there to say about photographs of the already dead? For photography and death share a history in the nineteenth-century United States. Posthumous photography—keepsake portraits of departed loved ones posed as if they were still alive—became popular as soon as the technology enabled it, in the 1840s.[57] Not long afterward, between September 18 and 22, 1862, Alexander Gardner and his assistant James Gibson photographed the aftermath of the Battle of Antietam for Mathew Brady's company, capturing images of the dead still strewn across the field. These were the first images of the battlefield dead to emerge from the war, and the first ever to appear before a larger public. Because of the technical difficulties associated with wet-plate photography (Brady's company used the collodion process), photographers could not easily capture the living, lethal dynamics of battle, but they could work with the aftermath.[58] The stilling effect of photography worked best on still forms in the mid-nineteenth century. The images reached the Northern public quickly: within a month they were exhibited in Brady's New York gallery and reproduced as woodcuts in the October 18 issue of *Harper's Weekly* (figs. 10–11). Brady titled the exhibition *The Dead of Antietam* and offered stereo views and cartes de visite for purchase through catalogues. These images were taken for commercial purposes.[59] William Frassanito tells us that "both the stereo view and the album card made their debut on the eve of the Civil War," ensuring that photographers would cover the war because they were certain to have a "ready-made mass-market" and because "they would be able to supply that demand with images that can be reproduced in unlimited quantities at a price almost everyone can afford."[60] Alan Trachtenberg also remarks upon the reciprocally enabling relationship between photography, mass communication, and the Civil War: "As a medium of communication, photography itself contributed to the modernizing process reflected in its own practices. The photographs offered a new public experience: eyewitness pictures almost immediately after the events. The *New York World* noted in November 1862 that 'Brady's Photographic Corps has been a feature as distinct and omnipresent as the corps of balloon, telegraph, and signal operators'—part of a vast, intricate network of military communication which laid the basis for the postwar burgeoning of telegraphic lines and print media."[61] The alignment of death and photography that Barthes recognizes and locates historically in the latter part of the nineteenth century surely has something to do not only with the way this medium creates death while seeking to preserve life, but also with the way it widely disseminates the fact of death, and especially the fact of mass death in wartime, in an irrefutable form.[62] By infiltrating, interacting with, and working through other mass media forms, photography changed perceptions of death and war, even as it changed perception itself.

For Barthes, photography distinguishes itself from other media because it refers directly and necessarily to "the real thing which has been placed before the lens." Photography not only represents; it refers itself to an indisputable original: "It can never be denied that the thing has been there." While the thing certainly was there, it just as certainly is there no longer, and this double effect generates a specific perception that is, for modern viewers, not repressed, exactly, but is "experienced with indifference, a feature which goes without saying."[63] In other words, we have become so accustomed to photography's ability to record vanished moments as if they continued to exist, we no longer find it astonishing. While Barthes seeks to excavate and re-enliven that experience, writers of the nineteenth century didn't have to, because it was still so novel to them. Instead, they worked to articulate the ways in which this new medium's doubleness informed modes of perception.

There are suggestions in her poems that Dickinson was aware of and contemplated these developments, though there is no evidence that she ever directly viewed the photographs. I propose that she found provocative the woodcuts of Brady's photos published in *Harper's Illustrated Weekly* as well as Oliver Wendell Holmes Sr.'s essays on photography and on Antietam, particularly "Doings of the Sunbeam," which appeared in the July 1863 issue of the *Atlantic Monthly*. Dickinson may well have seen the reproductions disseminated in *Harper's*, for her brother and sister-in-law, Austin and Susan Dickinson, subscribed to that periodical, and reading materials were exchanged between the households. Her longstanding interest in work published in the *Atlantic Monthly* is clear in her letters, which refer to essays by T. W. Higginson, and a story by Harriet Prescott Spofford, for example. Both Dickinson and Holmes grapple with the conjunction of modern warfare, photography, and mass information networks. While Holmes stresses the presence, truthfulness, and revelatory power of the photographic image, Dickinson insists that photography deadens not only the subject, but also the viewer. Photographs in circulation promise to convey a sense of death, but can do nothing to convey knowledge of the live individual. This makes it a compelling way to transmit the force of mass death in wartime to people on the home front.

Holmes anticipated the fusion of photographic and military interests, casting the conjunction in apocalyptic terms. In June 1859, two years before the U.S. Civil War broke out, he predicted that "the next European war will send us stereographs of battles. . . . The time is perhaps at hand when a flash of light, as sudden and brief as that of the lightning which shows a rolling wheel standing stock still, shall preserve the very instant of the shock of contact of the mighty armies that are even now gathering."[64] Though photography's flash could not capture the very instant of the shock of contact, Holmes neverthe-less predicted a conjunction between visual technologies and battlefield death that materialized much closer to home than he imagined. A passionate believer in the seamless union of religious, scientific, technological, and national prog-ress, and an optimistic observer and interpreter of the rise of mass information networks in the mid-nineteenth century, Holmes was a strong supporter of the Northern cause during the Civil War.

Holmes's passion for photography and his interest in the war came together in "Doings of the Sunbeam," in which he tried to convey the shock evoked by looking at the photographs of the dead at Antietam. He compared these impressions to his eyewitness account of the battlefield, occasioned by a search for his severely wounded son several days after the battle: "My Hunt After 'The Captain'" was published in the *Atlantic Monthly* in December of 1862. Having seen firsthand "the bloody cornfield of Antietam,"[65] Holmes apparently purchased the Antietam images from Brady, because he tells his readers in "Doings of the Sunbeam" that

> we have now before us a series of photographs showing the field of Antietam and the surrounding country, as they appeared after the great battle of the 17th of September. These terrible mementos of one of the most sanguinary conflicts of the war we owe to the enterprise of Mr. Brady of New York. We ourselves were on the field upon the Sunday following the Wednesday when the battle took place. It is not, however, for us to bear witness to the fidelity of views which the truthful sunbeam has delineated in all their dread reality. The photographs bear witness to the accuracy of some of our own sketches in a paper published in the December number of this magazine. The "ditch" is figured, still encumbered with the dead, construed, as we saw it in the neighboring fields, with fragments and tatters. The "colonel's gray horse" is given in another picture just as we saw him lying. Let him who wishes to know what war is look at this series of illustrations. These wrecks of manhood thrown together in careless heaps or ranged in ghastly rows for burial were alive but yesterday.[66]

Holmes is so fully transported by the photographs that a reader might not realize that he never saw the "wrecks of manhood . . . ranged in ghastly rows." Arriving on the scene after "the dead were nearly all buried," he tells us in his earlier essay, he saw instead the debris of the dead as he "wandered about in the cornfield": "The whole ground was strewed with fragments of clothing, haversacks, canteens, cap-boxes, cartridge boxes, cartridges, scraps of paper, portions of bread and meat. I saw two soldiers' caps that looked as though their owners had been shot through the head."[67] Though he notes a dead horse, Holmes doesn't mention seeing a single dead soldier on the Antietam battlefield; instead he saw "fragments," "scraps," and "portions" indicating where the bodies had been. But when he looks at the photos, he sees the dead he did not see, occupying the space in and among the traces of war. The photographs uncover what lies out of sight beneath the ground, forcing visibility of the bodies signified by the traces he had meticulously specified months before.

This revisiting of a scene populated by figures "ranged in ghastly rows" that he did not see recalls Dickinson's well-known poem "It was not Death, for I stood up," The speaker notes the cause of her indefinable, deathlike sensation as something that she saw, something that sounds like what Holmes saw:

> It was not Death, for I stood up,
> And all the Dead, lie down –
> It was not Night, for all the Bells
> Put out their Tongues, for Noon.
>
> It was not Frost, for on my Flesh
> I felt Siroccos – crawl –
> Nor Fire – for just my marble feet
> Could keep a Chancel, cool –
>
> And yet, it tasted, like them all,
> The Figures I have seen
> Set orderly, for Burial,
> Reminded me, of mine – [68]

"The Figures I have seen / Set orderly, for Burial" evokes Holmes's bodies "ranged in ghastly rows for burial." This is perhaps not coincidental, given that Dickinson avidly read the *Atlantic Monthly*, where "Doings of the Sunbeam" was published.[69] In the reading I would like to propose, the poem stages an

Figure 10. "Antietam, Md. Bodies of the Confederate dead gathered for burial."
Photograph by Alexander Gardner and James Gibson, September 1862. Courtesy
of the Library of Congress, Prints and Photographs Division, LC-B811-557.

encounter between a viewer and a photograph of a line of dead arranged for
burial. One dead body prepared for burial was common; but there are very
few catastrophic situations besides war that would generate a row of bodies,
"Figures . . . Set orderly, for Burial." The poem imagines what it is like to
see such images, foregrounding the role of mediation in what is a seemingly
immediate encounter between viewer and picture.

The speaker in the poem views not bodies, but "Figures" of the dead. The
abstraction suggests not only Dickinson's own poetry, but also the abstraction of photography. Both Dickinson's poem and Holmes's essay portray a
transference of the experience of death that is not quite the same as dying:
seeing the figures gives the viewer a temporary "taste" of the experience. The

Figure 11. One image in a collection of "Scenes on the Battlefield
of Antietam—From Photographs of Mr. M. B. Brady," *Harper's
Weekly*, October 18, 1862, 648. Courtesy of HarpWeek.

viewer's parallel form of deadness suggests that the images are contagious,
that they can convey an impression of an experience that the viewer didn't
personally have; her deathlike mood is the result. This same quality underpins
Holmes's assertion that he saw the Antietam dead with his own eyes, when
he only saw the afterimages through Alexander Gardner's photographs: the
"terrible mementos" were so compelling that "we buried them in the recesses
of our cabinet as we would have buried the mutilated remains of the dead
they too vividly represented."[70] Holmes felt compelled to bury the photographs because "it was so nearly like visiting the battlefield to look over these
views, that all the emotions excited by the actual sight of the stained and sor-
did scene, strewed with rags and wrecks, came back to us."[71] Transported and
transfixed by a scene he did not see the first time, Holmes relives a moment
that compels him to repress it. He experiences a desire for emotional erasure
brought on by and analogous to the physical erasure caused by the battle and
recorded by the photographs.

Dickinson analyzes this transference of a deathlike experience from the photo to the viewer in the last four stanzas of the poem. The speaker likens the experience of looking at a photograph to that of being a photograph: the mirroring effect (Holmes, among his contemporaries, describes photography as a "*mirror with a memory*."[72]) freezes the viewer rather than enlivening the subject. Seeing the Figures arranged for burial "reminded" her of her own interment that hasn't yet occurred:

> As if my life were shaven,
> And fitted to a frame,
> And could not breathe without a key,
> And 'twas like Midnight, some –
>
> When everything that ticked – has stopped –
> And space stares – all around –
> Or Grisly Frosts – first Autumn morns,
> Repeal the Beating Ground –
>
> But most, like Chaos – Stopless – cool –
> Without a Chance, or spar –
> Or even a Report of Land –
> To justify – Despair.[73]

The speaker marks a relation of similitude between her experience and that of the Figures she has seen. Looking makes her feel "shaven" and "fitted to a frame," as if she has been turned into a photographic portrait. The single confirmed daguerreotype of Dickinson was finished in a way typical for the period: "a sixth-plate portrait under glass, set in a velvet-lined leather case bearing a clasp."[74] Needing a key to breathe puts the speaker inside such a case, or a locked cabinet or drawer, where Holmes says the photos of the Antietam dead belong: "Many, having seen [this series] and dreamed of its horrors, would lock it up in some secret drawer."[75] Likewise, the horrors of seeing so fully absorb Dickinson's speaker that she cannot distinguish between the image that she looks at and her own perception of that image. She reminds us that the memory of the dead can only remain with the living; because the dead do not dream, the living are obligated to dream of death for them. The "Figures" "Set orderly" also establish a parallel between images of the battlefield dead and Dickinson's own carefully composed poem. Poetry, like photography, memorializes but cannot enliven, and this concept becomes newly fascinating during the Civil War, when poets and artists seek to commemorate the dead.

The experience of seeing the Figures—feeling breathless, shaven, locked, and framed—stops time for the speaker, as does the photographer's click of the shutter for the subject. The end of her ticking—both clocks and heart—evokes the dead of Antietam in particular. "Grisly Frosts" stop the "ground" from beating in "Autumn"; the phonetic link between "Autumn" and "Antietam" strengthens the association with the battlefield photographs, as does the fact that "Antietam" was known as "the Bloody Autumn." The "Grisly Frosts" are a horrible, inexorable killing force. ""Repeal" is a double-edged word that suggests either that the frost gives the animating force a reprieve by withdrawing, or that it annuls or removes that force: that the entire ground beats before it is forcibly stilled suggests that it is covered with life that is being ruthlessly extracted. The collection of images suggests that the ground is strewn with dead or dying men, and that the speaker's live burial within a locked frame results from seeing or imagining this image of mass suffering.[76] The circulation of verbal descriptions of visual images, multiply mediated representations of events, are the inspiration for a poem that treats the twinned subjects of imaging and imagining the dead, and their deadening effects.

In "about summer of 1862," according to Franklin's estimate, Dickinson wrote a number of poems about battlefield death as a specifically visual horror. That horror, as she characterizes it, while explicitly nonrepresentational, is nevertheless referential, like photography. Dickinson works through a range of ideas about the new medium's capacities and philosophical implications in order to convey the shock of mass death in warfare. Dickinson's war poems appropriate a mediated understanding of photographic technologies to a poetic perception of war: she competes with this new visual medium in an attempt to conceive not only of the enormity of the carnage, but of the way it is necessarily removed and distant from many "viewers," who gain their impressions secondhand but with new immediacy through newspaper and telegraph reports. Whether one scrutinizes the images of the dead or puts them away in a locked drawer, they implicate the viewer by reminding her of her lack of exposure to a conflict that is fought by proxy. Either the news of death numbs distant civilians, or they numb themselves to the news of death; either way, they lose a part of themselves. Dickinson's poems seek to make readers aware of the emotional cost of even unconscious or unwilling complicity.

Her poetic experiments show the signs of engaging with photography's knowledge not only to understand its ramifications for mediated viewing, but in order to surpass it. She suggests that poems can tell us things about war that photographs can't, regardless of their truth claim. In "The name – of it – is 'Autumn' –," for example, she experiments with monochromaticity, a capacity of representation that photography does not share with poetry. Here and elsewhere, Dickinson takes from photography the idea that stripping out superfluous color increases dramatic effect. According to Holmes, "we must, perhaps, sacrifice some luxury in the loss of color; but form and light and shade are the great things."[77] Photography distills and enhances the essentials of form through contrast. Demonstrating the rival capacities of poetry, in Poem #465F Dickinson creates in a single tint, "Scarlet,"—or the more painterly word, "Vermillion"—a picture with no contrast, one that would be indiscernible if it were not written in words. Notably, the poem is in vivid color, an impossibility for photography in the time. "The name – of it – is 'Autumn'– " offers a visualization that could not be rendered in a visual medium:

> The name – of it – is "Autumn" –
> The hue – of it – is Blood –
> An Artery – opon the Hill –
> A Vein – along the Road –
>
> Great Globules – in the Alleys –
> And Oh, the Shower of Stain –
> When Winds – upset the Basin –
> And spill the Scarlet Rain –
>
> It sprinkles Bonnets – far below –
> It gathers ruddy Pools –
> Then eddies like a Rose – away –
> Opon Vermillion Wheels – [78]

As David Cody and others have noted, Dickinson suggests that looking at New England autumn serves as an occasion to think about the inconceivable scene in Maryland. The speaker puts "Autumn" in quotes, as if the season has been tainted, or as if she's not really describing the color of New England leaves; here, more explicitly than in Poem #355A, "Autumn" recalls "Antietam." Indeed, the metaphoric referent overwhelms the object it is supposed to describe. By the second stanza it has become nearly impossible to retrieve the concept of "Autumn" from the bloody images that are supposed to describe it; instead, it becomes a figure for mass slaughter. Writing red on red, the poem makes present and immediate the horror of battle via a conspicuously mediated, painterly treatment that also alludes to photography's limitations.

Dickinson both evokes and trumps the photographic capacity to record the scene by eliminating the need for contrast, and by introducing motion, or circulation; she underscores the magnitude of the carnage by dissolving wounded bodies into a bloodbath that rains down on the people at home. She thus implicates her reader in a way that photographs can only indicate. We look at photographs of the dead and "feel" death; but Dickinson's poem warns readers that the slaughter on the battlefront sprinkles, soaks, and floods the people at home; blood isn't only on their hands, it is on their bonnets and in their streets. The essence of war, especially total war, according to the poem, is not written in black and white, as Holmes suggests, but in blood. That essence was revealed at Antietam, and symbolically inscribed in Dickinson's poem.

Dickinson's poems and Holmes's essays can extend an understanding of the influence of images of the dead on the perception of the living. What a comparison of these two distinctive writers adds to the contemporary critical picture is a sense of the ways in which nineteenth-century viewers gathered and synthesized information from multiple sources: from the history of art, from technical study of photographic processes, from literary history, from newspaper reports about the war, etc.[79] While photographs clearly captivate their viewers—and a number of scholars have critiqued the ideological components of wartime photography for that reason—the viewers are not restricted to that moment of captivation.[80] Instead, poetry and other media forms help them to analyze the relation between that experience and the moments before and after the momentary paralysis. By looking at the paralytic moment, Dickinson foregrounds the way photography enables a common understanding of the experience of death. This understanding in turn offers limited insight into the awareness of mass suffering occurring at a distance, on the war fronts. Even while the photograph and the poem can only offer multiply mediated glimpses into a distant reality elsewhere, remaining aware of that relation is one of the few ways that people on the home front can keep from becoming completely disengaged from the realities of war, whatever they may be.

In his recent study of "the long Civil War," Cody Marrs stresses the way Dickinson insistently removes her war poems from specific referents to a time or place.[81] In doing so, he brings out a key aspect of Dickinson's poems more generally. They resist being located, placed in a specific circumstance, and a reader who wants to contextualize them must supplement the logic of the poem itself. Even to identify a poem as "about" the Civil War, indeed, does that.[82] Dickinson both deprives us of external referents and encourages us to identify them, via her varied metaphors, her suggestive ellipses, her countless allusions to things known and unknown. In turning to the war, I have suggested that the "vortex" word ("one of those terms that organize and abbreviate broad cultural contexts") "Autumn" as well as the dynamic configurations surrounding that term summon a field of associations in the popular print culture of the day, firmly locating Dickinson within a larger social project of developing a language of emotional and ethical response to mass suffering at a distance.[83] This is a response situated through the uses of poetic language, not through direct reference to a particular location. The response to war in Dickinson is indeed, as Marrs astutely suggests, "a radical annulment that eludes history itself."[84] It cancels time. That cancellation becomes meaningful in the movement that surrounds it, as a moment of paralyzed shock that other writers—Holmes in particular—try to capture as well.

Marrs identifies Dickinson as a "transbellum" writer who continues to treat the war via a range of tropes throughout the years: her literary response to the war "continues to unfold through the 1870s and 1880s."[85] Indeed, her harvest poems from what R. W. Franklin designates as a later period retain their associations both with mass death and mediated suffering, as if the spectral presence of war continued to haunt the figure of autumn. "A Field of Stubble – lying sere" succinctly describes a harvested field, shorn of its abundance.[86] While the subject is straightforward, the diction and metaphors raise questions about how the speaker processes the scene. The poem is replete with suggestive variants:

A Field of Stubble – lying sere
Beneath the second sun
It's toils to Brindled nations tost –
It's triumphs – to the Bin –

Accosted by a timid Bird
Irresolute of Alms –
Is often seen – but seldom felt
On our New England Farms

3 toils] corn – 3 People] nations 3 tost] cast – *thrust
4 triumphs – to] Pumpkin to – [87]

The figures of people and nations are weighty entities for pigs, hens, or chick-ens—brindled, corn-fed animals—to assume, and under the burden of the adjective/noun combination, people and nations start seeming moblike in gathering for what is thrown their way. "Brindled" suggests a people divided in viewpoint, or a mixed-race nation. The poem's open possibilities summon the idea of the Civil War, in which "triumphs" aren't gains, and in which a "Field of Stubble – lying sere" resembles a battlefield, with a ghastly harvest that is tost/cast/thrust to a nation insensitive of the cost. The "second sun" of Indian summer doubles as a figure for the mediation of war not by print or other media, but by time: the speaker suggests that harvested fields summon the specter of the ghastly harvest, but only for those few that "feel" what they see.

The figure of the ghastly harvest circulates widely through print media, forming a community of poets who respond to untimely death and environ-mental devastation by renovating a tradition of autumn poetry. Recognizing this common condition, of witnessing mass suffering remotely, the adap-tations show a persistent tendency to fuse individual emotional states with expressions of shared feeling.[88] Romantic interiority adapts to the necessity of putting the imagination in the service of reaction to collective tragedy; poets accept that feelings are imposed from without rather than generated from within. The pressure of events troubles poetic figures as well, so that literal and metaphorical registers are conflated and the tenor and vehicle become diffi-cult to distinguish. Though the poetry I have discussed shares these common tendencies, the responses are highly varied. While "popular" poetry is usually aggregated by critics to show a generic commonality of viewpoint, it is clear that what is shared is not ideological perspective, but an aesthetic reservoir of literary traditions and practices that can be used for various forms of political and apolitical expression by a range of the period's poets. Though they are not popular poets, and though their aims are perhaps more transtemporal or philosophical than the immediate goals of much popular poetic expression, Whitman, Piatt, and Dickinson nevertheless share the same materials as other writers and respond acutely to the expressive field surrounding them.

Chapter 3

"To Signalize the Hour"

Memorialization and the Massachusetts 54th

Memorialization, by definition, happens after the fact, but in the case of the Massachusetts 54th, the first regiment of black Northerners, the process started even before the assault on Fort Wagner in July 18, 1863, turned the soldiers and their white commander, Robert Gould Shaw, into enduring symbols of Union martyrdom for the cause of freedom and racial equality. In his April 1863 call to arms, "Why Should a Colored Man Enlist," Frederick Douglass specifies the need for black martyrdom: "When time's ample curtain shall fall upon our national tragedy . . . and history shall record the names of heroes and martyrs—who bravely answered the call of patriotism and Liberty . . . let it not be said that in the long list of glory, composed of men of all nations— there appears the name of no colored man."[1] Representation on "the long list of glory," Douglass insisted, was a precondition for the recognition of full African American equality: men had to die for "patriotism and Liberty" in order for others to gain it.[2] Through a rhetoric of prediction, Douglass memorializes the 54th in advance of the regiment's formation as part of building it, guaranteeing the replacement of defamation and degradation with gratitude, applause, and a permanent place in collective memory.

The soldiers' enlistment was freighted with freedom's destiny, especially in the abolitionist press, and there were proclamations long before the Battle of Fort Wagner that the men of the 54th would have to die to gain full equality for enslaved and free blacks alike. The regiment fulfilled that prediction in the battle, when many of the enlisted men died in the assault along with Colonel Shaw. The July 18, 1863, frontal assault on a heavily armed, thirty-foot-high Confederate fort on Morris Island was ill planned (by Brigadier General

Quincy Gillmore), but the soldiers of the 54th showed tremendous courage under fire: many of the soldiers reached the parapet and engaged in hand-to-hand combat with the Confederate soldiers before they were repulsed.[3] The symbolization of the soldiers after the devastating loss was nearly instantaneous, largely due to the rapid production and circulation of newspaper reports, editorials, and poems that celebrated the soldiers' bravery under fire. Popular images such as the Currier and Ives print (fig. 12) commonly depicted the moment when Shaw stood at the top of the fort, urging his men forward, with soldier William Carney holding the American flag aloft (he was the first African American soldier awarded the Medal of Honor for retaining the American flag throughout the fight, despite suffering four wounds). The regiment's courage was sanctified unwittingly by the Confederates, who buried Shaw face down in a mass grave with some of his men. The gesture was intended as an insult to punish Shaw's betrayal of his race, but his family's insistence on the justness of his resting place encouraged the abolitionist press to translate the Confederate act of degradation into a sign of martyrdom.

This iconography was carried into the twentieth century via Augustus Saint-Gaudens's memorial to Shaw and his troops on the Boston Common: it is an equestrian frieze, with Shaw astride his horse, looking purposefully to the south, riding among his men. The monument, in turn, has inspired a number of poems, most memorably Robert Lowell's stunningly cynical "For the Union Dead" (1960), a musical composition by Charles Ives (1929),[4] and the film *Glory* (1989), starring Matthew Broderick, Denzel Washington, and Cary Elwes. Like the monument, these commemorations elevate Shaw's sacrifice above that of his men, who are represented as a dark collectivity following in the wake of their enlightened and courageous white leader. But this narrow, if predictable, end point, where a white man stands in for and all but replaces black agency, in no way represents the varied, sometimes boisterous and irreverent songs and tributes to the 54th initiated by the Emancipation Proclamation's call for black soldiers. Nor does it indicate the multiple, conflicting perspectives expressed in poems published throughout the nineteenth century. Saint-Gaudens's more well-known memorial project commemorates the heroic sacrifices at the Battle of Fort Wagner, but it also erases the complexities of the history it marks; in Dana Luciano's formulation, the public monument refuses "to concede the ambivalence of the national past."[5]

This chapter explores poetry's varied powers of memorialization as they work during the war and then serve as a vehicle to carry the Massachusetts 54th's legacy through time. Because the regiment from its inception was so

Figure 12. "The gallant charge of the fifty fourth Massachusetts (colored) regiment. On
the Rebel works at Fort Wagner, Morris Island, near Charleston, July 18th 1863, and
death of Colonel Robt. G. Shaw." Color lithograph, Currier and Ives, 1863. Courtesy
of Library of Congress, Prints and Photographs Division, LC-DIG-ppmsca-35357.

heavily freighted with the promise of black equality and the hope of overcoming racial discrimination, poets struggled to represent this unprecedented
potentiality through their responses. An analysis of their poems can show us
both the limitations and resiliencies of poetic form under conditions of cultural transformation, the competing claims of idealization and historical complexity in commemorative traditions, and the competition, convergence, and
divergence of African American and Anglo-American traditions.

Two commemorative traditions distinguished by racial affiliations arise
from the mustering of the Massachusetts 54th; interestingly, they are also distinguished by the distinctly different genres they travel through. Most poets
either write songs for the soldiers of the 54th or sonnets and odes eulogizing
Robert Gould Shaw. The force of song was powerful during the Civil War,
fueled by a collaborative relationship between voice and print: songs became
poems, poems became songs, and writers anticipated and capitalized on these
crossover possibilities. Faith Barrett tells us that "popular song and poetry
became more closely connected" during the war, "and this mingling of oral
and textual forms of circulation lent to poetry the ideological flexibility of

song."[6] Songs and the printed poems associated with them are animated by the collective force of marching and singing soldiers, while the sonnet and the commemorative ode, in contrast, are associated with epitaphs, graves, and monuments to the dead. In part because of their allegiance with living bodies, the song-poems are imbued with contemporary political commentary, while the sonnets and odes turn events into legendary icons that stand in for historical and political complexity. While the initial production of poetry surrounding the formation of the Massachusetts 54th was highly varied, by the end of the century, one tradition—the tradition associated with memorialization—ascended at the expense of the other—associated with the living body—overshadowing the energetic and prolonged competition over how to "signalize the hour," in one poet's phrase.[7]

"Give Us a Flag": Songs of the Massachusetts 54th

As the regiment was being formed, abolitionist writers composed song-poems for the black volunteers that celebrated collective experience and common destiny. Douglass's calls for enlistment in the 54th serve as a starting point in tracing an unacknowledged literary tradition focused on the black soldiers rather than their white leader. These poems, many of them by African Americans and at least three by soldiers in the regiment, are critical of the processes by which black men were finally accepted into the Union army. The focus of critique is not Southern racial oppression—a straightforward if formidable enemy—but more insidious political and ideological forms of Northern disenfranchisement. The poems follow in the footsteps of Douglass's complex justifications for enlistment, which interweave criticism of Northern prejudice with an insistence on African American autonomy in defining the stakes and goals of fighting the war. Indeed, Douglass gives the war an alternative name: rather than the "Secessionist War," it is the "war for Emancipation."[8] Taking the occasion of the mustering of the 54th to argue for black enlistment more generally, Douglass offers several tightly argued reasons: to prove manhood to those who believed blacks were work animals; to force their countrymen's hand in a bid for full equality; to "prevent the country from drifting back into the whirlpool of proslavery Compromise at the end of the war"; and to gain the equality of all black people, enslaved and free.[9] Douglass emphasizes the imperfection and incompleteness of the status of black equality at the time of, and even within the terms of, the Emancipation Proclamation. Even so, he urges African Americans to seize the moment and transform promises into realities: the men must fight the war for their own reasons, changing the terms of national interests in the process.

Poems following in this tradition of critical engagement appear in Union abolitionist publications from the Emancipation Proclamation forward. Former slave Fanny Jackson's caustic and complex "The Black Volunteers," published on the front page of the *Anglo-African* in May 1863, expresses both rage at America's long history of racial injustice and hope for a different future shaped by the Emancipation Proclamation and the black volunteers (fig. 13). The association with song is clear from the first line, when the collective speaker hails marching soldiers with a call for celebration:

> We welcome, we welcome, our brave volunteers,
> Fling your caps to the breeze, boys, and give them three cheers;
> They have proven their valor by many a scar,
> But their god-like endurance has been nobler by far.
> Think ye not that their brave hearts grew sick with delay
> When the battle-cry summoned their neighbors away;
> When their offers were spurned and their voices unheeded.
> And grim Prejudice vaunted their aid was not needed.[10]

Though the poem was probably not meant to be sung—the rhetorical logic is overly dense—the skipping anapestic tetrameter in perfectly rhymed couplets encourage the reader to "sing" rather than simply read the poem. The idea of singing puts the poem in the field of collective voicing, as does the scenario Jackson evokes of a soldiers' parade in the midst of a crowd, with the speaker encouraging others to cheer the passing procession. The subject is a "we," not an "I" or a "he," calling for solidarity; onlookers and soldiers share the mission of convincing their white "neighbors" of black equality. There are a number of ways that the poem's publication draws attention to its status as an extension of the deployment of the Massachusetts 54th. The poem was published on May 2; a list of the recruits follows the poem, indicating that the poem celebrates the enlistment. On May 13 the regiment was mustered into service; and on May 28, the Massachusetts 54th marched south through Boston, gathering a large crowd, before it embarked to the South Carolina Sea Islands.[11] Jackson summons the celebratory scene of African American soldiers marching toward the theater of war in anticipation of their Boston parade.

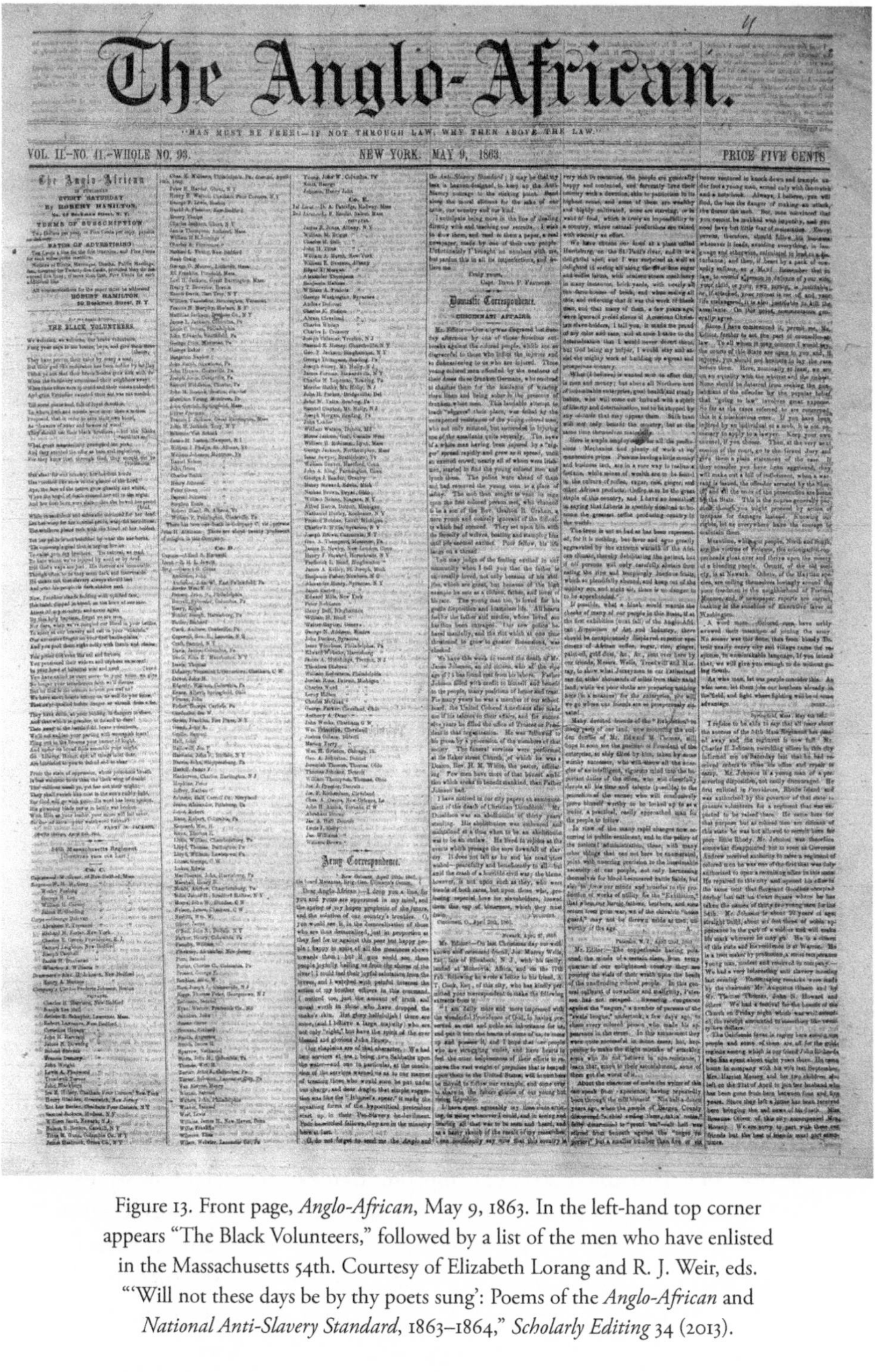
The Anglo-African.

"MAN MUST BE FREE!—IF NOT THROUGH LAW, WHY THEN ABOVE THE LAW."

VOL. II.—NO. 41.—WHOLE NO. 93. NEW YORK, MAY 9, 1863. PRICE FIVE CENTS

THE BLACK VOLUNTEERS.

54th Massachusetts Regiment.

Domestic Correspondence.

CINCINNATI AFFAIRS.

Army Correspondence.

Figure 13. Front page, *Anglo-African*, May 9, 1863. In the left-hand top corner appears "The Black Volunteers," followed by a list of the men who have enlisted in the Massachusetts 54th. Courtesy of Elizabeth Lorang and R. J. Weir, eds. "'Will not these days be by thy poets sung': Poems of the *Anglo-African* and *National Anti-Slavery Standard*, 1863–1864," *Scholarly Editing* 34 (2013).

The commemorative song tradition makes a point of noting hypocritical wartime political maneuvering, especially the refusal to allow blacks to enlist, sanctioned by Abraham Lincoln, which was only reversed when Union death tolls were mounting and more men were needed to fight. The catchy rhythm carries from the start both a celebration of the soldiers and an acknowledgement of the troubled history that brought African Americans to this moment. Even as the poem urges the soldiers onward, the speaker insists on noting Lincoln's earlier refusal to support black enlistment, as well as the broader "grim Prejudice" that underpinned his refusal.

Identifying a second violation of equality's ideal, Jackson suggests that whites want to reinscribe slavery within the army by enforcing a second class of soldiering for blacks, in which they serve their white comrades through physical labor. "Grim Prejudice" reigned,

> Till some pious soul full of loyal devotion,
> To whom flesh and muscle were more than a notion,
> Proposed, that in order to save their own blood,
> As "drawers of water and hewers of wood"
> They should use their black brothers;—but the blacks "couldn't see"
> What great magnanimity prompted the plea;
> And they scouted the offer as base and inglorious,
> For they knew that, through God, they would yet be victorious.

Jackson draws attention to the hypocrisy of the Emancipation Proclamation's motives: the deployment of black soldiers will save the blood of whites. The biblical phrase "drawers of water and hewers of wood" comes in the context of God condemning men to perpetual bondage.[12] Before the proclamation was issued, blacks were first used in a supporting labor capacity at Fortress Monroe, by Major General Benjamin F. Butler.[13] But even afterward black soldiers were often relegated to laboring behind the lines, while whites were assigned less degrading and physically arduous duties. After they had supposedly proved their manhood once and for all at the Battle of Fort Wagner, the Massachusetts 54th were assigned to dig ditches in the hot, swampy islands off the coast of Charleston; the bitter complaints of the men suggest how strongly they registered the insulting implications accompanying the tasks assigned them.[14] Jackson foregrounds the difference between white and black goals for black enlistment: "they" do not share her vision. Instead, she suggests, the "great magnanimity" is self-interest in disguise, fueled by entrenched racism.

Noah Webster's 1844 dictionary defines "scout" as "to sneer at; to treat with disdain and contempt."[15] The poem makes clear that black soldiers are aware of the imperfect conditions under which they have agreed to enlist. They do so anyway because they have decided it is the best way forward: "through God," not their country, the soldiers will win freedom and equality for their race.

Stressing the systemic and longstanding nature of institutionalized racism, Jackson indicates the possibility, as Douglass did, that blacks may be fighting for a country that will forget their contributions after the war and continue to treat them as second-class citizens:

> Now, Freedom stands holding with uplifted face,
> Her hand dipped in blood, on the brow of our race.
> Attest it! My country, and never again
> By this holy baptism forget we are *men*.
> Nor dare, when we've mingled our blood in your battles,
> To sneer at our bravery and call us your "chattels."
> Our ancestors fought on your first battle plains,
> And you paid them right nobly with insult and chains.

Through the voice of the black soldiers, Jackson reminds her country of the African Americans who fought in the Revolutionary War only to be "paid" with the continuation of slavery. She charges Northern whites to acknowledge their racism rather than congratulate themselves on their moral superiority.

Black soldiers spoke—and sang—on the same themes as Jackson, suggesting that the abolitionist community shared a common discursive field that emerged from reading abolitionist periodicals—such as the *National Anti-Slavery Standard*, the *Anglo-African*, and the *Liberator*—following the news, and critically observing the continued mistreatment of African Americans (fig. 14). Christian McWhirter notes that "The Fifty-Fourth Massachusetts was especially skilled at creating new versions of popular tunes."[16] One of the very first responses to the formation of the 54th was a song written by Private Frank Myers, published anonymously on the front page of the *Anglo-African* in June 1863. The epigraph explains that "the following song was written by a private in Co A 54th (colored) Regiment Massachusetts Volunteers and has been sent to us for publication by a friend of the regiment."[17]

"A Negro-Volunteer Song" catalogues the hypocrisies that preceded and informed the Emancipation Proclamation, which is so often cast as a noble, selfless act on the part of a visionary president:

Figure 14. Private Miles Moore, musician, carte de visite, circa 1863–1865. Photo. 103.37. 54th Massachusetts Volunteer Infantry Regiment carte de visite album. Visible image: 8.5 cm × 5 cm. Collection of the Massachusetts Historical Society.

> Fremont told them when the war it first begun,
> How to save the Union and the way it should be done
> But Kentucky swore so hard, and old Abe he had his fears,
> Till every hope was lost but the colored volunteers.[18]

The marching song carries a substantial burden of political information. John Charles Frémont took command of the Army of the West when the war broke out; in August 1861, he issued an edict to free the slaves in the divided state of Missouri in order to subdue Confederate opposition. This alarmed proslavery Unionists and threatened to undermine Lincoln's efforts to keep slave state Kentucky in the Union; for this reason Lincoln ordered his general to revoke the very sort of proclamation that he himself would make a year and a half later. Rather than occluding or erasing this cognitive dissonance, Myers foregrounds it, suggesting that it is possible to remember and evaluate the political contingencies and prejudices that permeate even the most enlightened moments of historical transformation, even while embracing their possibilities. That the men sang this song while preparing to fight for the government they critiqued offers a remarkable revision of the idea that fighting requires full, even "blind" commitment to an unalloyed patriotic ideal. The voiced ambivalence energizes the soldiers, who note their marginalized and precariously supported position even as they celebrate their fight to change it, consolidating their solidarity in the process.[19]

The song's refrain underscores the difference between the flag as it stands and the patriotic ideal the men are fighting for: while white soldiers may see the flag as representing their extant nation, "A Negro-Volunteer Song" asks for a flag that does not yet exist:

> O, give us a flag, all free without a slave,
> We'll fight to defend it as our Fathers did so brave,
> The gallant Comp'ny A will make the rebels dance,
> And we'll stand by the Union if we only have a chance.

The Emancipation Proclamation only freed the slaves in the Southern states; a "flag all free without a slave" is not the flag the men of the 54th are marching under. "O, give us" apostrophizes no one in particular, underscoring the difficulty of claiming a flag when so many dispersed social and political forces are against it. This is so even though black soldiers fought for an American flag during the Revolutionary War, only to have it taken away from them.

Again, the song draws on American democratic ideals while foregrounding their incomplete fulfillment rather than celebrating their existence.

The melodic scripting of "A Negro-Volunteer Song" is equally caustic in its criticism of Northern hypocrisies. The epigraph tells us that the words are to be sung to the "air" of "Hoist up the Flag," a popular Civil War song composed by Septimus Winner with lyrics by Billy Holmes, which sold as a broadside or in a longer, musically scored version.[20] Private Myers's version offers a rejoinder to the racist logic of the original. Here is the concluding stanza of "Hoist up the Flag":

> We'll fight for the Union, but just as it was,
> Nor care what secesh or Abe-o-lition does,
> We'll stand by the flag, the sword and the gun,
> To save from dishonor the land of Washington.[21]

In Holmes's version, white Union soldiers agree to fight in spite of, rather than for, "Abe-o-lition," which is just as bad as the "secesh" (a slang term for secessionists). They fight simply to avert the national dishonor of losing. In "Hoist up the Flag," validating white manhood is one of the primary stakes of the war. By singing Myers's revision, the men of the 54th challenged the exclusionary rhetoric and claimed black manhood. That the recognition of their comrades' racism fuels their march rather than halts it is evidence of the regiment's common conviction that they must be the agents of their destiny in spite of resistance from both sections.[22]

Myers was mustered out of the regiment because of a wound; a year later he republished his song in the *Anglo-African* after substantially rewriting it into a more literary song-poem hybrid. The title reflects the change: "A Negro-Volunteer Song" becomes "The Colored Volunteer."[23] The direction to sing to the "air—'Hoist Up the Flag'" has disappeared.[24] Rather than repeating after each verse, the "chorus" has become a stanza, heavily rewritten in more elevated diction. Myers adds additional stanzas with a recognizably "poetic" style that recount the story of the "gallant Fifty-fourth, roused by freedom's battle cry." At the same time, the poem retains full verses of the song. Even within the song verses, however, colloquialisms like the offensive command attributed to Major General George McClellan—"Keep back the niggers"— are rephrased; now he says "'Keep back the negroes, and the Union we will save.'"[25] While "song" persists in a significant residual form that recalls the earlier incarnation—a quality that Faith Barrett terms a "pentimento effect"—the revision also insists on the status of the new work as poetry on the page.[26] Now a veteran, Myers recasts himself as a poet while nevertheless retaining his status as songwriter and soldier of the 54th.

The transformation is significant and signals a partial shift from anticipation to retrospect, from preparation for battle to memorialization of courage. Myers adds three additional stanzas, two of which recount the battle he witnessed and participated in:

> Forth, with the flaunt of banners, and the drum's inspiring sound,
> We swept his treacherous hordes from freedom's holy ground.
> There were brave hearts among us, and we sent them to the rear;
> So that's why they hate us, the Colored Volunteer.
>
> The gallant Fifty-fourth! They're fearless and they're bold;
> May their courage never fail, and their ardor ne'er grow cold.
> Then rally round the flag for to us it is most dear,
> Bright stars of liberty to each Colored Volunteer.

In the first version Myers identified his song with Company A; now he broadens the identification so that he speaks for the entire Massachusetts 54th, marking their solidarity under fire; likewise, the "colored volunteers" of the first song are now the proper noun "Colored Volunteer," consolidated into a single, named entity. The poem is markedly less critical of the United States than its predecessor; the enemy is now the Confederacy, not the Union: "they" that "hate us" are the Confederate soldiers driven to the rear. The flag, which didn't belong to the volunteers in the earlier song, is now "most dear," and its stars bequeath "liberty to each Colored Volunteer." And now, in the final stanza, "The train is moving slowly on, never mind the past." Myers celebrates the country he had criticized heavily in the earlier version and expresses optimism about the future.

Myers's poem insists that the forceful spirit of the 54th did not abate, even after the Battle of Fort Wagner in which almost half of the enlisted men were killed, wounded, or missing. Though he commemorates the battle, the poem doesn't stop to mourn or even mention the dead. Instead he wishes the living soldiers Godspeed in future battles: "May their courage never fail, and their ardor ne'er grow cold." A song written after the battle, "The Fifty-Fourth Mass.," "Composed and Sung by Corporal Jos. A. Hall and Geo. Parker," as the manuscript, held by the Massachusetts Historical Society, proudly proclaims beneath the title, maintains the boisterous, critical tone of Myers's earlier "A Negro-Volunteer Song." The song absorbs the battle into its rhetoric to insist that white skepticism must now be solidly displaced by an incontrovertible example of black heroism. Like Jackson's poem and Myers's song, the first verse of "The Fifty-Fourth Mass." reminds listeners of the early part of the war when African Americans were not allowed to enlist. The song also distinctly echoes Myers's song in the stanzaic structure, iambic septameter four-line stanzas and return to the phrase "Colored Volunteer[s]" at the end of each stanza. The sharing of forms and phrases demonstrates a community held together by poetic repetition and variation, supported by periodical circulation:

> In sixty-one this War began, they 'listed far and near,
> But never would consent to take the Colored Volunteer,
> But since that time, how things have changed, their feelings
>   have drawn near
> So lately there has been a call for Colored Volunteers.[27]

The song moves quickly away from the time when all kinds of people "'listed," but "they" wouldn't "take the Colored Volunteer." In point of contrast to the collective white prejudice noted in the first verse, the following verses briskly commemorate the heroic support of the regiment's white officers, including Captain Luis Emilio of the 54th, who kept a copy of the song, which is among his papers at the Massachusetts Historical Society (my transcription of the song follows this manuscript, which is the only copy I have located):

> 2 There's Gov Andrew, our best friend, has labored for three years
>   At last he got the word to raise the Colored Volunteers.

> 3 God bless the name of Col Shaw, he fought without a fear
>   He led the van on Wagner with his Colored Volunteers.

> 4 Our Major was as brave a man, as you'd find far or near,
>   How gallant was he in "the Charge" with the Colored Volunteers.

> 5 Captain Emilio, we have not forgot, he bravely gave the cheers
>   Cried "now's the time to gain the name of Colored Volunteers."

6 The Copperheads way in the North no doubt would like to hear
   That every one of us are dead, in the Colored Volunteers.

7 To the fallen of our Regiment, we here will drop a tear,
   They were the "the bravest of the brave" those Colored
   Volunteers.

8 That we are of the Fifty Fourth, to you it will appear
   We both belong to Company "E" of the Colored Volunteers

In terse iambic septameter couplets (a modified form of the 4343 ballad), the song charts the history of the battle via the support provided by white leaders. It begins by acknowledging Massachusetts governor John Andrews's support for the regiment (though he wouldn't support the commissioning of black officers because he believed it was too controversial[28]) and moves through Shaw's charge on Fort Wagner to Captain Emilio's assumption of the regiment's leadership after all the other officers were killed or wounded. The courageous actions of these white individuals are contrasted pointedly with the mass of "Copperheads way in the North" who "no doubt would like to hear / That every one of us are dead, in the Colored Volunteers." This blunt comment is made even more devastating because many in the regiment had been killed in the battle, an indication that "wishing they were dead" is not simply an exaggerated turn of phrase. A tribute to the fallen of the 54th is offered in the penultimate stanza, but the quite animated voices of the authors and their fellow soldiers in Company E proudly conclude the poem.

After the Battle of Fort Wagner, the poem-song tradition persists in a more explicitly commemorative, elegiac mode. Frances Ellen Watkins Harper's "The Massachusetts Fifty-Fourth," published in the *Anglo-African* in October 1863, is one of the few poems published after the battle that remains focused solely on the heroism of the enlisted men; the poem doesn't mention Shaw.[29] The ballad meter aligns the poem with the animated collectivity of soldiers' marching songs, as does Harper's depiction of the men in action, assaulting the fort under heavy fire. But the emphasis on motion is counterbalanced by the stilling effects of a commemorative impulse:

Where storms of death were sweeping,
Wildly through the darkened sky,

Stood the bold but fated column,
Brave to do, to dare, and die.

With cheeks that knew no blanching,
And brows that would not pale
Where the bloody rain fell thickest
Mingled with the fiery hail.

Bearers of a high commission
To break each brother's chain;
With hearts aglow for freedom,
They bore the toil and pain.

And onward pressed though shot and shell
Swept fiercely round their path;
While batteries hissed with tongues of flame,
And bayonets flashed with wrath.

The first three stanzas freeze the men, who "stood," "bold and fated," while "storms of death were sweeping round them": strangely motionless under fire, the incongruency creates a visual imprint of a historically significant moment. Consolidating Douglass's anticipatory commemoration of the soldiers discussed earlier in the chapter, Harper monumentalizes the men as "bearers of a high commission" at the moment before their deaths. The insistence on the men's darkness—there is "no blanching"—not only stresses African American courage, it also offers a living image for future recollection. The statuary quality is counterbalanced in the fourth stanza, where the men finally rush forward through bullets and bayonets.

The poem balances iconic pictures of the living and the dead: after a single action-packed stanza, Harper returns to a description of stillness, this time among the fallen men. Here the poem's labor is intensively devoted to the work of commemoration:

Oh! not in vain those heroes fell,
Amid those hours of fearful strife;
Each dying heart poured out a balm
To heal the wounded nation's life.

And from the soil drenched with their blood,
The fairest flowers of peace shall bloom;
And history cull rich laurels there,
To deck each martyr hero's tomb.

And ages yet uncrossed with life,
As sacred urns, do hold each mound
Where sleep the loyal, true, and brave
In freedom's consecrated ground.

In a strangely circular process, laurels grow out of the men's own blood, commemorating their sacrifice even before they are "culled" to deck the tombs of the dead. Usually people, not personified history, deck men's tombs; the substitution suggests that Harper is uncertain whether the regiment's countrymen will honor the sacrifice. Insisting that the deaths not be forgotten, Harper piles commemorative images upon one another—the flowers, the laurel, the tomb, the urn, the mound. The insistence intimates a concern that in spite of her efforts, the men's deaths may not register indelibly in the country's history as they should.

Commemorating the Battle of Fort Wagner

While the commemorative song tradition persists after the Battle of Fort Wagner and at least up until the turn of the century,[30] a second tradition arose from that event that strains against the first. The burial of Shaw in a common grave with his men serves as the focal point for at least nine poems—and certainly more—published between 1863 and 1865.[31] While the song tradition stresses the collective force and agency of the enlisted men and rarely mentions the regiment's commanding officers, this predominantly Anglo-American tradition routinely elevates Shaw at the cost of his men, seeking to resurrect him from his place among a black collective, as if it were inconceivable that his body remain in a common grave, even as the poems insist on the righteousness of his resting place. The poems may honor all the men, but they usually create a two-tiered martyrdom, where Shaw is the central figure against a backdrop of common bravery. In contradistinction to song, these tributes assume more elevated forms—usually the sonnet or the blank verse elegiac ode—suited to eulogizing a heroic leader. They are published in the same abolitionist journals as the songs, and they share the same mixed-race readership.

But while this tradition consolidates sufficiently to persist into the twentieth century in a stable, recognizable form, a few exceptional poems centering on the burial from 1863 to the end of the war struggle to find a way to recognize both the heroism of the black regiment's fight for freedom and the leadership and heroism of Robert Gould Shaw, the "blue-eyed child of fortune," as William James later called him.[32] For some, the unprecedented collaboration of blacks and whites in the Massachusetts 54th at the Battle of Fort Wagner demanded a change in outlook, which in turn required experiments with poetic convention. Shaw's struggles with his own racism are clearly documented in his letters.[33] His growing admiration for his troops paralleled their increasing trust in him, evident in the reportage from the front by gifted African American soldier-journalist George Stephens who, writing about the Battle of Fort Wagner, said that "Colonel Shaw, our noble and lamented commander, was the bravest of the brave."[34] By the time the men fought at Fort Wagner they were a team, determined to prove black manhood under fire. The poems published after the tragic loss indicate that those observing the unfolding story had difficulty figuring out how to commemorate such a novel partnership. They struggled to credit both the valor of the enlisted men and that of their white leader, and those that managed gracefully were the exception. Registering the less common approaches to the subject are crucial, because they testify to the imaginative responses offered by individual poets who worked to adapt popular forms and conventions to a new situation. The poems that seek to convey a message of equality as well as solidarity in commemoration show that the terms of the "Shaw tradition" were not inevitable. Other forms of representation were possible, even if, given the complexity and awkwardness of the poems that take on this task—it may have been impossible that they become popular.

A. H. Hoyt, an unidentified author who published his "Storming of Fort Wagner" in the *Anglo-African* less than a month after the battle, identifies the representational challenges neatly in his insistence upon overcoming "clanish lines."[35] At the outset, however, the poem chooses the wrong metaphors for the task it stipulates, suggesting the difficulty of the representational challenge:

> Oh, speak not in this hour of grief
> Of clanish [*sic*] lines the selfish see,
> The horse who nobly bears his chief

Deserves the meed of chivalry;
So Africa, land of the sun,
Asks for the honor she has won.

Reprimanding those who enforce distinctions between white and black communities, the poet goes on to do just that, illustrating his point with an image of Shaw astride a horse, which in the metaphor is the Massachusetts 54th; the soldiers are further estranged from their humanity in the metonymic identification with "Africa, land of the sun." The next parallelism celebrates the accomplishments of the "chiefs," but those they "led" are strangely elided:

Hail to the chiefs! Who nobly led
Amid of arms the lurid flash,

That the denigration is unintentional is evident not only from the first two lines of the stanza, but also from the epigraph, which insists on the equality of the enlisted men with their leaders: "The colored regiment under Col. Shaw led the attack with the most determined spirit. A large number of its men fell with its leader."

The poem goes on to offer formulations that more successfully balance the bravery of Shaw and his men:

And hail the brave! Whose cold clay bed
Lies in the tide where billows dash . . .

Shaw and his men who share a common grave are joined in the single word "brave." Even more powerfully equalizing is the figure of God's list:

Hail to the names on that high scroll,
Imperishable of deathless fame!
Where every man that hath a soul
Shall boldly dare to write his name
As witness that no craven brand
Shall mark the brave of Afric's land.

The image of a deathless scroll recalls Douglass's "long list of glory," cited as a reason and incentive for black enlistment. This poem insists that the names of all men in the 54th appear there and moreover proclaims, rather oddly, that the names will be cosigned by "every man that hath a soul." The list within a list serves as a contract that prevents the feared reversion back to disenfranchisement: all men attesting before God to the bravery of the 54th will prevent the retrograde motion. But it seems that the names of the African American soldiers do not carry sufficient testimonial weight to stand alone.

A strange yet powerful poem by popular war poet Henry Howard Brownell demonstrates through its radical unsettling the inventiveness required for creating an image of solidarity and equality among the soldiers and their leader. Brownell served for a time under Admiral David Farragut; he gained fame and the status of a Civil War poet laureate when he published his versified rendition of Farragut's orders to his men (I discuss his work further in Chapter 5).[36] His poetry, difficult and dense, relies on ragged verse forms with disruptive rhythms and rhyme schemes, in part to dramatize the ways that the war challenges poetry to adapt to new conditions. In "Bury Them," published in the *Anglo-African* in February 1864, Brownell summons the men of the 54th who died and were buried in the sands of Morris Island around Fort Wagner by Confederate soldiers, in graves that were often uncovered again by the waves. The title recalls but does not complete the phrase "Bury him with his niggers," which was said to have been uttered by Confederate commander John Hagood when instructing his men to bury Shaw in a mass grave with his men.[37]

With violent force, Brownell's astonishing speaker assumes the place of the Confederate commander, demanding that the burial take place. The poem is spoken in the voice of the commander, but the oddness of the figurative language also unsettles that possibility and suggests to the reader that a more complex ventriloquism is being performed, and that the voicing may be intensely ironic:

> Bury the Dragon's teeth!
> Bury them deep and dark!
> The incisors swart and stark,
> The molars heavy and dark—
> And the one white fang underneath![38]

In a jagged trimeter composed of trochees, anapests, and iambs with no definite rhyme scheme, the speaker depicts the regiment as an ancient monstrosity, one that should be buried for good in the depths of the earth. In this image of a carnivore's teeth, Brownell evokes the army's coordinated destructive force in wartime. The image is both concise and surreal. Like a dentist, Brownell offers the technical names of teeth determined by their functions: incisors bite and tear, molars grind and chew. The "one white fang" makes the collection bestial and predatory and adds killing to its functions. That the fang is singular is the first sign of surreality in the poem: fangs, even in the mythical dragon's mouth, are a matched set. Also difficult to fathom is the blackness of the other teeth: no animal, real or legendary, has black teeth, especially if it also has a single white fang. The suggestion is that the soldiers were black to the bone. The monstrous image dehumanizes and demonizes the Massachusetts 54th and its leader, as if mixing colors had generated something inconceivably horrible.

In the long and intricate poem that follows, however, it becomes clear that Brownell is working from the Greek myth of Cadmus, whose men were killed by a dragon, which Cadmus then killed in turn. Athena instructed him to plant the dragon's teeth in the ground, from which sprung a race of fierce, armed men, some of whom helped Cadmus build the city of Thebes.[39] Brownell reconfigures the myth to intimate the ways that the Battle of Fort Wagner advanced American equality. We learn that the monster's name is Freedom and that this is what so enrages the Confederate speaker:

> Trample them, clod by clod,
> Stamp them in dust amain!
> The cuspids, cruent and red
> That the Monster, Freedom shed
> On the sacred, strong Slave sod—
> They never shall rise again!

The stamping and trampling is mimicked in the three-beat accentual meter and the monosyllabic masculine end rhymes. The initial image of burying teeth becomes even more grotesquely graphic in these lines: pounding bloody red teeth into the soil evokes a perverse form of burial where the violence of battle doesn't end with the annihilation of life. The speaker insists that freedom's opposite, slavery, will "stamp" the bodies down so thoroughly that free black people "never shall rise again." The voice of Confederate rage is most fully realized in its expression of a fervent wish to erase once and for all not only the Massachusetts 54th in its entirety, but all it stands for.

At this dismal point the poem takes an abrupt turn, rooted in the myth of Cadmus. The dragon's medieval power is reconfigured and magnified in the force of myriad steel weapons growing out of the soil and shocking the Confederate speaker:

> A crop of steel, on our oath!
> How the burnished stamen glance!—
> Spike, and anther, and blade
> How they burst from the bloody shade,
> And spindle to spear and lance!

Echoing the teeth, the "crop of steel" is both plantlike and technoindustrial, caricaturing and supplanting the georgic ideals of the South. Brownell is just as clinical in his description of the surreal botany-weaponry hybrid as he is with the dragon's teeth. The "anther" is the part of the plant that makes the pollen; the "blade" is the broad part of the leaf as well as the sharp side of a knife or sword. "Spike" is the term for flowers arranged singly along a stalk; it is also a poetic term for corn stalks, ubiquitous in southern poetry of the time; and it summons the point of a bayonet. The amassing of Union weaponry that grows from "the strong slave sod" supplants the agricultural ideals of Southern wartime poetry. Now "there are tassels of blood red maize— / How the horrible harvest grows!" Brownell celebrates the ascendance of the industrial North, whose production of steel weapons during the war far outstripped the resources and capacities of weapon making in the South.

The myriad weapons emerging from the soil are followed by the men who carry them, a thousand for every "one that we buried there." In this rebirth, Shaw has fully fused with his regiment:

> Ever, by door-stone and hearth,
> They break from the angry earth—
> And out of the crimson sand,
> Where the cold white Fang was laid,
> Rises a terrible Shade,
> The wrath of a sleepless Brand!

The "cold white Fang" no longer exists as a separate entity; Shaw and his men arise transformed into a single, yet multiple "terrible Shade" that breaks from the earth not only on the sands of Morrison beach, but from "doorstones and hearths" all over the South, destroying the domestic tranquility of civilians who supported and relied on slave labor. "Brand" carries multiple overlaid meanings. The branding of slaves is reconfigured into the image of a wrathful conflagration carried out by African American Shades but sanctioned by God's lightning. At the end of the poem the Confederate speaker finally sees that he fights not just against men; he is "fighting against Great God" and will surely lose. Brownell's extraordinary experiment in equal commemoration, wrought to inspire further action rather than elegiac sorrow, indicates the importance of noting the singularity of "popular" productions by unknown or little-known authors, rather than offering generalized conclusions about conventional norms. Brownell's poems were some of the most well known and popular of the war; many are also highly experimental. He continues to merit attention.

The Shaw Tradition

While the poems by Hoyt and Brownell seek a way to commemorate Shaw and his troops without subordinating one to the other and even to unify them in a single, biracial force, most other poems of the period choose between the two. Unlike Harper's poem, which imagines the burial of the enlisted men without the accompanying figure of Shaw, most of the poems commemorating the Battle of Fort Wagner routinely elevate Shaw at the cost of his men. Elizabeth Sedgwick's rhetorical strategies in "'Buried with His Niggers,'" published in *The National Anti-Slavery Standard* in 1863, are typical; Sedgwick takes as the title of her poem the rumored quotation of Fort Wagner's commander. In doing so, she replicates the racism she protests even as she ironizes it; she repeats the epithet that Brownell alludes to but omits. She honors all the men, but creates a two-tiered martyrdom where Shaw is the central figure against a backdrop of common bravery:

> Buried with the men God gave him,
> Those whom he was sent to save;
> Buried with the martyred heroes,
> He has found an honored grave.
>
> Buried where his dust so precious
> Makes the soil a hallowed spot;
> Buried where, by Christian patriot,
> He shall never be forgot.[40]

Shaw is the Christ figure, "sent to save" his African American soldiers. While
he is "honored" by his place among them, it is his "dust" that "makes the soil
a hallowed spot" and his burial that makes him unforgettable "by Christian
patriot." The sacrifice and suffering of the enlisted men fades into the background as Shaw becomes the central figure. Elizabeth Sedgwick was Catherine
Sedgwick's sister-in-law, a resident of Massachusetts, and an acquaintance of
Shaw, who called her "one of the most patriotic women I have ever seen"; the
regional and class-specific strain of commemoration emphasizes Shaw's bravery as a sign of civic duty suited to his social station.[41]

While Sedgwick's poem is affiliated with traditions of patriotic song,
many of the tributes to Shaw take more elevated forms suited to eulogizing
a heroic leader. A poem entitled "Colonel Shaw," published in the *Liberator*
and signed only "E. S." (perhaps Elizabeth Sedgwick?), is in blank verse with
elevated diction suited to the ode. The poem situates itself as having been
written "On hearing that the rebels had buried his body in a trench, under
a pile of twenty-five Negroes."[42] This poem resurrects Shaw at the cost of his
troops even in the epigraph, which may use more polite language than the
Confederate colonel, but nevertheless denigrates the enlisted men by figuring
them as "a pile" at the beginning of the poem. The rest of the poem is fully
centered on Shaw's heroic soul, which the speaker seeks to unearth and elevate
via apostrophe:

> O! young and sainted martyr, let them pile
> Whole hecatombs of dead upon thy ashes;
> They cannot bar God's angels from receiving
> Thy radiant spirit with divinest welcomes;
> They cannot cover from celestial eyes
> The sacrifice that bears thee close to Christ!

The men who share Shaw's grave are figured solely as obstacles to be overcome
by "celestial eyes" with supernatural vision that can penetrate even "hecatombs
of dead" to draw Shaw's "radiant spirit" to heaven. There is no mention of the
other men's spirits ascending; they are reduced to physical evidence of Shaw's
goodness. In this poem too the speaker locates Shaw's heroism locally, in Boston;
it captures the moment that Shaw marched through the streets with his troops:

> Did I not see thee on that day in spring
> Leading thy sable thousand through our streets?

Braving the scorn, and (what was worse) the pity
Of many backward hearts—yet cheered with bravos
From these who scanned the great significance
Of thy devoted daring—saw the crown
Behind the cross—behind the shame the glory—
Behind the imminent death the life immortal?

Deploying a logic of retrospective prospect shared by Harper and others, the speaker evokes the living Shaw only to emphasize his "imminent death." The embodiment of abolitionist righteousness, Shaw marches ahead of a "sable thousand" through the streets of Boston, validating not just a struggle for black equality, but the nation's redemption. The speaker has all but fully erased the African Americans who fought for freedom and equality by substituting the idealized purity of a democratic nation, purged of its sins.

A number of other poems, including the sonnet "To Robert Gould Shaw" published in The *Anglo-African* in October 1863, emphasize a set of similar figures and themes. This poem too summons the occasion of Shaw's burial "by South Carolinians under a pile of twenty-four Negroes" in the epigraph.[43] It too apostrophizes Shaw, "beneath the corpses hid of thy black braves"; in another version of the poem, the men become a "pyramid" under which the Egyptian king Shaw is entombed.[44] Here too, God summons Shaw, this time with a call: "come up higher." Again Shaw's resurrection is so certain it is unimpeded by the dead piled upon him; here too the ascendance of Shaw's men goes unremarked. The analysis of these representative poems indicates that the logic of this type of tribute is notably consistent, with few exceptions.

As with the tradition of song poems, the consistency suggests that a rhetorical field is consolidated through abolitionist print circulation. It indicates the ways that widespread circulation in the Northern press consolidates memorial conventions. Their iconography overwhelms the few more balanced tributes that work to validate the enlisted men's fight for their freedom. Poems in this "Shaw" tradition offer a stark contrast to the poem-song tradition, aligned with black soldiers' marching songs.

The Shaw tradition was carried through the end of the nineteenth century in distinguished writer and critic James Russell Lowell's "Memoriae Positum," a formal ode published in the *Atlantic Monthly* in January of 1864 that came to be considered the official commemoration of the event. Like Elizabeth Sedgwick, Lowell was a personal friend of the Shaw family; he wrote to Shaw's mother a few months before the poem was published: "I have been writing something about Robert, and if, after keeping a little while, it should turn out to be a poem, I shall print it; but not unless I think it some way worthy of what I feel, however far the best verse falls short of noble living and dying such as his."[45] Lowell's poem diminishes the presence of the soldiers of the Massachusetts 54th even more radically than most of the poems figuring the mass burial. In a ninety-line ode, Lowell doesn't once mention Shaw's men; nor does he describe the battle in any detail.[46] It is left to readers' memory of the event to know who was fighting with him and what "noble ends make dying sweet." Lowell depicts not Shaw's mass burial but the moment he was killed, in the most famous lines of the poem:

> Right in the van,
> On the red rampart's slippery swell,
> With heart that beat a charge, he fell
> Foeward, as fits a man;[47]

Even more extremely than in other odes and sonnets, Shaw's manhood swings free of history to become a more generalized image of dying nobly for a cause one believes in. Stephen Whitfield notes that "contemporary historians have classified such traits as the tradition of republican virtue."[48] Lowell's focus on the purity of Shaw's response to "Duty" erases the specificity of the cause he fought for and the men he fought with.[49]

The two poetic traditions I have delineated carry dramatically contrasting, racially coded commemorative logics, yet while the traditions are racialized, it cannot be said that they are completely separate, nor can they be distinguished entirely by the racial identity of the authors themselves—authors of both racial affiliations wrote in both traditions, and I will discuss some of these complex engagements.[50] The first plan for a Shaw memorial, for example, was developed by the surviving members of his regiment, in conjunction with another black regiment, the First South Carolina Volunteers, and the black citizens of Beaufort, South Carolina. They wanted to build a monument near Fort Wagner, but opposition by local whites and difficult terrain led to a cancellation of the plan: a school for freedmen in Charleston named after Shaw was founded instead.[51]

Soon after the Battle of Fort Wagner, two African American artists paid tribute to Shaw. Boston painter and abolitionist Edward Bannister contributed a portrait of Shaw to the Boston Colored Ladies Sanitary Commission's fair to raise money for black regiments in 1864 (the portrait is now lost); Boston sculptor Edmonia Lewis created a bust of Shaw in the same year. Marilyn Richardson notes that the "images of Bannister and Lewis brought considerable attention to the two black artists and served to further both of their careers."[52] It may well be that the popular power of the Shaw poetic tradition contributed both to the artists' interest in creating their works and to their warm reception. Richardson says that the artists recognized that "the possibilities of memorialization and historical immortality for the black men of the 54th were intrinsically bound up with the martyrdom of Shaw."[53] By themselves, she suggests, the black soldiers couldn't have registered in enduring public memory due to the racist logics of the time.

In a further twist of the cross-racial complexity of the tradition, both artworks inspired poems by white authors clearly aligned with the Shaw tradition; these poems responded not only to Shaw, but to African American depictions of his heroism. Though working in the same tradition, the poems posit radically different relations between the subject, the artist, and the poet. Boston Unitarian Martha Lowe's "The Picture of Colonel Shaw in Boston," published in the *Liberator* in 1864, was inspired by Bannister's painting, as the title clearly shows; yet the poem itself elides the painter's work and focuses on Shaw in the terms of the poems I have discussed earlier. The poem begins in a way that is by now familiar:

> Buried with his negroes in the trench!
> There he lies, a score of them around him;
> All the fires of bondage this shall quench;
> Could a monument so well have crowned him!
> Sight to make a father's bosom throb—
> There he stands upon a canvas glowing![54]

The resurrected Shaw bypasses the artist's craft simply to "stand upon a canvas glowing!" Just as Shaw's soldiers are reduced to "a score . . . around him," Bannister himself gets little credit for representing Shaw in a lifelike manner: Shaw is the source of his own animation. The poem cannot be said to be ekphrastic; instead it diminishes the art form to resurrect the man, in the process sidelining the African American artist's accomplishment.

A widely reprinted poem by another prominent Bostonian, Anna Quincy Waterston, offers a radically different use of inherited conventions; the poem sidesteps the recalcitrant logic reiterated in Lowe's poem in order to pay tribute to "Edmonia Lewis."[55] The artist's name titles the poem, and the epigraph identifies her as "The young colored woman who has successfully modeled the bust of Shaw." The poem acknowledges and praises the mediated representation: the sculpture offers "the mirror of her thought reflected clear," "a memory and a prophecy." Paying tribute to the transformative power of Lewis's art, Waterston "emphasized the artist and the artist's subject equally, championing the cause of that most improbable phenomenon—a young black woman aspiring to a career as a sculptor."[56] Expanding the circle of black accomplishment, Waterston finds a way to make the accomplishments of a black woman equal to Shaw's:

> . . . Neither power nor place
> Fashion or wealth, pride, custom, caste nor hue
> Can arrogantly claim what God doth lift
> Above these chances, and bestows on few.

Waterston refers directly here to Lewis's "genius," but aligns that genius with Shaw's inspired leadership. For Waterston, Lewis embodies and confirms the principles Shaw and his men fought for, and she carries them forward both through her representation of Shaw and her work as an artist. Waterston's poem, like Brownell's, demonstrates that while traditions can be recalcitrant and persistent, they can also be modified. The exceptions can reveal potentialities and possibilities that are elsewhere shut down.

A sign of poetry's power to carry commemorative logics across time, the tradition of Shaw's martyrdom crystallized in Augustus Saint-Gaudens's monument and the discourse surrounding the occasion of its unveiling, which brought back to public notice the events at Fort Wagner. Unveiled in 1897, the famous frieze on the Boston Common has become the iconic representation of this event (fig. 15). The commander dominates the scene, his horse in the foreground, his soldiers surrounding him on three sides. Though Shaw and his horse are highlighted against a black collectivity, however, the depictions of the enlisted men are not generalized or caricatured: the men are scrupulously delineated; it is said to be the first time a monument depicted African Americans realistically and not as stereotypes.[57] But while Saint-Gaudens meticulously worked from photographs to depict Shaw's likeness, he hired black men to pose for him in his studio, rather than working from the many photographs of the regiment men that were available—he was more interested in figuring a range of types than the soldiers of the 54th.[58]

Figure 15. Augustus Saint-Gaudens, sculptor, Shaw Memorial, Boston Common, Boston, Massachusetts. Between 1900 and 1915. Photograph. Detroit Publishing Co. Courtesy of the Library of Congress LC-D4-90157.

In the same retrospective prospect that marks many of the earlier tributes, Shaw and his men march southward, leaning forward toward the battle that will take many of their lives. The Massachusetts 54th marched through Boston in May 1863 before it left for South Carolina. In the first black history of the Civil War, published in 1867, William Wells Brown depicts the scene: "The Regiment marched down State Street to the tune of 'John Brown' and was vociferously cheered by the vast crowds that covered the sidewalks and filled the windows."[59] Saint-Gaudens had been at one of those windows, and he talked about how the scene imprinted itself on his memory. Saint-Gaudens would have been fifteen when the 54th marched by his window, and he memorialized this moment in a monument to living energies surging toward the moment of sacrificial death. He describes his experience of déjà vu on the day of the monument's unveiling, when the black veterans marched in front of the monument and saluted their representation: "The impression of those old soldiers, passing the very spot where they left for the war so many years before, thrills me even as I write these words. They faced and saluted the relief, with the music playing 'John Brown's Body,' a recall of what I had heard and seen thirty years before from my cameo-cutter's window."[60] In a stunning formulation, Saint-Gaudens summons two sets of the same marching soldiers more than thirty years apart; the second group salutes the image of its earlier self, which is more symbolically whole than their living, partial presence. Not incidentally, a marching song animates both scenes, superimposing the two moments: "John Brown's Body" figures prominently in descriptions of both events. The doubling of the soldiers draws attention not only to the war's decimation of youthful wholeness, but also to Shaw's absent singularity, which cannot be duplicated.

The day after the unveiling there were dedicatory speeches at the Boston Music Hall; Harvard philosopher William James delivered the primary oration, in which he plumbed the significance of the frieze.[61] James momentarily returns the regiment to life through his use of the present tense and his rhetorical gesture of pointing to the statue as if he were pointing to the May 1863 procession: "There they march, warm-blooded champions of a better day for man. There on horseback, among them, in his very habit as he lived, sits the blue-eyed child of fortune, upon whose happy youth every divinity had smiled. Onward they move together, a single resolution kindled in their eyes, and animating their otherwise so different frames. The bronze that makes their memory eternal betrays the very soul and secret of those awful years."[62] The animating power of art brings a symbolic life to the statue that contrasts with and overshadows the living veterans on stage. It is "a single resolution" breathing through "otherwise so different frames." The monument reveals the unconscious reality of the animating spirit of the regiment.

James, along with the monument he commemorates, creates the sense of inevitability that he claims to describe: the "blue-eyed child of fortune" rides among—but also above and before—the dark collectivity of "warm-blooded champions of a better day." Again Shaw's privileged white manhood stands in synechdochal relation to a black collectivity: the many become the righteous one. That one is a white officer: not a common man, but a Boston Brahmin. Shaw fights not for his own freedom, but for the freedom of others. That abstracted notion of duty and moral self-sacrifice—republican virtue—is at the center of the memorial. It is notable that while the survivors of the regiment marched during the unveiling, and a number of veterans sat on the stage during the speeches, not a single black veteran spoke, though Sergeant William Carney, the first black soldier to win the Medal of Honor for carrying the regimental flag during the assault, was on the stage. Booker T. Washington gave a short concluding speech.

The monument carries the commemorative weight of the historical event unevenly, a topic explored in a number of critical discussions that arrive at a range of conclusions.[63] Interpretations range from exposure of unalloyed racism (Albert Boime) to explications of an unprecedented depiction of hopes for racial equality (David Blight, Kirk Savage). Certainly the Saint-Gaudens monument participates in the Shaw tradition I have traced. Only the names of the white officers were etched on the monument; the names of the African American soldiers were added in 1981, almost a century later. Though the formal title of the monument is *Memorial to Robert Gould Shaw and the Massachusetts 54th Regiment*, it is popularly known, and even listed on the National Park Service website, as *The Robert Gould Shaw Monument*, or simply the *Shaw Memorial*. In his memoir, Saint-Gaudens tells us that he originally had no intention of depicting the black soldiers. He had envisioned an equestrian statue with Shaw alone, but "the family objected on the ground that, although Shaw was of a noble type . . . still he had not been a great commander, and only men of the highest rank should be so honored. . . . Accordingly, in casting about for some manner of reconciling my desire with their ideas, I fell upon a plan of associating him directly with his troops in a bas-relief, and thereby reducing his importance."[64] In its "reduction," Shaw's importance only grows, his individualized humility and self-sacrifice set in dramatic contrast to the black collective he represents.

Through this logic of memorialization, the devastating loss at the Battle of Fort Wagner signifies the epitome of a fight for liberal ideals, coded as white. James sums up the idea, no longer through a gesture to the bronze soldiers marching, but through a direct address to the two groups of veterans Shaw fought with, one white and one black: "What we really need the poet's and orator's help to keep alive in us is not, then, the common and gregarious courage which Robert Shaw showed when he marched with you, men of the Seventh Regiment. It is that more lonely courage which he showed when he dropped his warm commission in the glorious Second to head your dubious fortunes, negroes of the Fifty-fourth."[65] James's primary point is that there are kinds of courage, some easier and more socially sanctioned than others;

Shaw's courage in leading the 54th was more difficult. He makes the point, however, at the expense of the men Shaw fought with by collapsing past and present: the "negroes" still have dubious fortunes in spite of the fact that they fought at Fort Wagner for the better future that the monument is supposed to be celebrating. Shaw stands with and for his men, but also for a surplus that is not simply the "courage" he shares with them. He embodies "what we really need the poet's and orator's help to keep alive": that "more lonely courage" of conviction. The soldiers themselves are emptied of moral agency, which then resides in Shaw alone in a distilled, noble, universal principle.

Poets and orators certainly did lend their help in this alchemic conversion. The passage from James Russell Lowell's "Memoriae Positum" discussed earlier emerges from the past to again commemorate the event in a different age, with the lines etched beneath the bronze image of Shaw and his men:

> RIGHT IN THE VAN ON THE RED RAMPART'S
>   SLIPPERY SWELL
> WITH HEART THAT BEAT A CHARGE HE FELL
> FOEWARD AS FITS A MAN:
> BUT THE HIGH SOUL BURNS ON TO LIGHT MEN'S FEET
> WHERE DEATH FOR NOBLE ENDS MAKES DYING
>   SWEET.[66]

Shaw's high soul departs from the embodied historical circumstances surrounding his death to become a beacon for mankind. Though his men are meticulously depicted in the frieze, the poetic epigraph renders the statue legible as a depiction of Shaw surrounded by incidental figures whose presence grounds a singular courage.

The historical elisions consolidated in the monument convey a sense of inevitability, as if the critical spirit of the earlier soldiers' songs and affiliated song-poems had been entirely erased from commemorative traditions. But a sign of the resiliency of the counter-strain emerges in a number of unexpected places, not least in the monument itself. For while Shaw certainly dominates the scene, Saint-Gaudens's incorporation of the black soldiers is unprecedented. The memorial is noted for its innovative structure: he elevated the frieze, which was usually on the base of European statues, by integrating it with the equestrian statue.[67] Kirk Savage explains that "it was the first monument in the nation to show African American soldiers in full uniform, and it was a uniquely artful solution to the whole problem of the war memorial—in effect synthesizing the great officer monument and the common soldier monument into one startlingly new depiction of a cohesive military unit."[68] The presence of the African American soldiers seemingly could not be diminished, in spite of Saint-Gaudens's reluctance to acknowledge them: "the negroes assumed far more importance than I had originally intended."[69] The result is a visual equivalent of an attempt to bring together the African American tradition of commemorative song—Saint-Gaudens noted his memory of the Massachusetts regiment singing "John Brown's Body," while marching through Boston—with the Anglo-American tradition of odes and sonnets to Shaw. The ongoing discussion and annotation of the statue continues to allow new interpretations of the monument to emerge. In response to Saint-Gaudens's decision to work from models rather than the actual likenesses of the men, for example, Sarah Greenough and Nancy K. Anderson have compiled the photographs of as many of the soldiers of the 54th as possible in a book entitled *Tell It with Pride: The 54th Regiment and Augustus Saint-Gaudens' Shaw Memorial.*[70]

Thomas Wentworth Higginson, Commander of the First South Carolina Colored Troops, the first black regiment to be mustered after the Emancipation Proclamation, identifies the logic of commemoration reiterated by Lowell and James, stressing its ubiquity and durability. In his essay on the history of African American soldiers during the war, included in a series of essays on the Saint-Gaudens monument, Higginson depicts Shaw as a monument even before he died. His formulation neatly encapsulates the temporal strangeness of the memorialization process surrounding Shaw and the 54th: "The attack on Fort Wagner, with the picturesque and gallant death of young Colonel Shaw, made a great impression on the North, and did more than anything else, perhaps, to convince the public that negro troops could fight well . . . in line of battle." Higginson imagines Shaw's death on the parapet of Fort Wagner as a scene composed for future admiration, "picturesque and gallant." But while noting the power of the image, he goes on to indicate the injustice of the way this specific picturesque event, with the stunning figure of the "blue-eyed child of fortune" leading his troops into an almost certain defeat, stands in for countless lesser-known and forgotten acts of bravery by African American soldiers and their white leaders: at the Battle of Olustee, Fort Pillow, and elsewhere. Higginson embeds the battle of Fort Wagner in this longer narrative, and he follows his depiction of the iconic event by noting flatly: "the early stages of a movement always call for more fullness of narration than later ones."[71] The comment calls for public attention to move beyond the easily apprehended image of Shaw leading the 54th into battle, and to take into account the broader history of African Americans' multiple and varied military contributions to the Union.

A Countertradition

Also writing at the turn of the century, Paul Laurence Dunbar extends Higginson's criticism. Composing a song-poem for "The Colored Soldiers" and a sonnet to "Robert Gould Shaw," Dunbar demonstrates a canny knowledge of both the history of black participation in the Civil War and of the bifurcated literary traditions emerging from it. Most scholars who have analyzed the commemorative tradition of the Massachusetts 54th have treated only the sonnet, inadvertently reiterating the logic of commemoration that elevates Shaw above his troops.[72] The focus derives from the way that the Saint-Gaudens memorial has come to serve as the means for understanding both the Battle of Fort Wagner and its earlier commemorative traditions. Published in *Lyrics of Lowly Life* in 1895, "The Colored Soldiers" precedes the unveiling of the monument by two years. The poem positions itself instead in relation to the earlier tradition of black soldier songs; the alternative focus may well be enabled by the fact that the Shaw memorial did not yet exist in the cultural imagination. The poem's ballad form, regular meter, simple phrasing, and rhetorical formulations link Dunbar's 1897 poem to the critical tradition of Civil War–era abolitionist song-poems. Like the works of Fanny Jackson, Private Myers, Frances Ellen Watkins Harper, and others, Dunbar reminds readers of unpleasant historical details that don't fit into a progressive narrative, particularly the refusal to accept black volunteers before the Emancipation Proclamation:

> In the early days you scorned them,
> And with many a flip and flout
> Said "These battles are the white man's,
> And the whites will fight them out."
> Up the hills you fought and faltered,
> In the vales you strove and bled,
> While your ears still heard the thunder
> Of the foes' advancing tread.[73]

The racist quotation indicates that Dunbar has studied the history of African Americans during the war. Though it surely echoes a range of responses to the idea of black soldiers joining the fight, it is more particularly a paraphrase of Ohio congressman Chilton A. White's well-known declaration: "This is a government of white men, made by white men for white men, to be administered, protected, defended, and maintained by white men."[74] Dunbar's shifting apostrophe moves readers' attention quickly away from the racist discourse of the naysayers to the courage of the black volunteers, curtailing the one and elevating the other. The remaining seven stanzas document the bravery of the men "in the thickest of the fray, / And where'er the fight was hottest." Like the songs it recalls, Dunbar's poem emphasizes the collective nature of the accomplishments, celebrating the bravery not only of the 54th regiment at Fort Wagner, but of all the black soldiers who fought in the war: he specifically notes the battles of Olustee, Wagner, and Fort Pillow, where Confederate soldiers targeted African Americans, killing them in much greater numbers than white Union soldiers.

In keeping with the critical tradition of black patriotic soldier songs, Dunbar celebrates the flag but calls attention to the unfulfilled promise of equality. Responding to earlier fears that attitudes of whites would backslide after the war, Dunbar confirms that the situation has indeed come about. He musters the courageous sacrifice of the volunteers not to celebrate equality but to mark its failure:

> They were comrades then and brothers,
> Are they more or less to-day?
> They were good to stop a bullet
> And to front the fearful fray.
> They were citizens and soldiers,
> When rebellion raised its head;
> And the traits that made them worthy,—
> Ah! those virtues are not dead.

By putting in the past tense the usually permanent condition of "comrades" "brothers," and "citizens," Dunbar creates a cognitive dissonance that results from a severe social disorder. He charges the United States for using men as cannon fodder. Though the soldiers' "virtues are not dead," Dunbar suggests they are being denied; he alludes to increasing institutionalization of black inequality in the 1890s, epitomized by the *Plessy v. Ferguson* decision the year before the poem was published.

The poem's apostrophe shifts again to address white readers, pointedly contrasting their shortcomings with his praise of black bravery; Dunbar charges them with hypocrisy and a lack of civic virtue by reminding them of the equal burden blacks shared during the war:

> They have shared your nightly vigils,
> They have shared your daily toil;
> And their blood with yours commingling
> Has enriched the Southern soil.
>
> They have slept and marched and suffered
> 'Neath the same dark skies as you,
> They have met as fierce a foeman,
> And have been as brave and true.

Though one might expect a call for political change to emerge from the caustic charges, Dunbar declines to issue one, dropping his apostrophic address in favor of blunt assertion. Giving up on convincing his white readers, he insists instead that regardless of the betrayal of the legacy of black soldiers, the men will nevertheless receive their due:

> And their deeds shall find a record
> In the registry of Fame;
> For their blood has cleansed completely
> Every blot of Slavery's shame.
>
> So all honor and all glory
> To those noble sons of Ham—
> The gallant colored soldiers
> Who fought for Uncle Sam!

Perhaps because it is inconceivable that the "registry of fame" will lie within the American national imagination, it remains unlocalized. This is compelling and tragic in part because it recalls the earlier optimism of the soldier songs, the boisterous call to "give us a flag, all free without a slave." Whether or not the nation claims them now, the soldiers fought for the idea of America, embodied here in "Uncle Sam." Concluding with a celebration of black agency rather than a call for white leadership, Dunbar's clear allegiance with an African American critical tradition shows that, though it is harder to find, that earlier legacy is not forgotten, and it continues to mobilize a more caustic criticism suited to the turn of the century.

Dunbar also responded to the Shaw tradition, demonstrating his awareness of the bifurcation of the two lines of commemorative response. Published three years after "The Colored Soldiers," in the *Atlantic Monthly*, Dunbar's "Robert Gould Shaw" contrasts neatly with the earlier poem-song. The sonnet participates in the discursive field surrounding the Saint-Gaudens monument. But the poem dramatically departs from that tradition in expressing a hopelessness akin to that expressed in "The Colored Soldiers," here even more all-encompassing and catastrophic:

> Why was it that the thunder voice of Fate
> Should call thee, studious, from the classic groves,
> Where calm-eyed Pallas with still footstep roves,
> And charge thee seek the turmoil of the state?
> What bade thee hear the voice and rise elate,
> Leave home and kindred and thy spicy loaves,
> To lead th' unlettered and despised droves
> To manhood's home and thunder at the gate?
>
> Far better the slow blaze of Learning's light,
> The cool and quiet of her dearer fane,
> Than this hot terror of a hopeless fight,
> This cold endurance of the final pain,—
> Since thou and those who with thee died for right
> Have died, the Present teaches, but in vain![75]

Dunbar offers a lamentation for wasted talent, portraying Shaw as one who sacrificed a scholarly and material comfort to join "a hopeless fight." While the image bears a tenuous relation to Shaw's biography—he attended Harvard briefly before dropping out—it nevertheless pits the life of the mind against national military engagement and finds the latter useless in this particular case. Dunbar curtails any description of courage under fire, reducing battle to the "hot terror of a hopeless fight." While the sonnet follows in the Shaw tradition by elevating Shaw to idealized heights of moral virtue, it does so to stress

in an unprecedented way the futility of his sacrifice. But the most remarkable innovation comes in the way Dunbar doubles the poem's speaker—the
African American poet—with Shaw. Shaw may not have been a scholar, but
Dunbar surely was; his poems attest to ample knowledge of American history, especially African American history, and of literary traditions, especially
poetic traditions. The image of light signifies poetic inspiration as well as intellectual pursuit. Pallas Athena is the goddess of war, wisdom, and the arts,
fields the poem holds in play. Dunbar offers a self-portrait that mirrors Shaw's
image; both engage in the same futile fight for "right," one by pen and one by
sword. This doubling suggests that the poem is not only about futility after
all, but about ethical commitment to a seemingly impossible cause.[76] Dunbar,
like Shaw, has committed to fighting for black equality, the "hot terror of a
hopeless fight," rather than, or perhaps in addition to, writing less politically
engaged, more intellectually removed poems in "the cool and quiet of her
dearer fane." He does so because he, like Shaw, continues to believe that the
fight itself is necessary whether it can be won or not.

Placing Dunbar's "The Colored Soldiers" alongside "Robert Gould Shaw"
offers an occasion to think about ways to consider the popular, the conventional, the elite, the formal, and the innovative in complex, dynamic relations.
Only when understanding that Dunbar allies his poetic practice with African
American soldier songs in some poems can we understand that the turn to the
sonnet is one of many conscious choices, and one that Dunbar knows bears
a historical significance in the context of the memorialization of the Battle of
Fort Wagner. As one of the few poets who has written in both traditions, Dunbar calls us to consider them in relation to one another, to compare the collective critical voicing of African American solidarity with the solitary figuration
of Shaw's futile sacrifice as a twin of Dunbar's writing practices, both displaced
from song's companionship. It is only by bringing together consideration of
song and sonnet that we can appreciate that Dunbar expresses solidarity with
Shaw in a way that also elevates his "popular" poetic endeavor of song. Dunbar
asks the reader to pull away from the sonnet form and feel estranged from it,
feel the limitations it imposes and the isolation it enacts—the sonnet distances
itself from the song, just as the song's solidarity repudiates the solitude of
the sonnet. Considering these two non-dialect poems that deeply engage the
ongoing problem of American race relations offers a way of parsing Dunbar's
poems along alternative lines to the familiar critical tendency to distinguish
between dialect and standard English poems.[77] Dunbar interjects his political
critique in a tradition of political sonnets that push against "the cool and quiet

of her dearer fane": William Wordsworth's "London 1802" or "To Toussaint L'Ouverture" similarly disrupt the sonnet's cool remove, its insistence on psychological interiorities and individual intimate relations. In doing so, Dunbar foregrounds the limitations of the sonnet form and of the Shaw tradition that it helped to carry. Tracing the Shaw tradition alone wouldn't allow us to see Dunbar's crosstraditional interventions, nor would it show us the longstanding cultural power of both of the traditions he engages.

Conclusion

Writers of both races affiliated themselves in complex ways with these two racialized traditions that arose from a single, unprecedented event. The formal configurations of each tradition are distinct and resilient; each enables some structures of affiliation while disabling others. The African American song-poems afford collective voicing of trenchant political criticism as well as the celebration of common convictions. The form's invocation of animated solidarity—singing together—enables collaborations and identifications that endure over time with the recollection of the wartime reality of marching, singing soldiers. Openly critical of racial injustice even in seemingly progressive, liberal political actions, these poems carry a historical awareness that has been neglected in favor of attending to the Shaw tradition.

Commemorations that focus on the figure of Shaw, in contrast, are carried in poetic forms long identified with the power to elevate individual accomplishment. The elegiac ode and the sonnet tend to assign special affective attachment to a lost loved one, who is singled out for individual praise and attention.[78] These forms are often understood to be poetry itself, while song, as a point of contrast, is assigned the ephemeral traits of embodied voice; popular songs of previous historical periods, it is assumed, belong to the "voices that are gone," the title of a study of nineteenth-century American song by Joel Finson.[79] But as we have seen, poets of the nineteenth century did not distinguish so strictly between song and poem. Song, they understood, is a genre that invokes voicing but doesn't have to be voiced; it carries the spectral presence of singing people across time and place, invoking them precisely where they are not and cannot be: at the breakfast table over the morning newspaper during the war, for example. With the increased attention to a broader understanding of the extensive and varied field of nineteenth-century American poetry, critics could be even more attentive to the politics of form—to the formal choices of nineteenth-century writers, and to those of contemporary critics. [80]

Considering these two commemorative traditions in their complex relations affirms Dana Luciano's claim that though "the postmodern countermonument might be a recent cultural development," nineteenth-century American writers were no strangers to both the "countermonumental *vision*— the assurance that past, present, and future are linked not in a single linear narrative but in an ever evolving array, and the countermonumental *impulse*— the demand for historical memory to work through this linkage without relying on amnesia or subscribing to a redemptionist teleology."[81] The song-poem tradition pushes against the amnesia of the commemorative sonnet and ode, and it opens to analysis the Shaw tradition's tenacious impulse to create a legible set of cultural ideals through a limiting mythology that is mistaken for history. Tracing the "ever-evolving array" of commemorative impulses asks that we resist monumental forms of idealization that cover up the nuances, complexities, accidents, and embarrassing moral failures that play a central role in even the most remarkable and positive social transformations. To leave that part out is to collude in a misrecognition of familiar stories as histories, of more familiar poetic forms as the most culturally significant ones . . . and of the most easily legible forms—the popular song—as the least innovative.

Chapter 4

Poetry Under Siege

Charleston Harbor's Talking Guns

In other chapters I have explored the ways that Northern poets have sought to respond sympathetically to remote suffering. But there are also antipathetic ways to imagine negotiating the distance between the home front and the battlefront. This chapter focuses on patriotic rage against the enemy as the animus for crossing the distance. Poets on both sides used their pens to join the fight. As James Dawes notes, "wars are born and sustained in rivers of language about what it means to serve the cause, to kill the enemy, and to die with dignity"; poetry in particular "was part of war's arsenal as surely as uniforms and training camps."[1] This was especially true for the Civil War, when poetry held such a central place in the circulation of print through mass media networks. The popular trope of the talking gun was one of the most extreme weapons in that arsenal: it conveyed the widespread fantasy that words could kill. The figure acknowledges the distance that separates people from the fighting, and it seeks to close the gap through a strongly willed imaginative act. In poems of the period, killing messages fly from weapons' mouths to their targets with deadly accuracy. In "The Gun," for example, the cannon urges its makers to finish up quickly and wheel it "Southward" so it can begin its mission of killing. Its speech is perfected when it can finally "talk" to the enemy:

> Ah! I see—quick with a shell
> In my throat—boom—there it goes,
> With a long-tailed, fiery yell,
> Right among the thickest foes.[2]

Here metaphor is collapsed as completely as possible: it speaks for itself without interference from the poet. The tenor is the desire to kill, and the vehicle is the material means of killing. The fervent hope is that the poem can turn into a literal gun. The impulse to physicalize the shell's trajectory is evident in the heavy trochaic tetrameter, with many other syllables that could count as heavy beats. This poem was published in *Harper's Weekly* on July 4, 1863, as if the gun were not just speaking for itself, but for the nation. The talking weapon perspicaciously distinguishes between "comrades' tears" and its own emotion:

> But for me is only joy—
> Iron joy at victory won;
> I was fashioned to destroy—
> Ho! I am the conquering gun.

The gun expresses only pleasure and happiness over killing the enemy and winning the battle. In these poems there is no room for personal, individualized feelings; the gun speaks state-sanctioned violence, and it is entirely one with the national mission.

In his groundbreaking study *On War*, Carl von Clausewitz insists that war is not a failure of political action, but an extension of it: it is "an instrument of policy." "A continuation of political intercourse by other means," fighting and killing carry out the ends of the state after linguistic negotiations fail. If war is "just another form of speech or writing," poetry can put itself in service to the state in order to give words to that other form of speech.[3] Talking-gun poems operate at the logical end of these forms of language dedicated to sustaining war. Positioned at a point beyond offering ideological justifications of violence, they have only one thing to say: they speak death to the enemy. Bent on the desire to kill, propelled by raw feeling, they take in their targets and will destruction. The carrier of these violent fantasies is a collapsed metaphor—speech is weaponized and weapons speak—so that there are usually two speakers in the poem: the poet and his instrument of destruction.

Focusing on the prolonged siege of Charleston, which took place over the last three years of the war, this chapter will explore the exchange of killing words that accompanied the military engagement.[4] The Union siege engaged both the forts around the harbor and the people of Charleston in one of the first incendiary bombings of a civilian population in wartime. In spite of their radically different circumstances, Northern poets at a distance and the Charleston poets under siege responded in kind, by sending poetic death wishes in the newspapers across a physically unbridgeable gap. During the siege those voices entered into a highly polarized exchange that is tautological and destructive of the value of human life. At the site of a major military engagement, Union and Confederate poetry forms an expressive system that helps us to understand the massive violence of which it was such an integral part. The chapter charts poetry's response to developing events in Charleston Harbor, tracing the intensification of violent language as the conflict builds, from the blockade, to attacks on the forts, to the direct bombing of Charleston. At the end of the chapter I turn to two poets who searched for ways to avoid the end game of killing words. They use poetry instead to seek ethical positions in the face of the violence surrounding them: Northern poet Herman Melville and Southern poet Henry Timrod; Timrod is known for his poems supportive of the Confederacy (which I discussed in Chapter 1), but his perspective on the war shifted radically as the war progressed, and I will chart this unusual shift throughout the chapter alongside the more entrenched Confederate poems.

"The Song of the Shell"

Charleston's intense symbolic significance made it an important focus for poets of both sides throughout the war. The first state to secede and nearly the last to surrender, South Carolina, and particularly Charleston and its harbor, held acute importance for both the Union and the Confederacy. Charleston was repeatedly identified by Northerners and Southerners alike as the "heart" or the "brain" of the Confederacy. A seaport and center of trade, Charleston was a hub for the domestic slave trade even after international trafficking had been abolished; it had the largest slave population of all the states at the start of the war. Many Northerners blamed Charleston for causing the war. For these reasons, it was a focal point for Union fantasies of revenge. The *New York Tribune* declared: "If there is any city deserving of holocaustic infamy, it is Charleston." And U.S. naval officer Gustavus Fox wrote to Rear Admiral Samuel Du Pont, "The fall of Charleston is the Fall of Satan's kingdom."[5]

As the Union blockade of Charleston's port intensified in the spring of 1862, the city's cosmopolitan self-identity shrank and became explicitly defensive. The sense of curtailment is evident in the poems Henry Timrod published in the *Charleston Mercury* about this time. In "Charleston," he addresses not the world, as he had in earlier poems, promoting enlistment in the Confederate cause, but the people of his city, who watch the Union ships on the horizon and wonder when there will be an attack. He celebrates international trade as a means of establishing the Confederacy as an ambassadorial nation among nations, but the Union ships constrain and circumscribe his vision. The international trade routes are centripetal, moving inward (the ships bound for Charleston are running the Union blockade):

> Thus girt without and garrisoned at home,
> Day patient following day,
> Old Charleston looks from roof, and spire, and dome,
> Across her tranquil bay.

> Ships, through a hundred foes, from Saxon lands
> And spicy Indian ports,
> Bring Saxon steel and iron to her hands,
> And summer to her courts

> But still, along yon dim Atlantic line,
> The only hostile smoke
> Creeps like a harmless mist above the brine,
> From some frail, floating oak.[6]

Rather than flowing outward generously and abundantly toward the rest of the world, as in Timrod's earlier poems "Ethnogenesis" and "The Cotton Boll," trade now flows inward, sustaining the everyday life of Charleston. The poem balances anxious vigilance with studied nonchalance. Spectators have eyes trained on the horizon with such a strong common feeling that they become one, a personified city, trying to assess the danger of an inscrutable threat. Still, ships of trade manage to run the blockade and provide the city not only with sustenance, but luxuries. "Saxon" steel and iron are singled out because they are raw materials for arms and ammunition from England, the nation with which the Confederacy identified most closely; in repeating the word "Saxon," Timrod also underscores a fantasy of Confederate racial heritage. These crucial imports are strangely coupled with decadent goods from Asia that fortify Charleston's sense of itself as a leisured, pleasure-loving, courtly society. Timrod reduces the blockade to a "hostile" wisp of smoke and some inconsequential driftwood, but it is clear from the foreboding he simultaneously charts that his wishful thinking cannot reduce the material threat from the Federal navy.

Because the city was the location of the siege, poetry and journalism become one in Charleston. Poets report on and editorialize about experiences witnessed and shared by everyone in the city, who hardly needed to read newspapers to know what was happening, though of course the papers—especially the *Charleston Courier* and the *Charleston Mercury*—were full of accounts of the events unfolding around them; newspapers served as a crucial means of sustaining community during the conflict. Observing the people walking the streets, Timrod portrays a population whose sensibilities are transformed by the war; the poet seems startled at new hints of aggressivity that threaten his vision of a peace-loving nation:

> Meanwhile through the streets still echoing with trade
> Walk grave and thoughtful men,
> Whose hands may one day yield the patriot's blade
> As lightly as the pen.
>
> And maidens with such eyes as would grow dim
> Over a bleeding hound,
> Seem each one to have caught the strength of him
> Whose sword she sadly bound.

Sober businessmen may soon turn their hand to killing, and women's sympathies transfer from wounded dogs to wounding men. Timrod neglects to celebrate these developments, as many of his contemporaries did. All he can muster is observation.

The contemplative quality of Timrod's poetry throughout the conflict is almost completely anomalous; Paul Hamilton Hayne's poem "Charleston!" offers a more typical viewpoint, responding aggressively to the attacks on the city rather than contemplating them. Addressing the Union ships in the harbor, Hayne fights fire with fiery words:

> Aye! Launch your red lightnings, blaspheme in your wrath,
> Shock earth, wave, and heaven with the blasts of your ire;—
> But she seizes your death-bolts, yet hot from their path,
> And hurls back your lightnings, and mocks at the fire
> Of your fruitless desire.[7]

Hayne manages to make Charleston both the victim of violent aggression and an equally lethal opponent, who throws back whatever it receives. His abstraction depends on the concrete image of Charleston Harbor, ringed by forts that protect the city—"a fierce circlet of flame"—exchanging fire with the Union ships. "She" who seizes and returns the death bolts along with her mockery is Charleston personified; she does not need to be named, she is so fully present. Hayne's address mimics the forts' bombardment of the Union ships, neatly inscribing the tautological thinking that accompanies wartime hostilities: seeking to reciprocate the Union attack in kind, he summons words to perform the work of guns. The direct address to Union combatants bears a certain weight of futility, however. Given the blockade and the severance of postal communications between the sections, there is no certainty that the *Charleston Mercury* will end up in the hands of the men on the Union ships or of Northern civilians at a greater distance. (It is surprising, nevertheless, how much traffic in poetry and news there is between the sections; Union officers stationed around the Harbor note reading the Charleston papers; columns in Northern newspapers reprint Southern poetry; Southern poets are clearly aware of the poems published in Northern papers). Hayne's first readership is the people of Charleston who find an outlet for their rage in his communications to an enemy who may or may not receive the message; the expression itself serves a cathartic purpose during the siege.

In addition to tightening the blockade, the Federal navy moved aggressively to take over the forts in Charleston Harbor, and poets responded attentively to unfolding events. On April 7, 1863, eight Union ironclads commanded by Rear Admiral Samuel Du Pont attacked Fort Sumter and were repulsed, demonstrating, Du Pont believed, that Charleston could not be taken by naval forces alone.[8] Commentators on both sides imagined the battle in terms of tradition and modernity, technological invention that dwarfed and antiquated the human scale. Freighted with symbolism as well as some of the most advanced weaponry of the war, for Unionists, the ironclad fleet aligned modern mechanized warfare's killing power with the moral justice of the Northern cause. A sketch that appeared in the *New York Illustrated News* on April 25 depicts the attack (fig. 16). Impervious to the ammunition raining down on them, the ships are uniformly parallel in effortless military formation. Devoid of human presence, led onward by the American flag, they are a mechanized killing force that signifies the technological dominance of the Union. Seemingly impenetrable and invincible, they epitomize modern warfare.

Figure 16. "The attack of the federal ironclads on Fort Sumter and the Rebel batteries commanding the entrance to Charleston Harbor, on the 7th of April 1863," *New York Illustrated News*, April 25, 1863, 392–393. Courtesy of HarpWeek.

For Confederates in this particular battle—because it didn't involve their ships—the ironclads signified a sinister, even evil, killing force. In the Confederate-sympathetic *Illustrated London News*, reporter Frank Vizetelly's sketches of the event champion the human scale (fig. 17). In his April 5 report about the impending battle, Vizetelly calls the ships "mail-clad monsters."[9] On April 7, he opts to sketch the "ladies of Charleston" watching the fight from the edge of the harbor with "no undue fear for the result of the attack, which, if successful, would place their homes at the mercy of an exasperated foe."[10] The sketch shows not just ladies, but a mingled crowd of women, men, and children, black and white, all watching the battle from the edge of their home city. Depicting the diverse group as a community with a common concern, Vizetelly foregrounds their peaceful, vulnerable collectivity.

The failure of the ships to subdue Sumter dealt a blow to the mythology of infallible Northern power. Du Pont's ship *Ironsides* was heavily damaged by

Figure 17. [Frank Vizetelly], "The Civil War in America: Attack by the federal ironclads on the harbour defences of Charleston, 3pm of the 7th of April. From a sketch by our special artist," *Illustrated London News*, May 16, 1863, 532–533. Courtesy of HarpWeek.

Fort Sumter's guns, and the new, experimental ironclad *Keokuk* was sunk. The poets of Charleston celebrated the event. In "Our City by the Sea," William Gilmore Simms charts the battle from the position of an eyewitness. First "spoke an eager gun / From the walls of Moultrie," then:

> Full a hundred cannon roared
> The dread welcome to the foe,
> And his felon spirit cowered
> As he crouched beneath the blow!
> As each side opened wide
> To the iron and the tide,
> He lost his faith in armor and in art;
> And with the loss of faith
> Came the dread of wounds and scars—
> And the felon fear of death
> Wrung his heart![11]

Simms's words are one with the cannons' roar, delivering "vengeance sharp and hot" and elaborating on the guns' nonverbal message of ripping into metal and sinking the ship. The speaker revels in imagining the enemy's transformation of emotions, from confidence in a technological and strategic advantage—"armor and art"—; to the loss of faith; and finally to fears of pain and death. He works through the process of suffering delivered by the gun's roar, dwelling particularly on the destruction of the *Keokuk*: their leader sinks with the ship, "choking with the cry— / 'Keokuk!'" The verbalization of human despair meets the guns' roar and is defeated. In reality, the commander did not sink with the ship; Simms's counterfactual account heightens the Union loss through a death wish that is poetically fulfilled.

There were other victories for the Confederacy at the time, and Timrod celebrated this high point in a poem entitled "Carmen Triumphale," published on June 7, 1863, in Richmond's *Southern Illustrated News*.[12] It is the last time that Timrod imagines his nation in relation to a broader international community; a spark of his initial idealism ignites in the poem, illuminating the sky in technicolor:

> Our foes are fallen! Flash, ye wires!
> The mighty tidings far and nigh!
> Ye cities! write them on the sky
> In purple and in emerald fires![13]

Timrod imagines broad transmission of the recent Confederate successes. Charleston Harbor was indeed a focus of international attention in the summer and fall of 1863; journalists from both sections and abroad reported the victories, expressing surprise that Confederate forces could defend themselves against superior military strength for so long. Nevertheless, Timrod's striking, impossible image acknowledges its own roots in wish-fulfilling fantasy. The speaker encourages cities everywhere to extend the telegraph's electrical power into supernatural forms of global communication that take the form of "purple and emerald" sky writing. His joyful vision seems improbable, and indeed it is soon eclipsed.

The Confederate celebration contrasts starkly with the vengeful fantasies of destruction that the series of losses inspired in popular Northern poetry of this period. In "June" for example, published in *Frank Leslie's Illustrated Newspaper*, Amanda Jones—a particularly bellicose Union poet—calls on nature to join with the Union forces to ensure the annihilation of everyone living in Charleston:

> Shine, sun of the summer! blow wind of the West!
> And hurl these black battle-clouds back to the wave,
> Where, with seals of destruction on forehead and breast—
> The scourge of our nation, that shame of the brave—
> Charleston cowers by her grave![14]

Jones imagines nature itself as an enormous weapon and commands it to destroy the people of Charleston, who are already marked by doom. The Union's aggrieved sense of damage and loss, and the impulse to blame the war on Charleston as a metonymic representation of the Confederacy, deepened and intensified after Confederate troops repelled a larger Union force at the Battle of Fort Wagner, in Charleston Harbor, on July 18, 1863.

Soon, however, the Union gained an advantage in the war and greater traction in the harbor. After Union forces successfully took over Fort Wagner in a third attempt, General Quincy Adams Gillmore, then head of the Union's naval operations in Charleston Harbor, devised a plan to bombard the city with incendiary shells. By mid-August of 1863, Union soldiers had completed a floating battery near Morris Island to hold "The Swamp Angel," the nickname given by Union soldiers to a 16,500-pound rifled Parrott cannon with an eight-inch bore (fig. 18). Gillmore sent a message to General P. G. T. Beauregard, demanding that the Confederates evacuate Morris Island and

Sumter immediately or he would begin shelling the city. Beauregard didn't receive the message in time, and early on the morning of August 22, using a compass reading on St. Michael's Church steeple, Union troops fired the first shell 7,900 yards across the harbor into Charleston, panicking and perplexing the city's residents. Outraged, Beauregard charged Gillmore with violating the rules of combat. He wrote: "It would appear, sir, that despairing of reducing these works, you now resort to the novel measure of turning your guns against the old men, the women and children and the hospitals of a sleeping city."[15] Gillmore granted a brief respite and then resumed the shelling on the evening of August 23, when the Swamp Angel exploded while firing its thirty-sixth round. Though that particular gun had exploded, the bombardment of the city from the marsh battery continued throughout the war, and thousands of incendiary shells were fired into the city. Though only a few people were killed or injured due to the shelling, the siege destroyed much of downtown Charleston and forced civilian evacuation south of Broad Street. Gillmore argued—rightly, historians agree—that Charleston was a legitimate military target because, according to Craig Symonds, "it was effectively an armed camp"; in addition, however, "it was evident to all that his actions were designed to punish the city."[16]

This unprecedented action—it was the first time a compass was used to direct an artillery firing, the longest distance a shell had ever traveled, as well as one of the first incendiary bombings of a civilian population—intensified the war of words to a stark new level on both sides.[17] Union poets celebrated the attack, casting the shells as the only kind of language that might make the residents of Charleston understand the evils of their ways. The Swamp Angel's very name derived from this idea; one of the Union soldiers who helped construct the marsh battery reportedly said, "We're building a pulpit on which a Swamp Angel will preach."[18] Perhaps the name emerged in part because some of the soldiers who constructed the "pulpit" were African Americans: Gillmore had integrated his forces by the time the men were working on Morris Island.[19] Responding to the intensive coverage of the event, a remarkable poem published in *Harper's Weekly* develops this logic. Justifying the bombardment in a religious context, the poem posits a calculus of angels. The "angel of the dark swamp"—a counterpoint to St. Michael, the guardian angel of Charleston's church—comforts and defends all runaway slaves who have hidden in the swamps to escape from the men and bloodhounds tracking them. The speaker explains that angels can be, or can seem to be, like demons to those who commit evil acts: "frequent the good angels are the bane / Of evil men, who name

Figure 18. "The Siege of Charleston—The Swamp Angel. Sketched by Mr. Theodore R. Davis," *Harper's Weekly*, September 19, 1863, 597. Courtesy of HarpWeek.

them evil things." It is only fitting that the white residents of Charleston, who have so long forced African Americans into a position of terrified suffering, feel the tables reversed:

> Before the wicked city's traitor hold
> Stands a swamp angel all unangel wise;
> Perhaps some bondman's prayer has made it bold,
> Thus to put off its old and unseen guise.
>
> And it sends back the hound's deep-throated tone
> Full with the message of rebounding ill:
> And the pale hunters curse it with a groan,
> For the swamp angel is a demon still.[20]

Morally equivocal, filled with rage, the Swamp Angel matches the violence of slavery with an equal and opposite retribution: "it sends back the hound's deep-throated tone." The bombardment derives from dark angelic impulses that assume the form of a Parrott gun's voice: it is the Swamp Angel's fiery retribution for the "wicked city's traitors." The speaker hypothesizes that "some bondman's prayer" has caused the angel-demon to emerge and speak its violence.

Another Union poem, also entitled "The Swamp Angel," sanctifies the gun's shells by portraying their arc of travel as an ascent to the heavens; the shells are naturalized and spiritualized before descending to their target:

> At night this angel raiseth her voice,
> And her cry is "woe" and not "rejoice."
> She sendeth far her meteor shell,
> And it soareth up as if to dwell
> With the twinkling stars in the fadeless blue;
> There poiseth itself for the mighty blow,
> Then downward shoots like a bolt from God
> Crushes the dwelling and crimsons the sod[21]

Inevitable as the stars, the shell's cry of "woe" brings total destruction in the name of God, whose other name is Union:

> Hear ye in the Angel the Northern call,
> Thundered on Sumter's broken wall,
> Echoed in Charleston's silent street,
> Shouted in Treason's proud retreat:
>
> "Freemen must share with you the land!
> Choose olive leaf—or blazing brand;
> Choose peaceful Commerce's flag of stars,
> Or rifled guns and monitors!"

This shell serves explicitly as a representative of the North, who speaks for the people by delivering death after all verbal discourse has ceased. The missile's message is translated as an ultimatum: give up slavery or receive the "blazing brand." Again the poem calls for balanced, if catastrophic, retribution: a burning city for the branding of slaves.

In an even more violent fantasy of retribution, J. Warren Newcomb's "The Song of the Shell," also published in *Frank Leslie's Illustrated Newspaper* during the siege, doesn't mention the sin of slavery, dwelling rather on the treachery of secession. The moral violation of the Union justifies unbridled vengeance. "The 'Swamp Angel' flies and sings":

> It sings of the death of the traitorous town,
> It sings of red-handed rebellion crushed down.
> Sharp are its cadences, harsh its song,
> It shrieks for the right and it crushes the wrong;
> And never a blast, shaking nethermost hell,
> Cried vengeance and wrath like the song of the shell.[22]

Straining metaphor, the poem's voice collapses the distance between language and physical violence as completely as possible. Shrieking for the right is hard to comprehend because it seems oxymoronic; people in the right don't need to shriek, and it wouldn't be an effective form of persuasion anyway. But this shriek is the sound of a shell cutting through the air, and that reality takes precedence over the figure of human rhetorical persuasion. This physical act of persuasion cannot help but be felt: under the conditions of war, the shriek of a lethal shell is a legitimate form of speech, one that is translated via poetry's figure of the talking weapon.

As the world narrows under the conditions of violence to immediate circumstances for the Charleston poets, the bombardment visibly proves the virtue of the Confederacy and the vice of the Union. Stressing their status as victims, the poets of Charleston summon their own angels to retaliate against the assault. Paul Hamilton Hayne's "Invocation from the Besieged," "referring to the present condition of Charleston," addresses not the Union, but God, condemning the ongoing "homicide" and praying for an end to the destruction. The poem centers on the residents' "wail on the wo-burdened air [*sic*]" that is so loud and urgent it penetrates the celestial sphere and summons the help of heavenly beings:

> In the darkness, the tempest, the fire,
> In the stress of our anguished desire,
> We are lifting wild voices to *Thee*!
> O God! strike the homicides gory,
> With our hearts' blood outpoured in its glory,
> To the uttermost depths of the sea![23]

The plea, garbled by anxiety, rage, and a desire for revenge, is not that God keep the citizens of Charleston safe. Rather Charleston pleads for God to strike the Union murderers dead at the willing cost of a sea of Confederate blood.

William Gilmore Simms addresses the Union forces targeting the city with a force equal and opposed to that of a poem like "The Song of the Shell." Simms doesn't assume the voice of the gun, perhaps because the conditions of the siege disallow it: the people are not armed, and even if they were, the Union forces are beyond reach. Instead, he uses his words like bullets, returning blow for blow the enemy's fire in his taunt; the exclamation points suggest how far beyond words the feelings of rage extend:

> Shell the old city! Shell!
> Ye myrmidons of Hell;
> Ye serve your master well,
> With hellish arts!
> Hurl down, with bolt and fire,
> The grand old shrines, the spire;
> But know, your demon ire
> Subdues no hearts![24]

The first line mimics a bombardment with its substitution of a trochee for the first iamb, the preponderance of heavy stresses, and the mimetic repetition of the monosyllabic word "shell," punctuated by exclamation points. Rather than seeking relief from suffering, Simms encourages Union forces to destroy the city. He declares that the perpetrators' violence is a sign even before death that they are already hell's minions, without any possibility of redemption, resigned to eternal suffering by their own actions. The poem's weight of rage generates incoherence, however; though the Union troops may already be in hell, that doesn't prevent Simms from insisting on killing them:

> Shell the old city—shell!
> But, with each rooftree's knell,
> Vows of deep vengeance fell,
> Fire in soul and eye!
> With every tear that falls
> Above our stricken walls

Each heart more fiercely calls,
"Avenge or die!"

While insisting that the people of Charleston are innocent victims of an evil
act, Simms vows that the people of the South will seek retribution at all costs.
Fueled by tears, their hearts are weaponized, devoted to preparing for future
assault.

As if in answer to Simms's verbal taunt, the shelling intensified. Shortly
after midnight on Christmas day, 1863, Gillmore's troops opened fire, aiming
again at St Michael's steeple, in the most severe bombardment the city had
yet experienced. The timing was clearly intended to incense the residents of
the city, to assault their religious sensibilities as well as their buildings. Simms
responded in "The Angel of the Church," published in the *Charleston Mercury*. Voicing righteous, enraged defiance, Simms pits St. Michael against the
unseen forces of the Swamp Angel, taunting them to do their worst, for nothing would convince Charleston or the Confederacy to surrender:

Think not, though long his anger stays,
His justice sleeps—His wrath is spent;
The arm of vengeance but delays,
To make more dread the punishment!
Each impious hand that lights the torch
Shall wither ere the bolt shall fall;
And the bright Angel of the Church
With seraph shield avert the ball![25]

Simms adds the force of God to the force of the Confederacy, insisting that St.
Michael is on their side and will eventually seek vengeance.

As the bombardment wears on, the belligerent rhetoric reaches a standoff. Both sides justify killing on moral grounds: the Union seeks to punish
Charleston for secession and the sin of slavery; the Charleston poets insist that
God will punish the unwarranted attack on an unarmed city. On the Union
side, patriots writing from a safe distance, inspired by the news coverage, exert
every energy to make poetry an extension of the physical assault on the city;
the poems refuse to think of the people of Charleston as anything other than
targets who deserve to die. Their remote expressions of violence echo the position of the Union soldiers firing on the city; five miles across the harbor, they

are out of range of seeing the consequences of the bombardment. The righteous rage of the poets of Charleston, on the other hand, leaves no room for the contemplation of their own moral violations: the poets never acknowledge that slavery or secession is at issue. Summoning God's wrath and directing it toward their enemies, they seem to wish to expedite their own destruction by aggravating their attackers and encouraging them to rain more fire on the city. Reflection is nonexistent in many of these poems; it evaporates under fire. They come as close to automatic physical response as words are able to.

Thinking Through Violence

Concluding the discussion here would suggest that there is no way out of the escalating force of violent destruction, and that citizen-poets necessarily serve as unquestioning extensions of national rhetorics of violence in wartime, especially when the fighting is located at an ideological epicenter. But turning to poems by Melville and Timrod will show that even under these extreme conditions, poetry does not have to serve as an automatic part of war's arsenal; it can create room to consider the relation of violence to ethics rather than foreclosing the possibility of contemplation.

A composition grounded in radical intertextuality, Melville's "The Swamp Angel" engages intensively not with any single poem about the conflict but with the remarkably unified rhetorical field surrounding the event that I have just discussed. He synthesizes and ventriloquizes the literary and journalistic responses to the bombardment of Charleston in order to consider the impulsive desires mobilized with the siege and weigh them alongside the human costs and moral consequences of the action. Though written with the benefit of hindsight, at a temporal distance that helps enable philosophical thought, the poem is set in the present moment of the bombardment. Like the popular poems I've just discussed, Melville's speaker allies himself with the Union perspective, casting the cannon as a vengeful angel who speaks on behalf of slave suffering:

> There is a coal-black Angel
>   With a thick Afric lip,
> And he dwells (like the hunted and harried)
>   In a swamp where the green frogs dip.

But his face is against a City
>   Which is over a bay of the sea,
And he breathes with a breath that is blastment,
>   And dooms by a far decree.[26]

The poem closely follows the logics of the other poems I have discussed: seeking righteous vengeance, the Swamp Angel speaks his justice in the language of violence upon Charleston. But the phrasing raises unformulated questions as well. The gun's "thick Afric lip" alludes to the metal lip of the Parrott gun, but it does so via a caricature, to an unclear end: is Melville revealing his own racism? Is he drawing attention to the ways white poets use an African American figure to deliver their own vengeance by proxy? The emphasis on the gun's distance—the city "is over a bay" and is doomed by a "far decree"—not only evokes God's descending wrath but also foregrounds the vulnerability of the citizen population. An undercurrent of ambivalence infuses a poem that emulates and seems to ally itself with the poems of unalloyed aggression it evokes.

Unlike the Union poems of vengeance he clearly draws upon, Melville's poem foregrounds Charleston's civilians' vulnerability in its body. While stopping short of expressions of sympathy or alliance, Melville recognizes the suffering of the people of the city:

By night there is fear in the City,
>   Through the darkness a star soareth on;
There's a scream that screams up to the zenith,
>   Then the poise of a meteor lone—
Lighting far the pale fright of the faces,
>   And downward the coming is seen;
Then the rush, and the burst, and the havoc,
>   And wails and shrieks between.

Melville paraphrases T. N. J.'s "The Swamp Angel," evoking the same image of a shell soaring up to the heavens to be infused with the inevitability of astronomical bodies—but the moral justice of God's wrath is withheld, and instead Melville substitutes the image of frightened faces, illuminated from an aerial view by the suspended shell. The perspective suddenly shifts to the human scale. The "scream" of the shell gives way to the "wails and shrieks" from the bewildered citizens who are the target of the attacks. The displacement raises questions about the moral compass of the "shell who shrieks for right."

The image Melville summons in this stanza bears a relation to a sketch by Frank Vizetelly—who was in Charleston during the bombardment—published in the *Illustrated London News* (fig. 19). The stanza begins by portraying the moment preceding the illustration, when the meteoric projectile, poised above its target, illuminates the upturned faces before it falls and explodes among them, creating the "havoc" depicted in Vizetelly's sketch. The poem adds sound to the image, adding another dimension to the suffering. But though the poem insists on replaying the scene vividly to summon that suffering, it does not condemn the attack. Instead it raises the question of the costs and stakes of political violence, asking us whether the ends justify the means, and whether this is the best way to convince people of wrongdoing. The poem continues to dwell on the effects of the bombing:

> They live in a sleepless spell
> That wizens, and withers, and whitens;
>   It ages the young, and the bloom
> Of the maiden is ashes of roses—
>   The Swamp Angel broods in his gloom.

The Swamp Angel is insatiable in his revenge, destroying the young and the innocent, pushing the boundaries of destruction ever further: "And weed follows weed through the Town." Melville exaggerates the destruction in his depiction; anticipating the continued bombardment, the people of Charleston deserted that part of the city and moved out of reach of the attacks. In capturing the siege in process, Melville foregrounds the ethical questions surrounding civilian bombardment without foreclosing them.

The poem pans out from its focus on individual human suffering in the penultimate stanza in order to evaluate the justness of the bombardment in abstract moral terms. Aligning himself closely with the Unionist sentiments expressed in the popular poems, the speaker seems to determine that punishment has been meted out appropriately:

> Is this the proud City? the scorner
> Which never would yield the ground?
> Which mocked at the coal-black Angel?
> The cup of despair goes round.

Figure 19. [Frank Vizetelly], "The War in America: The federals shelling the city of Charleston—shell bursting in the streets. From a sketch by our special artist," *Illustrated London News*, December 5, 1863. Courtesy of HarpWeek.

Vainly she calls upon Michael
(The white man's seraph was he),
For Michael has fled from his tower
To the Angel over the sea.

Calling on Proverb 16:18—"Pride goeth before destruction, and an haughty spirit before a fall"—the speaker declares that Charleston's pride has brought on a suitable retribution. The city's refusal to cede ground and its indifference to human suffering has made it necessary for "the cup of despair" to come round; only then might it realize its wrongs. Charleston is even forsaken by its guardian angel, embodied in St. Michael's Church, which has "fled" Charleston and allied itself with the Swamp Angel. Black and white angels have combined forces to avenge the wrongs of slavery. Just as strongly as Melville has previously articulated the questionable nature of mass violence in the service of national goals, he now seems to advocate for it.

The poem doesn't end on this note, however, as its popular sources did. Instead, Melville adds a coda that offers two unusual formulations:

Who weeps for the woeful City
Let him weep for our guilty kind;
Who joys at her wild despairing—
Christ, the Forgiver, convert his mind.

Reflecting on the scenarios formally staged in the poem, this stanza from an impartial speaker offers a double aphorism of the moral mandates of the event. Rather than insisting that the South's sins are discrete and that the North is a purely virtuous force working in the service of God, Melville insists on collective sin and shared guilt. Pushing back against an enormous sea of patriotic rhetoric, he implies that all people are complicit with or at least capable of crimes against humanity; those who weep for Charleston should acknowledge their own sins within the context of universal guilt. One of those crimes, he suggests in the final two lines, is taking pleasure in the suffering of the people of Charleston, as the other talking-gun poems clearly have. Drawing into a calculus of suffering and moral accountability both slavery and the death tolls of the war, Melville's conclusion is stark: Southerners require lethal punishment to convince them to abandon slavery and secession, but Northerners who revel in their pain are sinners.

Melville's meditations on war's justice in Charleston have an unlikely counterpoint in the poetry of Henry Timrod. A native of Charleston, Timrod moved his family to Columbia during the siege hoping it would be safer and began writing a column for the *Daily South Carolinian*. (He was wrong; in just a few months Columbia would be burned during William Tecumseh Sherman's march, and the office of the *South Carolinian* would be destroyed.) Though Timrod is remembered almost solely for his two celebrations of the Confederacy written in 1861, "The Cotton Boll" and "Ethnogenesis," as well as his later ode to the Confederate dead, several of the poems Timrod published toward the end of the war express doubt about the Confederate cause. Unlike the poems of Hayne and Simms, which become increasingly partisan under siege conditions, Timrod's poems turn away from battle scenes to question the moral grounds for the conflict and to mourn the dead.

Indeed, in a number of his later war poems, rather than offering support of the war, Timrod offers prayers for peace. A hymn that was "sung at a sacred concert at Columbia, SC" and published in the *Daily South Carolinian* in

November 1864 expresses confidence that God will hear the "gentle voice of prayer" even if it is nearly drowned out by the "wild sounds" of war:

> Not all the darkness of the land
> Can hide the lifted eye and Hand;
> Nor need the clanging conflict cease,
> To make thee hear our cries for peace.[27]

Timrod calls not for "victory," but for "peace," which can come whether one wins or loses. Reversing the logic of the talking-gun poems on both the Union and the Confederate sides, Timrod elevates the human voice to intelligibility, and de-animates the weapons, reducing them to interfering noise. The meaning of prayer is no longer restricted—and arguably perverted—to a plea to God to kill the enemy. Timrod's prayer doesn't single out one group at the expense of another, but asks for universal respite from violence. As early as December 1862, in the *Charleston Mercury*, Timrod had called for peace, but in a way that was still inflected by sectional limits:

> Peace on the farthest seas,
> Peace in our sheltered bays and ample streams,
> Peace whereso-er our starry garland gleams,
> And peace in every breeze![28]

If it weren't for "our starry garland," this earlier prayer for peace would seem to blanket the entire world, and the intense desire for cessation of hostilities is underscored by the fact that the relatively brief poem uses the word "peace" over twenty times, as if chanting the word could bring about the reality. But Timrod does insert the Confederate flag, delimiting peace and reserving it for his section. This distinction disappears by 1864.

Timrod expressed enduring support for the Confederate cause for the last time in a public commemorative poem, "Ode, Sung on the Occasion of Decorating the Graves of the Confederate Dead"; the poem was recalled to attention in the twentieth century by Allen Tate's "Ode to the Confederate Dead" (1928), which speaks to the earlier poem. In the same year, however, in a forgotten poem entitled "1866," Timrod stresses the futility of 1865's tremendous bloodshed, condemning mass violence in unequivocally moral terms, devoid of political affiliation. He addresses 1865:

In dark Plutonian caves,
Beneath the lowest deep, go, hide thy head;
Or earth thee where the blood that thou has shed
May trickle on thee from thy countless graves.[29]

Unable to fathom or justify the massive loss of the period, Timrod demands that it all be buried. In a bizarre formulation, he wants the idea of the war to bury itself beneath the dead, so that the men's blood can drip down upon the concept and make it feel its accountability. The image is cryptic: what guilt does a year carry? Where should the guilt reside? Timrod thinks through the war in his poetry, sometimes expressing bafflement, sometimes contradicting himself. Over time, his perspectives transform, rather than remaining statically devoted to a single viewpoint. "1866" is not written by the patriotic poet of "Ethnogenesis"; in the later poem, violence is stripped down to its bare conditions and held before the eye, as in Melville's "Swamp Angel." It differs from Melville's poem by holding the war dead apart from political justifications and simply contemplating the overwhelming enormity of the fact of the dead.

After seven stanzas of lamentation, however, Timrod does turn his eye to the nation. Surprisingly, however, it is not the Confederacy, but the United States. He expresses fidelity to the coming year and the reunited country:

A time of peaceful prayer,
Of law, love, labor, honest loss and gain—
These are the visions of the coming reign
Now floating to them on the wintry air.

The "wintry air" has always been the North in Timrod's poetry, but instead of finding it repellent, he now welcomes it as invigorating. Professing obedience to the new "law" and the "coming reign" ("reign" does not suggest tyranny in Timrod's consistently aristocratic diction), he expresses a desire for peace and a willingness to work for the reunited country.

Timrod died soon afterward of tuberculosis. Not long after his death, a remarkable poem, "Storm and Calm" was published; it charts his turn of allegiance from South to North, even suggesting, as Melville's poem does, that Southerners needed the war to force them to confront their moral wrongs. He casts the South before the war as complacently mired in sensuality:

Sweet are these kisses of the South,
As dropped from woman's rosiest mouth,
And tenderer are those azure skies
Than this world's tenderest pair of eyes?

But ah! Beneath such influence
Thought is too often lost in Sense;
And Action, faltering as we thrill,
Sinks in the unnerved arms of will[30]

Whereas in "The Cotton Boll" and other earlier poems Timrod had cast the South's tropical warmth as the basis for congenial international exchange and beneficent goodness, here it is illusory, a seduction that enervates the bodies of white Southerners, kills thought, and drains the will. Overly sensual, enchanted by beauty, the South needs the North to shake it into reality through violence:

Awake, thou stormy North, and blast
The subtle spells around us cast;
Beat from our limbs these flowery chains
With the sharp scourges of thy rains!

Bring with thee from thy Polar cave
All the wild songs of wind and wave,
Of toppling berg and grinding floe
And the dread avalanche of snow!

Wrap us in Arctic night and clouds!
Yell like a fiend amid the shrouds
Of some slow-sinking vessel, when
He hears the shrieks of drowning men!

Like Simms and Hayne, Timrod summons righteous violence and wrath, but remarkably, he calls on it to punish the South rather than the North. As in his previous poems the North is a polar force of sublime proportions, but whereas he had earlier defended the Confederacy from this aggressive force, now he opens the South to the blast and encourages the North winds to do their worst. Though Timrod still doesn't name slavery as one of the sins that requires divine punishment, it is nearly explicit in the inverted image of the "flowery chains" that he begs the North to "beat" from white Southerners, and in the "sharp scourges of the rain." The poem implies that white Southerners should suffer a pain commensurate with that the slaves experienced at their hands, and Timrod frames the justness of Northern violence in these terms, nearly the same terms we see in the Union poems of the Charleston siege. With some ambivalence, Timrod views the violence, in spite of its enormous costs in human life, along with the "terror and despair" that accompanies it, as justified. The viewpoint's tragedy is clear in the image of a "fiend" yelling in response to the "shrieks" of drowning men: the image is diabolical, yet it stands.

In the final stanza, Timrod's messages are fully explicit. He condenses his calls for punishment into unambiguous maxims at the end of the poem:

> Sting our weak hearts with bitter shame,
> Bear us along with thee like flame;
> And prove that even to destroy
> More God-like may be than to toy
> And rust or rot in idle joy!

While leisure had been valued positively in Timrod's earlier poem, "The Cotton Boll," here it is equated with evil, and it is a path to certain destruction. The phrasing leaves open the possibility that the primary sin is sloth rather than slavery, but the two are linked through the concept of labor: white Southerners held leisure as a positive value supported by slavery. Timrod insists that white Southerners need to confront and accept their "bitter shame," assume humility, and let the North lead them on the right path. His "idle joy" corresponds to Melville's joy in despair: Southerners must be brought to feel shame for the joy they have experienced at the expense of others, while Northerners must refrain from taking pleasure in the suffering of the repentant South.

Timrod's response serves as a counterpoint to the majority of Southern writers at the end of the war, who mourn the loss of life and lament the war's loss, but almost never accept moral failings or explicitly retract allegiance to secession or slavery. More common and influential is the response of William Gilmore Simms, who gathered the poems of the war in an anthology, entitled *War Poetry of the South*, in order to honor the contributions of Southerners to the Confederate war effort and to integrate their story of the Civil War into the story of a reunited nation. In his preface to the volume, Simms compares the poems to captured artillery, which he bequeaths with some ceremony to the conquering powers, expressing the certainty that they will become part of the literary history of the united nation.

> Though sectional in its character, and indicative of a temper and a feeling which were in conflict with nationality, yet, now that the States of the Union have been resolved into one nation, this collection is essentially as much the property of the whole as are the captured cannon which were employed against it during the progress of the late war. It belongs to the national literature, and will hereafter be regarded as constituting a proper part of it, just as legitimately to be recognized by the nation as are the rival ballads of the cavaliers and roundheads, by the English, in the great civil conflict of their country.[31]

Simms's vision of a reunited literature didn't come to pass; none of the poems in the volume entered the national canon in any substantial way, though several of the songs continue to serve as state anthems (J. R. Randall's "My Maryland" and Henry Timrod's "Carolina!") or hold a minor place in popular culture. But the terms by which Simms frames his surrender are familiar, and they support the ways that a reunion between Northern and Southern whites came at the expense of black equality.[32] Notably, Simms never says the South was wrong on any score; he simply accepts its loss and highlights the bravery, the tenaciousness, and the dignity of the people of the Confederacy. The painstaking care with which Simms collected the poems from newspapers and magazines around the South suggests an intense desire to chronicle and preserve the Confederacy for historical memory. He insists that it is important to capture the "true *animus* of the action," and that poetry is a key place to find that animus.[33] The collection unapologetically includes selections that are intensely hostile to the Union, including more than a dozen poems focusing on Charleston, among them Hayne's "Charleston" and Simms's "Shell the Old City." Simms justifies the inclusions by valorizing the way "sentiment and opinion have sustained their people through a war unexampled in its horrors in modern times," and indeed, I have offered the same reason for discussing the poems in this chapter. But Simms stops there; he doesn't include poems of regret or renunciation or of a change of mind (he does include several poems dedicated to peace). Simms's selection implicitly valorizes the lost cause along with the contemporary sentiments of the people during a brutal war; his investment in Confederate ideals remains intact.

An exception, Timrod seems to take seriously the ubiquitous rhetoric of the war, embraced by both sides, that God is on the side of right and that therefore the right must be victorious, and conversely, the victorious must be right. After the war, that argument evaporates for most Southerners; though they lost, they don't accept the logical conclusion that if God is on the side of right, and the right side won, then they must be wrong. The Union, of course, could embrace this rhetoric without dissonance and with a sense of righteousness. But Timrod too embraces the logic, reversing his previously held convictions. Terminally ill from advanced tuberculosis, his family close to starvation, Timrod wrote to influential editor R. H. Stoddard in July 1865, inquiring after the dubious possibility of working in the North. He tells Stoddard that he feels he must be honest about his political position: "In the late civil conflict I was a Secessionist in opinion, though the state of my health precluded my bearing arms. But the logic of events has made me once more a citizen of the United States; I begin to see (darkly) behind that Divine political economy which has ended in the extinction of slavery and the preservation of the Union; and I am prepared to discharge in good faith the obligations which I assumed upon taking the oath."[34] Timrod's profession of allegiance may be strategic and perfunctory, of course, but it also may be sincere, for Timrod took "good faith" seriously. His citation of Corinthians 13:12 suggests that he is working through a difficult process of acceptance and understanding, with the help of his faith: "For now we see through a glass, darkly; but then face to face: now I know in part; but then shall I know even as also I am known." There are several indications during the two years Timrod lived after the war that he became increasingly convinced his side was in the wrong. Timrod's sister-in-law told Hayne, for example, that the last lines Timrod ever read to her before he died were from John Greenleaf Whittier's "Snow-Bound." Composed in 1866, the poem, though conciliatory and amnesiac, celebrates the Union's triumph as God's victory over slavery and treason. If the political economy is divinely designed, as he came to believe, the war's outcome could not be a mistake, and the "extinction of slavery" and the "preservation of the Union" were part of God's plan. Though they also seek reconciliation with their Northern literary counterparts after the war, neither Simms nor Hayne show any indication of this sort of meditative transformation.

In just a few years, Timrod moves from being a poet of war to a poet of peace, and from a champion of the Confederacy to a willing citizen in the reunited nation. His work indicates how rapidly catastrophic events can transform poetic practice and perspective, if a writer is receptive to change. Unlike many poets on either side of the war, but particularly on the losing side, Timrod is receptive to change. Poetry during the war served as more than a mode of propaganda or a vehicle of solace; it also served as a means of thinking for some poets, as a way to work through serious ethical problems even when immersed in violent, unpredictable circumstances. In the end, poetry apparently helped Timrod change his mind in a rather extraordinary turnaround, one that cuts against the grain of the very lines of communication he had been putting down.

Timrod was singled out for praise after the war by leading northern writers, foremost among them John Greenleaf Whittier, but also Oliver Wendell Holmes, Henry Wadsworth Longfellow, and R. H. Stoddard.[35] Highly unusual for a Southern poet of the war era, his poems were collected and published by Houghton-Mifflin in 1899.[36] Timrod was not simply a spokesman for the Confederacy. It is perhaps more important to know that he changed his positions as the war progressed. For it is when people admit responsibility for their wrongs and profess to a new set of commitments—to peace, and to the end of slavery, in this case—that a different history might emerge, one that bears a greater sense of accountability for the past.

This chapter started with a consideration of the power of the desire to kill in the name of the state in the poetry emerging from the siege of Charleston. Poetry, it is clear, could serve as an almost mindless, automatic expression of desire for the perpetuation of violence on both sides of the war. Poems in this mode bear particular traits in their figurative language: notably, the collapse of metaphor works to bring language close to the physical urge to kill, creating a powerful fantasy of a physical possibility that both expresses and generates patriotic rage. Melville and Timrod offer counterpoints to this impasse, opening in their poetry a space for contemplation, but under quite different conditions. With the benefit of hindsight and temporal distance, Melville marshals the rhetoric of the siege in order to examine the ways language sanctions violence by summoning divine justice. Rather than simply embracing and reiterating this formulation, which repudiates introspection, Melville asks readers to look at the consequences of such rhetoric in the physical and psychic damage it inflicts. Timrod also uses poetry as a space of contemplation, in the midst of circumstances that would seem to prevent it. The poets surrounding him join forces in a collective project to condemn and doom the enemy by bombarding them with death wishes. Timrod nevertheless finds a way to turn poetic vision to the mission of peace and mourning, moving from his earlier patriotic rhetoric to an increasingly introspective examination of the South's position on slavery and secession. In considering Union and Confederate poetry together, we note the vast range of purposes poetry can serve in wartime, some of which hinge on the dynamics of violence between the two sections, some of which serve as a means of opening up ways of thinking about the relation of violence to morality, even in the most difficult circumstances.

Chapter 5

Poetry at Sea

Naval Ballads and the Battle of Mobile Bay

The antebellum ballad often carried with it a certain metrical looseness within a fairly recognizable stanzaic form—often 4-3-4-3 quatrains—associated with song.[1] Within that form, someone may call us to remember a historical event as if it were a myth, or a myth as if it were a historical event, confounding the two. Henry Wadsworth Longfellow's "Paul Revere's Ride," for example, created the hero it purported to recall from history. According to historian David Hackett Fisher, Longfellow "appealed to the evidence of history as a source of patriotic inspiration but was utterly without scruple in his manipulation of historical fact": the poem is "grossly, systematically and deliberately inaccurate."[2] That said, there would be no Paul Revere's ride or heroic Paul Revere if it weren't for Longfellow's poem, which has carried the story "through the night wind of the past" on its galloping tetrameter lines.[3] What that ballad carried in its nostalgic fantasy of the Revolutionary past was the image of an everyman, anachronistically ready to fight for his not-yet-extant country. That country existed when Longfellow published "Paul Revere's Ride" in the *Atlantic Monthly* in January 1861, but it was threatening to split in two. The poem is a call to arms that cultivates a specifically northeastern patriotic fervor summoned by the Battle at Lexington and Concord in order to encourage readers to join in the imminent war effort. The ballad's conflation of history and myth, especially before the Civil War, may work in the service of unfolding political events, but the relation between poem and context is often obscured, nearly unarticulated, so that readers not of that moment can easily miss the point. Longfellow leaves the "midnight message" of Paul Revere unspecified, so it can be both "the British are coming"—that funny rendition of a phrase that would not have been uttered during the American Revolution—or, to borrow a line from another Civil War ballad, "We are coming, Father Abraham, three hundred thousand more."[4]

After the first year, when casualty counts mounted into the tens of thousands, even in a single battle, and there was no hint of a resolution, the ballad form diversified its modes of mediating the conflict in fascinating ways. Writers of the time recognized something modern about the engagement, in terms of both the killing technologies and the consolidating information networks, and they explored how to adapt poetic expression to accommodate and express these transformations. Because the ballad was so strongly codified in the antebellum period as a means for developing national mythologies, it makes sense that writers would mobilize the form to think about the crisis in national identity with its accompanying changes in the practice of warfare and communication; the crisis registers in the ballad form itself, I suggest, and we can begin to see how that happens in the many ballads about naval battles, particularly those in which wooden war sloops are pitted against a new warship, the ironclad.

In these poems, by returning to a less emphasized set of associations with the form, the writers are trying to remake the ballad into something more akin to a news report that can both recount and mythologize current events and thus render them historically and ideologically meaningful, even before anyone knows the outcome of the war.[5] This is an inherently unstable endeavor, and the instability registers both formally and symbolically. While it would be easier if the symbolic world aligned seamlessly with events, the facts, which the poets feel newly obligated to honor, keep challenging this framework. Facts alone are not sufficient; poets are interested in the ways they are mediated by human subjectivity in order to create the "sense of the times." Poets seek to capture the emotional traces of the unfolding events of the war. At the same time, they try to shape the reception of those events, known to a broad audience through newspaper reportage, by infusing them with idealized, ideological, or moral meaning.

In depicting these battles—on the Mississippi River, off the Southeastern coast, in Mobile Bay—writers are thrown into uncertainty about, for example, what symbolic valence to attribute to battleships. On the one hand, Northern writers want wooden sloops to align with earlier times, the outdated South, and the traditional ballad (a fantasy form). The newly invented ironclads, in contrast, would then signify Northern industrialism, progress, and poetic experimentation. One of the obvious challenges writers faced in reconciling naval events during the war with idealized national sentiment is that they imagined the ironclad as a marvel of modernity for its superior killing force, the ability to deliver lethal destruction while remaining impervious. That is not an aspect of progress that easily fits into the vision of the Union as morally superior and more highly civilized than the barbaric South. A second problem is that the Confederates also had the technology and actually developed and used it first, at the Battle of Hampton Roads, where the CSS *Virginia* rammed and sank the USS *Cumberland*. In this case it was necessary to turn the ironclad into a prehistoric monstrosity and to cast the wooden ship as the more civilized vessel. A third problem is that the ironclads weren't actually impervious and lost more than once to wooden ships. In the Battle of Mobile Bay, for example, a Union ironclad was punctured by mines and sank, entombing everyone aboard. In that battle, Admiral David Farragut led a victory while lashed to the mast of a wooden ship; his ship rammed a Confederate ironclad, disabling it. Blurring the line between wooden ships and ironclads was the fact that the wooden sloops were themselves "modern," newly powered by steam engines and equipped with the latest guns—Parrotts and Dahlgrens.[6]

Given all these variables, poets couldn't simply align one kind of ship with progress, moral goodness, and modernity and the other with the romantic past or the dark ages. Depending on the circumstances of the battle, they had to radically alter the valences of the tropes, which were used to describe different sides under different circumstances, creating a vertiginous sense of relativity. A study of the instability of the symbolic assignments in relation to this fidelity to facts allows us to explore the ways that poets integrated events into poems. The stakes of the endeavor were not just the making of legends that would project and shape the values of the postwar nation; the poems also incorporated an awareness of the fragility of the myths they forged, dependent as they were on unfolding events. There is a persistent sense of doubt in the poems, veiled or otherwise, about the power of patriotic rhetoric to frame the war in unambiguous moral terms. I'll trace these poetic labors through two of the most significant naval battles of the war: the Battle of Hampton Roads in March 1862 and the Battle of Mobile Bay in August 1864. The first section will chart the range of poetic responses to the sinking of the *Cumberland*, marking the newly important role of facticity with its accompanying portrayals of empirical observation. The second section will analyze Henry Howard Brownell's experimental treatment of the Battle of Mobile Bay, which he recorded in poetic form as an observer and officer aboard the Union sloop *Hartford*; I will then turn to Herman Melville's engagements with Brownell's unusual experiment. In contrast to the earlier poet, Melville draws on eye-witness accounting at second hand in order to explore both the question of chance in the unfolding of events and the place of poetry in a technologically driven age.

On Board the *Cumberland*

At the Battle of Hampton Roads, the first encounter between an ironclad and a wooden ship, the monitor CSS *Virginia* attacked the USS *Cumberland* off the coast of Virginia. The battle is quite simple to tell. As Frank Day puts it succinctly, "The *Merrimac* [the original name of the *Virginia*] simply bore in on the *Cumberland*, ignoring the shots, and rammed her so that she sank."[7] The flag on the ship's mast remained above water. While the ship was sinking, the crew continued to fire at the largely impervious ironclad; more than half the men died. Numerous poems recounted this landmark event, largely from the crews' perspective. In Longfellow's "The Cumberland," published in the *Atlantic Monthly* soon after the battle and reprinted widely, a sailor aboard the sloop recounts the battle with attention to the accuracy of events, which are cast in an antiquated language that elevates and renders them legendary and timeless. The speaker casts the Confederate ironclad as a demonic force:

> Then, like a kraken, huge and black,
> She crushed our ribs in her iron grasp!
> Down went the Cumberland all a wrack,
> With a sudden shudder of death,
> And the cannon's breath
> For her dying gasp.[8]

The appearance of ironclads shocked first-time viewers, for unlike wooden sloops, whose sails towered high above the water, ironclads were largely submerged except for their steam spouts and gun turrets. Longfellow figures this vessel as an ancient, evil sea monster, void of humanity, bent on destruction. He bequeaths vulnerable, crushable human qualities to the Union ship, the qualities we should want to preserve, he suggests. The wracking of the *Cumberland*, a distinguished sloop in service since 1842, troubles the ballad form, which dies with a dimeter gasp because Longfellow breaks the final tetrameter line in two. That doesn't mean the form is dying, of course; it means Longfellow is performing the strain exerted on the ballad's long tradition of telling stories about wooden, wind-powered sailing ships.

The change in Longfellow's balladic practice becomes more evident in a comparison to his earlier poem "The Wreck of the Hesperus" (1840), in which a foolhardy and stubborn skipper takes his daughter out in an impending storm, which kills them both:

> It was the schooner Hesperus,
>   That sailed the wintry sea;
> And the skipper had taken his little daughtèr,
>   To bear him company.[9]

The story is dislocated from time, place, and specific event; and indeed, Longfellow drew from an amalgam of events to create the poem; the moral tale takes precedence over fidelity to any specific incident.[10] Though there is still an intense idealization, Longfellow locates "The Cumberland" in a specific time, place, and event by naming the ship, its commanding officer, and the battle. He charts events even though they are not in favor of the Union: the rebounding of the shot from the ironclad's impermeable sides, the ramming of the *Cumberland*, and the rapid sinking of the ship. While "The Wreck of the Hesperus" operates as a moral fable, "The Cumberland" retells a specific current event, transforming the event into a nationalist historical moment.

Other poems were far more aggressive in their adaptations of the ballad in order to offer a detailed news report in addition to a celebration of patriotism. War poet George Henry Boker's "On Board the Cumberland" was perhaps the most popular Union commemoration of the battle (fig. 20). It manages to make the abrupt and complete loss into a prolonged, dramatic fight. Told from a common sailor's perspective, the first part of the poem focuses on the introduction of the ironclad. The sailor's perspective moves from ridicule, to horror, to disbelief: "What thing is that, I say?" is his response to the first sighting.[11] Soon the sailors recognize the threat and describe the ship as a "silent monster" and a "sea boar" with vicious and effective tusks. The remainder of the poem—eighteen stanzas—focuses on the crew who continue to fight against an invulnerable enemy even though they know their ship is sinking, they've lost the battle, and they're risking their lives to no avail. Though according to convention it would be more heroic if they all went down with the ship, Boker describes the evacuation of the lower level, which was taking in water quickly:

> We turned,—we did not like to go;
> Yet staying seemed in vain.
> Knee-deep in water; so we left;
> Some swore, some groaned with pain.

Acknowledging the futility rather than the heroism of their potential deaths, the sailors unceremoniously "left." On deck, they continued fighting, managing to get a single shot through a porthole of the *Virginia* before the *Cumberland* sank. Compensating for the loss, the poem concludes with the flag, "the noblest constellation set / Against our northern sky":

> A sign that we who live may claim
> The peerage of the brave;
> A monument that needs no scroll,
> For those beneath the wave.

Working from the materials he has, Boker crafts a poem that remains faithful to events but nevertheless pays tribute to the men who fought in a battle that isn't suited to conventional stories of heroism. The flag integrates the loss into an ongoing narrative of Union perseverance.

Henry Howard Brownell offers an even more conspicuously modernized ballad that dramatizes the ways that events encourage formal adaptation. With the date of the battle as the epigraph, "Hearts of Oak—An Epitaph" situates the reader as an eyewitness. Brownell chooses Acting Commanding Officer Lieutenant George Upham Morris as his speaker; the poem is a series of commands to the crew infused with rousing encouragement and disparaging characterizations of the enemy:

> How the hog-back's snout comes on us!
> Give it again to 'em, boys!
> Ah, there's a crash at our counter,
> Can be heard through all the noise!
>
> 'Tis like pitching of peas and pebbles—
> No matter for that, my men;
> Stand by to send them another—
> Ah! I think we hulled her then![12]

SINKING OF THE CUMBERLAND

On Board the Cumberland, March 7, 1862.

BY GEORGE H. BOKER.

"Stand to your guns, men!" Morris cried.
  Small need to pass the word;
Our men at quarters ranged themselves
  Before the drum was heard.

And then began the sailors' jests:
  "What thing is that, I say?"
"A long-shore meeting-house adrift
  Is standing down the bay!"

A frown came over Morris' face;
  The strange, dark craft he knew;
"That is the iron *Merrimac*,
  Manned by a rebel crew.

"So shot your guns, and point them straight;
  Before this day goes by,
We'll try of what her metal's made."
  A cheer was our reply.

"Remember, boys, this flag of ours
  Has seldom left its place;
And where it falls, the deck it strikes
  Is covered with disgrace.

"I ask but this, or sink or swim,
  Or live or nobly die,
My last sight upon earth may be
  To see that ensign fly!"

Meanwhile the shapeless iron mass
  Came moving o'er the wave,
As gloomy as a passing hearse,
  As silent as the grave.

9

Figure 20. George H. Boker, "On Board the Cumberland, March 7, 1862," *Lyrics of the War* (Philadelphia: Barclay & Co., 1864). Wilson Library, University of North Carolina Chapel Hill. Boker's poem was widely reprinted, including in this illustrated poetry pamphlet.

The recreation of the event combines journalistic detail with imaginative dramatization; Brownell locates the reader on the ship, in hearing distance of its commanding officer, who delivers orders in a stylized rendition of natural speech. The stanzas chart a precise moment in the battle when the *Virginia* rammed the *Cumberland* but before it started taking in water. The moment is decidedly unheroic: Brownell portrays the Union crew as boys impotently throwing pebbles while their own ship sinks. The idiosyncratic, colloquial, emphatically oral language and the pronounced marks of immediacy strain against the uniform, archaicized diction and legendary timelessness of the literary ballad that continue to inflect Longfellow's poem, which reduces the scene to "the cannon's breath" and the ship's "dying gasp." Brownell adapts the ballad's narrative form and investments in historicity to chart events in all their currency, noting particularities that would normally be left out, bringing the news alive for readers.

As he charts the battle, Brownell works to champion Union manhood in a way that remains faithful to the facts. He finds heroism in the men who continued firing on the *Virginia* as the wardroom filled with water, a moment that Boker also captures. Morris orders the men onto the deck, where he urges them to keep firing even though the ship is sinking:

> Sinking, my hearts, at an anchor—
> But never say die till it's o'er!
> Are you ready there on the spar-deck?
> We'll give them one round more.

"My hearts" alludes to the "hearts of oak" of the title, which are never otherwise mentioned. It associates the bravery of the men with the materials the ship is made of and suggests that their courage is natural, enduring, and traditional. The title underscores the poem's negotiations between old and new technologies of ships and songs: it is a phrase long used for British sailing ships, which were usually made of oak, and for the men who sailed on these ships. The official march of the Royal Navy, composed by David Garrick in 1759, bears the title "Heart of Oak."[13]

Published after the war in his collection *Battle-Pieces* (1866) rather than in the midst of unfolding events, Melville's "The Cumberland" makes its subject the processes of commemoration and balladic transformation evident in the poems by Longfellow, Boker, and Brownell. Like his peers, Melville ponders the question of how to turn events into memorable story while retaining factuality. The difference that the temporal gap allows is that the question of commemoration can be more important than the actual story. Instead of enhancing the drama of the event and foregrounding the bravery of the Union crew, Melville strangely deflates his account, drawing attention to the anticlimactic quality of the events that the other poems try to minimize and compensate for. He formulates the problem of commemoration in such an unpromising situation rather cryptically at first, through a meditation on the name of the ship, whose syllabics pose a challenge for ballad meter:

> Some names there are of telling sound,
> Whose voweled syllables free
> Are pledge that they should ever live renowned;
> Such seem to be
> A Frigate's name (by present glory spanned)—
> The Cumberland.[14]

The poem starts with a definite assertion that is then undercut in the fourth line; while there certainly are "names of telling sound," it remains to be seen whether "Cumberland" is one, or just "seems" to be one. The doubt is underscored with the way the expected final line of a ballad quatrain is cut in two by an intervening line, leaving "The Cumberland" alone at the end of the stanza. The refrain augments the uncertainty with its awkward syllabification:

> Sounding name as ere was sung,
> Flowing, rolling on the tongue—
> Cumberland! Cumberland!

A heavy stress, light stress, and heavy stress sequence repeated twice, "Cumberland! Cumberland!" does not flow and roll on the tongue; it interrupts the trochaic consistency of the first two lines (and a trochee is not a foot that lends itself to flowing; anapests, more common in ballad, tend to carry that function). The metrical variation, repetition of the name, and exclamation point cut the line in half. The clunkiness of the line combined with the assertion of mellifluousness raises questions about the project of commemoration: Is Melville trying to immortalize the name and the story it summons? Or is he exploring the challenges to the commemorative process? The poems in *Battle-Pieces* have remarkably diverse aims and approaches, so that it is difficult and perhaps unwise to generalize about intention, perspective, or point; but "The

Cumberland" is certainly interested in the challenges posed when facts must be accounted for by poems.

As with the uncertain refrain, the poem charts events with a less than fully enthusiastic attempt to immortalize them in song:

> She warred and sank. There's no denying
> That she was ended—quelled.
> And yet her flag above her fate is flying,
> As when it swelled
> Unswallowed by the swallowing sea: so grand—
> The Cumberland.

"Ended—quelled," the *Cumberland* doesn't seem to be able to rise again in story, even if the flag that marks its grave keeps flying. The flag in this poem is doubled: there is the flag that swells above the water and the metaphorical flag that flies above "her fate." Because the flag is not marked in any particular way, however—as a Union banner—it is unclear what it is signaling. When Melville says that the *Cumberland* is "so grand," he may also be referring to the swallowing sea. The dash, the dimeter ending of the stanza with the interruption of the fourth line, and the lack of a final exclamation point contribute to a sense of anticlimax.

If the ship's commemoration is ambivalent, the men who fought fare no better:

> What need to tell how she was fought—
> The sinking flaming gun—
> The gunner leaping out the port—
> Washed back, undone!
> Her dead unconquerably manned
> The Cumberland.

Melville deprives the ship of agency in the passive construction of the first line: "she was fought." In the same line he declines to retell the story in detail, perhaps alluding to the fact that it has already been done—even overdone—by his contemporaries; perhaps suggesting that everyone already knows the story; but also perhaps implying that the story isn't worth telling. The one attempt at action by the gunner is ineffective; water rushes in and drowns him as he tries to leap out of the port.[15] In Longfellow, Boker, and Brownell, the way to justify the men's loss is to find a way to render it heroic. Melville is ambivalent about affirming or negating the sailors' manhood; he may simply be stating the facts. The dead indeed had "manned" the *Cumberland*: they were the crew of the ship. But were they also made men in the course of the battle? That the dead were "unconquerably manned" suggests that something has dominated them. Rather than turning them into men, perhaps the battle took away their masculinity along with their lives.

Melville's peers demonstrate the many ways possible to commemorate the sinking of the *Cumberland*: by demonizing the new technology, by emphasizing the tenacity of the men, by dramatizing the fight to make it appear more than a pedestrian and inevitable loss. While Melville acknowledges these other poets via his participation in the tradition, he refrains from mobilizing those strategies. Instead his poem poses questions about how to adapt commemoration to the conditions of an era in which facts rival idealizations. Melville doesn't dissolve ballad in "The Cumberland," nor does he suggest that it is antiquated. But more than his fellow memorialists, he sinks the ballad into an unsettled rhythm, breaking the refrain off into a separate three-line verse, so that it indicates song, but is not singable. His retoolings foreground questions about the possibilities of mythic history in a mundane age. By the end of the war, it seems, ballads are not just a mode of transport for legend that energizes and informs the current moment, they capture the present moment while also carrying the unresolved qualities of that moment into the future. Melville in particular encourages future readers to probe the past by burying something before our eyes so that we want to uncover it and to learn more about the multiform ways ballads tell us about Civil War events. In that way, we recognize the ballad's power to hold a key to history, but not to unlock its meaning.

Balladizing the Battle of Mobile Bay

The last major naval engagement of the war, the Battle of Mobile Bay was more involved than the Battle of Hampton Roads.[16] In spite of its intricacy, most poets distilled the narrative down to a timely legend of heroism. Aboard the wooden sloop *Hartford*, Admiral Farragut led his fleet through dangerous waters to victory; lashed to the mast, he won the fight through courage and strong leadership. An exception to this template, Henry Howard Brownell's "The Bay Fight" is perhaps the most unusual and celebrated attempt at combining eyewitness reportage and poetry during the war. The admiral's personal secretary, Brownell composed the poem during the battle, recording the events as they unfolded regardless of their import, which could not be assessed until afterward. This experiment in poetic immediacy pushes to the extreme the interest in the power of facts that the *Cumberland* ballads display. "The Battle for the Bay" reveals a fascination with chance, reversal, accident, and all those disruptions that are usually culled during processes of balladic myth making. Herman Melville engages this unusual poem in order to pursue a rigorous inquiry into the way experience relates to design in both poetry and war.

Brownell had already shown an interest in recounting battles at first hand in "Hearts of Oak," and his later publications indicate that he was fascinated with the idea of turning ordinary military language into poetry under conditions of battle stress. He first encountered widespread recognition after his poetic rendition of Admiral Farragut's general orders to his fleet before the river battle over New Orleans appeared in the Hartford *Evening Press*.[17] Farragut advised his men on how to tend to the ship, beat the enemy, and survive the assault. Brownell adhered to the sense of Farragut's orders while condensing and fitting them to ballad form. Farragut advised the crew, for example, how to prepare for the possibility of fire and thirst: "You see that force and other pumps and engine hose are in good order.". . . "Have many tubs of water about the decks, both for the purpose of extinguishing fire and for drinking."[18] Brownell paraphrases, in accentual trimeter:

> Look well to your pumps and hose—
> Have water tubs, fore and aft,
> For quenching flame in your craft
> And the gun-crews' fiery thirst—[19]

This translation of urgently utilitarian advice came to the attention of the admiral, who admired the poem so much he invited the writer to join his crew aboard the flagship *Hartford*; Brownell became Farragut's personal secretary on the strength of the poem and was placed in charge of taking notes on the military actions. After the Battle of Mobile Bay, Farragut's official report to the Department of the Navy said that Brownell performed his duty "with coolness and accuracy."[20]

A rare eyewitness poem emerged from this engagement; Brownell was said to have written the poem on the same pages as the official notes, and completed it while still on the battleship before the day ended.[21] Whether or not this is entirely true, the poem circulated with this understanding; Brownell noted the date and location of composition—"U.S. Flagship Hartford, August, 1864, U.S. Navy"—at the end of the poem, which was first published in *Harper's Monthly* in December 1864 and then collected in *Lyrics of a Day: or News-Paper Poetry. By a Volunteer in the United States Service* (1864).[22] The poem was reprinted widely and enthusiastically embraced as the truest poetic expression of military valor to emerge from the war. A sign that the scene of Farragut in the rigging with an observant Brownell close by became iconic is a painting from later in the century by William Overend (fig. 21) that depicts "Brownell, leaning eagerly forward as he watches the fight, and fully exposed to the storm of shot and shell, holding in one hand a piece of paper—perhaps the notes for 'The Bay Fight,' some stanzas of which were actually written on the spot."[23]

If there weren't a Brownell, someone would have had to invent him. Throughout the war people eagerly pored over newspapers and magazines searching for "true" reports of the war wherever they might find them. "True" doesn't simply mean descriptively accurate, but also passionately felt and effectively communicated. The "truth" of Brownell's expression derived from both his poetic sensibility and nerve to experience a battle at first hand; Oliver Wendell Holmes tells us he accurately fired a cannon at an enemy fort in the midst of writing the poem.[24] Crediting Brownell with poetic originality and fidelity of detail, he praised the "vigorous pictures . . . fresh from the terrible original."[25] We are familiar with the cliché that great writing emerges from direct observation and firsthand experience, but we don't usually associate it with war poets before World War I. Hailing Brownell as "Our Battle Laureate" in the *Atlantic Monthly*, Holmes hyperbolically placed Brownell's "The Bay Fight" above any other war poem written to date for this reason: "If Drayton had fought at Agincourt, if Campbell had held a sabre at Hohenlinden, if Scott had been in the saddle with Marmion, if Tennyson had charged with the 600 at Balaklava, each of these poets might possibly have pictured what he said as faithfully and as fearfully as Mr. Brownell has painted the sea-fights in which he took part as a combatant. But no man can tell a story at second hand with the truth of incident which belongs to an eye-witness who was part of what he saw."[26] While Drayton, Campbell, and Tennyson offer emotional intensity, they cannot do so "faithfully," since they worked from "second hand." Brownell can offer "truth of incident" because he possesses both the powers of imagination and the experience necessary to create a great poem. This valorization of experience is not new with the war; Ralph Waldo Emerson stresses the need for the poet to know nature, and Walt Whitman emphasizes

Figure 21. William Overend, English, 1851–1898. *An August Morning with Farragut; the Battle of Mobile Bay, August 5, 1864.* 1883. Oil on canvas, 77.5 in. × 120 in. (196.9 cm × 304.8 cm). Brownell is near Farragut, leaning forward with a paper in one hand, watching events unfold. That this scene was portrayed in 1883 attests to the enduring power of the story of Brownell and Farragut in the nineteenth century. Wadsworth Athenaeum Museum of Art, Hartford, Connecticut. Gift of Citizens of Hartford by Subscription, 1886.1. Photograph credit: Allen Philips/Wadsworth Atheneum.

his role of observer of humanity in the 1855 edition of *Leaves of Grass.*[27] But neither stresses the exactitude of specific incident—especially violent political incident—as it unfolds the way Brownell does. Holmes marvels that "he took minutes of everything as it happened during the contest, so that the simple record and the poetical delineation run into each other."[28] During the war, it seemed as if the smallest fact might carry momentous significance, and critics admired Brownell's willingness to record these details and illuminate that significance, not in relation to the poet's sensibility, but to the impersonal aesthetic of war itself. Brownell himself claimed that his poetry had less to do with expressing his own thoughts than with expressing the spirit of war; he said that his poems "are spray, as it were, flung up by the strong Tide-Rip of Public Trouble, and present the Time more nearly, perhaps, than they do the writer."[29] Reviewers also describe the work in these terms. A review in the *New Englander* proclaims that "his lines are instinct with true impassioned poetic fire, and breathe the very spirit of that hour when Farragut in the maintop fought the battle of Mobile Bay."[30]

Farragut himself validated Brownell's claim to expressing the "very spirit" of the battle. When the poet wrote to ask if he could dedicate his volume of war lyrics to the admiral, he replied:

> I have always esteemed it one of the happy events of my life that I was able to gratify your enthusiastic desire to witness the grandest as well as the most terrible of all nautical events, a great sea-fight! And you were particularly fortunate in its being one in which all the ingenuity of our country had been employed to render it more terrible by the use of almost every implement of destruction known in the world, from the old-fashioned smooth-bore gun to the most diabolical con-trivances for the destruction of human life. And permit me to assure you I have fully realized all my anticipations that your pen would faithfully delineate the scene and do justice to the subject.[31]

Farragut cites the massive deployment of new killing technologies as a pri-mary motivation for seeking a new poem: the cumulative power of Dahl-grens, Parrotts, ironclads, torpedoes, and other weapons, many of them first deployed in the Civil War. Invoking the sublime, Farragut suggests that the terror of this modern mechanized warfare has changed fighting so extremely that it requires new forms of expression, which he believes Brownell offers. Reviewers agree, and once again Holmes is most eloquent and suggestive on the topic: "The War of Freedom against Slavery has created a devilish enginery of its own: iron for wood, steam for wind and muscle, 'Swamp-Angels' and thousand pounders in the place of the armaments that gained the Battle of the Nile. . . . New modes of warfare thundered their demand for a new poet to describe them; and Nature has answered in the voice of our Battle-Laureate, Henry Howard Brownell."[32] Both Farragut and Holmes associate the enginery of mass death with the devil—it is "diabolical" and "devilish"—but they ultimately attribute the use of this power to God. Incomprehensibly, somehow, moral forces propelled these killing forces of iron and steam into being, and the same superhuman intelligence that forged these death-delivering powers motivates Brownell's expression. "Original" is the word reviewers use, and "The Bay Fight" is the premier example of what they identify as a new kind of poetic practice that derives from this particular form of possession rooted in the actual empirical details of the war. It is a possession not by the people, exactly, but by a God-blessed, overawing Union. The Northern people need the violence to speak, to explain and justify itself, and to assure them that it comes from God; that is Brownell's assigned job as Farragut's personal poet.

Brownell, in other words, is possessed by moral forces of total destruction, and his poetry bears the record. If it stopped here, his practice would be comparable to Julia Ward Howe's, whose "The Battle Hymn of the Republic" proclaims a deadly vision of Christian righteousness. The journalistic impulse in Brownell distinguishes them. Howe's poem envisions "a fiery gospel writ in burnished rows of steel"; the vision is firmly rooted in apocalyptic end time, words and weapons are completely identified.[33] Brownell, however, situates his words in the midst of unfolding events, and the end is not entirely clear. He offers emotion not recollected in tranquility, but in the midst of its physiological emergence, "hot from the heart," as one later reviewer says.[34] Holmes declares that "the words themselves have the weight and the rush of shot and shell, and the verses seem aflame with the passion of the conflict. . . . No one can fail to be struck with the freedom and robustness of the language, the irregular strength of the rhythm, the audacious felicities of the rhyme."[35] The lines bear the traces of Brownell's physical response to the sights and sounds of battle and convey them to the readers. "Veritable children of the war," as another commentator calls them, they carry the tragedy of the event with them in their shocked, disheveled forms.[36] Ripped from the event even before it becomes headlines, they come to the reader bellowing, stumbling, and bleeding.

In "The Bay Fight," Brownell intertwines the story of the battle with the story of what the battle is doing to his poem as he tries to write it. Not an allegory of writing, not an analogy, the poem offers a record or trace of transformations in language practice that occur in the collision and collusion with violent events. "The Bay Fight" has the fidelity of an eyewitness report that does not pick and choose its details, and so runs on to many pages of minute and chaotic description. But the poem begins familiarly enough, in untroubled, familiar ballad stanzas. Brownell charts the ship's course south through tranquil, tropical waters, around the coast of Florida, to Mobile Bay. The ballad stanzas are seemingly as endless and undulating as the sea itself:

> Yet, coast-wise as we cruised or lay,
> The land-breeze still at nightfall bore,
> By beach and fortress-guarded bay,
> Sweet odors from the enemy's shore,
>
> Fresh from the forest solitudes,
> Unchallenged of his sentry lines—
> The bursting of his cypress buds,
> And the warm fragrance of his pines.[37]

The iambic tetrameter lines end in perfect abab rhymes; they summon a tradition of sea ballads that link the ocean's waves with a predictable, repetitive form. Foreshadowing what is to come, however, the poem cites the lack of enemy encroachment as the reason for the regularity; because it is "unchallenged of his sentry lines," its own lines have no need to bristle.

While the trip along the Gulf Coast is recalled in smooth, regular quatrains, once the Confederate ships and forts around the bay engage the Union fleet, the formal structure of the ballad is disrupted. As soon as the battle starts the lines are shortened to trimeter and the meter turns irregular:

> Ah, how poor the prate
> Of statute and state
> We once held with these fellows—
> Here, on the flood's pale-green,
> Hark how he bellows,
> Each bluff old Sea-Lawyer!
> Talk to them, Dahlgren,
> Parrott, and Sawyer!

Brownell compares prewar legal negotiations with the law of force spoken by the *Hartford*'s cannons. The poem registers that new persuasive force with shortened lines full of short words, heavy stresses, and what must have been construed as the barbaric use of alliteration and rhyme that defies predictable pattern. Brownell speaks with the guns, adapting the poem's form to attend to their bluff bellows.

The poem charts the consequences of the combined force of two modes of speech working together: the deadly language of the guns and the ship's officers' verbal management of violence (Brownell's "we" counts himself among the officers, and indeed he was one):

> But soon, as once and agen [*sic*]
> Fore and aft we sped,
> (The firing to guide or check,)
> You could hardly choose but tread
> On the ghastly human wreck,
> (Dreadful gobbet and shred
> That a minute ago were men!)

Officers' words guide or check the firing, even as they must confront the physical consequences of these verbal directions by stepping among the wounded and dead as they run along the decks. A gobbet is a "part, portion, piece, or fragment of anything which is divided, cut, or broken."[38] Brownell was struck by how few dead men could constitute such a horrifying scene within the close space of a battleship; he wrote to Holmes that "Though we had only 25 killed and 28 wounded . . . on that day, yet numbers were torn into fragments, (men with their muscles tense, subjected to violent concussion, seem as brittle as glass), causing the deck and its surroundings to present a most strange spectacle."[39]

Shattered men and Brownell's metrical experimentation are both aptly described by "numbers torn into fragments." Immersed in the chaos, seeking to capture the carnage, Brownell's lines are in unpredictable accentual trimeter: a mix of iambs, trochees, and anapests in no particular sequence, a curtailed, unsettled ballad form. The monosyllabic end rhymes follow something of a pattern—abcbcba—but they also present as a series of partial rhymes, varied only by the last letter. With no word more than two syllables, the phrasing is curt and curtailed. The words seem to be uttered under the constraints of action. Brownell infuses journalistic immediacy into poetic language in order to record events and express their ambivalent impact, both of which, in his view, should occupy a place in historical record.

Faithful to details, Brownell's narrative includes but does not capitalize on the moments that would become iconographic in other ballads about the battle. Primary among these is the image of Farragut tied to the mast. In order to have a clear view of unfolding events unobstructed by smoke, and in order to make sure he didn't fall in the midst of the fight, Farragut ordered the men to tie him to the mast of the *Hartford*; from that position he commanded the Union forces. W. E. Channing's poem makes this heroic image the center of his ballad "Lashed to the Mast":

> It was the brave old Farragut,
> And he these words did say,—
> Now lash me to the foremast fast,
> And then boys fire away;
> They robbed our forts, our arms, our ships,
> Our sailors' hearts remain,
> Take back your own and break their whips,
> And free the doomed from pain.[40]

There is no indication in histories of the battle that Farragut made such an eloquent, pointedly ideological speech; Channing uses the occasion to stage an oratorical performance that espouses patriotic rhetoric inspiring the soldiers and celebrating the Union as a moral force seeking to abolish slavery.

In contrast, Brownell's poem mirrors the utilitarianism of the admiral's position, without mentioning the lashing. The figure of Farragut at the mast is rendered in just five lines that form part of a scene of battle action:

> High in the mizzen shroud
> (Lest the smoke of the sight oe'er whelm),
> Our Admiral's voice rang loud,
> "Hard a starboard your helm!
> Starboard, and run him down!"

Brownell's admiral is bent on winning the battle and restricts his comments to practical orders driven by strategy. The admiral's competency is emphasized, courageous, but devoid of ideological motivation. Brownell's eyewitness poem estranges a standard feature of other Civil War ballads: the framing of every action in highly symbolic, predictable patriotic iconography.

In spite of the powerful Unionist conclusion of the poem, which explains the legitimacy of the carnage through God and the Union, Brownell meticulously records accidents, mistakes, and reversals in the course of the narrative that disrupt a strong, familiar heroic narrative. He recounts, for example, the accidental collision of two Union ships that wreaks momentary havoc; the event could easily have been omitted in order to streamline the poem and further glorify the military prowess of the Federal navy. A more serious challenge to a purely heroic narrative of commemoration was the sudden sinking of the Union ironclad *Tecumseh*, which took everyone by surprise because no one expected ironclads to be so vulnerable. Advancing to engage Confederate troops, the ship hit a Confederate mine and sank immediately; the men had no time to escape. Brownell depicts the shocking transformation of the warship into a "great iron coffin":

> Caught by the under-death,
> In the drawing of a breath,
> Down went the dauntless Craven
> He and his hundred!
>
> A moment we saw her turret,
> A little heel she gave,
> And a thin white spray went o'er her,
> Like the crest of a breaking wave—
> In that great iron coffin,
> The channel for their grave.

"In the drawing of a breath," all the men on board sank. Striking is their complete impotence and invisibility. Brownell charts an unprecedented form of battle death excruciatingly devoid of human agency; enclosed in a steel case, the men are powerless to do anything but accept their fate. In the course of the poem, this event seems like a brief aside, noted and then forgotten as attention turns to the fiery sea battle. The shift of attention is necessary under battle conditions: the survivors must fully attend to the ongoing fight, and Brownell adheres to the necessity in the poem.

But after the Confederate surrender, he quickly returns to the image of the men slowly asphyxiating at the bottom of the ocean. Brownell imagines them cheering on their comrades with their last breaths. He compares the swift death of the sailors on deck with the sunken men:

> Our dead lay cold and stark,
> But our dying, down in the dark,
> Answered as best they might—
> Lifting their poor lost arms,
> And cheering for God and right

Brownell may be trying to summon patriotism in a fantasy of the men cheering at the bottom of the ocean while awaiting their death, but the image remains merely horrifying. The earlier fragmentation of the dead men on the deck returns in the figure of the sunken men's "poor lost arms." The phrase cannot function as metonymy after Brownell's insistent, prolonged description of physical dismemberment throughout the poem. Of the dying men aboveboard, for example, he says "we . . . held their hands to the last / (Those that had hands to hold)." The poor lost arms tossed upward instead summon the futility of human energies in the face of this new technological creation and its challenge to human agency. Lashed to the mast in the old-fashioned way, Farragut won the fight on a wooden ship, supported by other sloops and ironclads. Incoherently, the old-fashioned figure of heroism remains the memorable shorthand for the fight.[41] But the primary sense the poem conveys is not that ironclads have gained ascendance with all the accompanying implications, nor that the "hearts of oak" are sturdier and more heroic, but the prominence of accident and chance.[42] The meticulous detail with which Brownell charts the battle raises serious questions, however inadvertent, about governing forces like fate or divinity.

Brownell passionately formulates the power of chance, reconciling it with the presence of God:

Fear? A forgotten form!
Death? A dream of the eyes!
We were atoms in God's great storm
That roared through the angry skies.

As atoms in God's great storm, Brownell and his companions could not predict individual events; thrown around by the chaos of violence, they could nevertheless be sure of God's guiding hand. That is the point Brownell certainly wants to make, but the image challenges divine agency by summoning the field of scientific inquiry via the concept of the atom. The figure of atoms in a storm suggests that he isn't sure precisely what the men are instruments of, or what the final outcome will be. Even when working within a mode where the rhetorical rules are unambiguous, propaganda for the Union cause, Brownell does not express absolute certainty whether the Union is a force of good or something more neutral, like physics.

At the close of the poem, Brownell curtails poetic experimentation and returns to a classic patriotic ballad or hymn. Set in regular iambic tetrameter, the final stanzas are set apart from the narrative and begin with an address to the "Mother Land." Brownell accounts for the battle's violence in the familiar terms of God and country. Even here, however, "Dread Nature" raises questions about the formula:

> Ah, ever, when with storm sublime
> Dread Nature clears our murky air,
> Thus in the crash of falling crime
> Some lesser guilt must share

The stanza is difficult to reconcile with the rest of the section. While Brownell ultimately asserts that the "Dahlgren and the drum / Are dread apostles of God's name," here he suggests that perhaps the moral calculus isn't so clear. The phrase "some lesser guilt must share" struggles for attribution. There's no clear subject, the guilt hovers, and nature, not God, presides over an uncertain scenario. Watching the battle's often arbitrary events, seeing men torn apart, and attempting to capture it all in poetic form has created for Brownell a situation in which material circumstances threaten to override idealizations of war.

Several poems were written about the Battle of Mobile Bay, but none of them resemble Brownell's or raise questions about fate, destiny, and the possibility of accident or chaos as a primary governing force of human experience. For the most part, the poems celebrate the old-fashioned heroism of Farragut, whose quick decision to move forward through the minefield after the sinking of the *Tecumseh* inspired admiration. That, combined with his forward position in battle, tied to the mast of a wooden ship, made him a powerful figure for heroicization. Channing's "Lashed to the Mast," an anonymous poem entitled "'We'll Fight It Out,'" John Hay's "'After You, Pilot,'" and others take the traditional ballad form and select images that monumentalize the admiral and celebrate the Union victory.[43] Seamless in their legend-making processes, they don't allow for the complexities of Brownell's uneven but brilliant account. Only Melville's "Battle for the Bay" shares Brownell's novel practices, and I suggest that "The Bay Fight" in a primary intertext for Melville's poem.[44] Certainly Melville was aware of Brownell's work: "The Bay Fight" was first published in *Harper's Monthly*, the same magazine in which five of Melville's poems appeared in advance of the publication of *Battle-Pieces*; the popularity of "The Bay Fight" along with its critical acclaim made it difficult for a contemporary aspiring to capture the sense of the war to overlook. A sign of their common ambitions, both poets published a collection of war poems in

1866 with distinguished presses: Brownell's *War-Lyrics and Other Poems* was published by Ticknor and Fields and *Battle-Pieces* was published by Harper and Bros.[45] Reviews of *Battle-Pieces* frequently compare Melville's poems with Brownell's. From another angle, Frank Day notes that Farragut's account of the battle was one of Melville's primary sources.[46] If Brownell was assigned by Farragut the task of documenting the battle, it stands to reason that Farragut's account draws on Brownell's notes, which is another way that Melville's poem is affiliated with Brownell's writings. The story of Brownell's dual role of note taker and poet was well known, and Melville's poems indicate an interest in studying the form of poetic eyewitnessing that Brownell practiced.

In their comparisons of Brownell and Melville, contemporary critics tend to identify originality of form as a shared trait: roughness of language and rhythm and an emphasis on journalistic detail that captures the spirit of battle. Evaluations are reversed in two reviews: The *Philadelphia Inquirer* finds "Melville preferable to Brownell, possessing all the powers of the warrior poet, without his fault of detailing minutely all the accessories of an action." The *Boston Commercial Bulletin*, on the other hand, says that they share "the quality of Brusqueness," but "with more polish and less freedom than Brownell, Mr Melville writes what he thinks rather than what he feels." A third review identifies the central quality in both as originality. Melville's poetry "is as original as the poetry of Mr. Brownell . . . and often as obscure in his mysterious, orphic utterances."[47] Fidelity to event, an interest in empiricism, and cryptic or prophetic meditations are the unlikely collection of traits identified in the verse of both poets.

Along with Holmes and Farragut, both poets believed that facts are only discernible through their emotional life; they sought to capture the "aspects of war" that derive from novel killing technologies, journalistic coverage, and intensive strategizing. They demonstrate a belief that language could physically register the seismic shocks of war and hold them in cultural memory in a shared poetic archive that goes beyond what individual poets intended to say or could consciously know. But there are significant differences as well. While Brownell saturates his poem in immediate experience, Melville foregrounds his poetic mediation of that immediacy. Brownell seeks to register shock firsthand, while Melville tracks the aftershock—what happens to cataclysmic events at a distance from immediate experience, and how or whether they can be conveyed beyond their own time. What traces remain after the dust settles seems to be Melville's central question. Melville enters into dialogue with Brownell's poem to explore this question.

Melville does indeed intellectualize or abstract the events that Brownell renders more concretely, as one of the reviewers notes as a criticism: but this is not a flaw. Melville distills essences of events, seeking to articulate verity. Condensation is one of the most visible differences in the two poems. While Brownell's poem runs to over sixty stanzas, Melville compacts his narrative into fourteen. While Brownell's poem devotes seven stanzas to the tropical tranquility aboard the ships that precedes the battle, Melville has one:

> Beyond the bar the land-wind dies,
> The prows becharmed at anchor swim:
> A summer night; the stars withdrawn look down—
> Fair eve of battle grim.
> The sentries pace, bonetas glide;
> Below, the sleeping sailors swing,
> And in their dreams to quarters spring,
> Or cheer their flag, or breast a stormy tide.[48]

Brownell describes the sentries' tedium ("weary was the long patrol") and the sense of stasis in a tropical wonderland, but the figure of the sleeping sailor is Melville's alone. There he concentrates a languid well-being that saturates even the unconsciousness of the sailor, dramatizing the contrast between peaceful rest and the anticipated chaos of battle. The "fair eve of battle grim" finds the crew in an almost mesmerized state, infused with the tranquility of the natural surroundings. The sentries pace while bonetas (Melville's spelling for bonito, a kind of fish) glide, harmoniously fulfilling their forms of mobility. The ships don't need their anchors, because the water calmly holds them.

With the other poets of his time, Melville renders Farragut symbolic, but not of the Union cause. Instead the admiral serves as an inspiration and guiding force for his men. Crystallizing Brownell's depiction of utilitarian competence and concern for his crew, Melville casts Farragut as a beacon whose single vision governs the men:

> The Admiral—yielding to the love
> Which held his life and ship so dear—
> Sailed second in the long fleet's midmost line;
> Yet thwarted all their care:
> He lashed himself aloft, and shone
> Star of the fight, with influence sent

> Throughout the dusk embattlement;
> And so they neared the strait and walls of stone.[49]

"Star of the fight," Farragut joins the other celestial imagery in *Battle-Pieces* that aligns the Union with fated movements on an inscrutable, inhuman scale. There is no mention of punishing the Confederacy for its crimes, however, or of divine justice at work. As in Brownell's poem, Farragut is centered on the practical tasks of commanding his men throughout the poem, sending his "influence" through them to coordinate the men's efforts. Like Brownell, in spite of the coherence of the figuration, Melville doesn't elide inconvenient facts. While it would be more fitting for a beacon to hold the first place in the line, Farragut initially stayed behind—moving to the front after the *Tecumseh* sank; Melville acknowledges that "he sailed second," an awkward location for a beacon.

In Brownell's poem the expected narrative that would chart an inexorable movement toward Union victory is punctuated by random occurrences that generate reversals, interruptions, anticlimax, and the element of chance. Melville distills this quality in a few prominent examples that forcefully disrupt conventional naval ballads of heroism. An example of anticlimax arises in the middle of the poem, where it seems that the battle is suddenly over and the Union has won:

> The strong-holds past: assailed, they run;
> The Selma strikes, and the work is done:
> The dropping anchor the achievement seals.[50]

As in Brownell's poem but far more tersely, Melville describes the lull in the battle and the retreating Confederate ships: the small ironclad CSS *Selma* strikes a final time before it is captured, and the Union fleet anchors. The perception of victory is short-lived, however, because the Confederate ironclad *Tennessee* shifts its path and approaches the Union fleet: "But no, she turns—the Tennessee!" Melville could have easily elided the momentary misperception. Retaining it underscores the uncertainty of battle. He juxtaposes the desire to commemorate events: "the work is done," "the achievement seal[ed]"—with the shifting of events before the commemoration even has a chance to gain traction. Even the moment of premature commemoration, however, does not describe a heroic victor and a cowardly foe; the description of victory continues to emphasize utilitarian competency rather than heroism.

A second, more extreme example of arbitrary reversal, which is central to Brownell's poem as well, is the sinking of the *Tecumseh*. Melville includes a mystical prelude that heightens by contrast the rapidity of catastrophe, which takes up a single line:

> But what delays? 'mid wounds above
> Dim buoys give hint of death below—
> Sea-ambuscades, where evil art had aped
> Hecla that hides in snow.
> The centre-van, entangled, trips;
> The starboard leader holds straight on:
> A cheer for the Tecumseh!—nay,
> Before their eyes the turreted ship goes down![51]

With foreknowledge, Melville elaborately describes the mines and obstructions that the Confederates have sunk, summoning the volcano Hecla covered in snow before it erupts. The "starboard leader" seems to have succeeded in bringing the ships through the intricate dangers, but in a shocking reversal, revealed in the last five words of the stanza, "the turreted ship goes down." "Turreted" is the only suggestion that the ship is an ironclad and should have been invulnerable. The premature celebration—"A cheer for the Tecumseh"— suggests that viewers would like to tout the ironclad's invincibility, but the ship's sinking radically curtails that desire. Mimicking the crew's inability to process the shock of the unanticipated tragedy, Melville barely describes the reaction to the event; he simply notes Farragut moving forward "ere the horror ran" through the onlookers. As in Brownell's poem, no more is said about the men trapped at the bottom of the ocean until after the battle is won.

Like Brownell, Melville refrains from any mention of the men buried alive until it seems as if they will go unnoticed in the victory celebration; but then he concludes the poem with a tribute. Here there is a significant difference between the two poems. Whereas Brownell mourns the loss for four stanzas, he then turns away to cap the poem with a patriotic hymn of nine stanzas; the effect is to submerge and rationalize the deaths of the men within the poem's final celebration of the righteousness of the Union cause. Melville, on the other hand, concludes the poem with the equivocal image of the dead men:

> And quiet far below the wave,
> Where never cheers shall move their sleep

> Some who did boldly nobly earn them lie
> Charmed children of the deep.
> But decks that are now in the seed
> And cannon yet within the mine
> Shall thrill the deeper, gun and pine
> Because of the Tecumseh's glorious deed.[52]

Instead of commemorating the loss and stressing the importance of the men's sacrifices for the Union, Melville summons the men as if they were suspended in time, floating, enchanted. The image recalls the tranquil sleep on the ship before the battle began, but it is eerily displaced from natural contexts, raising questions about the relation between war and nature. Melville points out that the men are impervious, suggesting that cheers are not worth much if they can't reach those who earned them. Pushed to its conclusion, the logic suggests that the iron is happy to be mined and the pine trees are happy to grow so that they can create the means—weapons, warships—for people to be entombed alive, like raw metal or seeds. The image foregrounds the stark difference between the unnaturalness of men suffocating in a metal pod at the bottom of the ocean and a seed that will break open and grow, while proposing an alternative viewpoint, also discomfiting, that nature supports human cycles that return always to war.[53]

The final line underscores the doubts raised about the value of war, for the *Tecumseh*'s "glorious deed" was to sink. The ship ran over a mine even before it could fight and sank in what must have been seconds ("In the drawing of a breath"). The event couldn't have been more unexpected, tragic, or anticlimactic. Brownell's image of the men cheering for a victory that they can't see or know at the bottom of the ocean "with their poor arms" encapsulates that sense, perhaps unintentionally. Melville, however, foregrounds the ambivalence. He captures both the desire to make the sacrifices meaningful and legible in moral terms and the grave doubts over whether these new wartime circumstances can be assimilated to that frame.

Both Brownell and Melville infuse journalistic immediacy into poetic language in order to record events and express their impact on human consciousness. Making sense of that project in more than broad delineations requires "reading in detail" (Naomi Schor's phrase), as I have begun to do here.[54] Recent readings of Melville's *Battle-Pieces* have tended to attend to his philosophical formulations without taking into account his meticulous attention to facts, even seemingly inconsequential events, in some of the poems (certainly not all). Disregarding the details in Melville's Civil War poems, along with his engagements with other poets, leaves significant lacunae. While critics have offered important insights into Melville's awareness of the operations of historical time and his disenchantment with war and industrialization, for example, they often leave unnoted the simultaneous unsettling of these ideas, his sense of unpredictability, immediacy, and entropy that derive from and emerge in relation to his attentiveness to historical fact.[55]

These aspects of *Battle-Pieces* become more visible when considered in relation to the dialogues Melville enters with his contemporaries. Brownell's poems, as immersed as they are in the faith that filtering events through a poetic sensibility will convey the truth of war, perhaps unwittingly registers a sense that the war is filled with accidents, not design; that chaos can rule in battle; that there is no clear association of wooden ships with stolid morality or iron ships with evil, or with progress. The doubts, along with the violent upheavals that cause them, register formally, in the rough rhythms, terse lines, and varying stanza length of "The Bay Fight." Entering into dialogue with Brownell's practices, Melville offers more philosophical speculations on the Battle of Mobile Bay that are grounded in events. He foregrounds passing disruptions of Unionist narratives and in doing so emphasizes the possibility of the atomization of consciousness. Melville balances this speculation with other more settled ideas: that God governs events and that his guiding hand led the Union to win the fight. He holds the question in the balance.

The model embraced by Holmes, Farragut, Brownell, and Melville might be understood as one of direct, albeit multiply mediated transmission and translation that runs from physical clash, to the poet's physical and mental absorption of that shock, to the pen's marks on the paper, to the reader's absorption of the repercussions. This view of poetry as the register and therefore the reservoir of the impact of war posits a theory of language in which language itself is physically altered—disfigured, distorted, fragmented—by the shock of war.[56] We can therefore read war's legacy formally as well as thematically in the poetry that emerges from the Civil War era. A part of that legacy is inscribed in the poetry of both Melville and Brownell.

Writing's Wars

Stephen Crane's Poetry
and the Postbellum Turn to the Page

Kerry Larson has identified "the priority of the social whole in the imaginative life of the democratic subject" in the antebellum period; that priority made the "idea of a representative experience so fundamental and so pervasive that interest in personal, purely subjective expression [was] effectively outlawed."[1] Holding the many in the one, the poet feels obligated to suppress his own subjectivity in the service of the people; his charge is to express "the precise spirit of the average mass." Ironically, that sense of the social whole was perhaps never so intense as during the Civil War, when the nation split in two.

Oliver Wendell Holmes's description of the Union as a "national nervous system," forged into a "single living body" by communications technologies, captures the intensity of the sensation of living within a social whole.[2] Abnegating self-expression, poets worked to circulate ideas and feelings through this body, making affective sense of the conflict for their readership. Civil War poets understood themselves as part of a networked system of relations that included soldiers, journalists, policy makers, and civilians; they spoke as part of and for that national community, binding it together through a constant flow of ephemeral print media.

Poets lost that single-minded purpose after the war because no cause was so catastrophically consequential for the nation, and because poetry didn't circulate as broadly and promiscuously in national magazines and newspapers by the turn of the century. Edmund Clarence Stedman, in his introduction to his *American Anthology, 1787–1900* (1900), describes the shifting literary terrain: by 1900, "prose fiction, instead of verse, is the characteristic imaginative product," in contrast to the middle years of the century when "poetry led other forms of our literature."[3] Comparing it to the Spanish-American War, Stedman notes the particular sense of urgency and unity of poetic output during the Civil War: "As for our poetry of the Spanish War, I think that sufficient will be found in my closing pages to indicate that our quickstep was enlivened by a reasonable measure of prosody. The Civil War was a different matter—preceded by years of excitement, and at last waged with gigantic conflicts and countless tragic interludes, until every home was desolate, North or South. Men and women still survive who—with [Henry Howard] Brownell, [Forceythe] Willson, and others of the dead—made songs and ballads that, as I have said, were known the world over."[4] The "gigantic" nature of the conflict gave rise to far more than a "reasonable measure of prosody." Not only Americans but people "the world over" were brought together by the same songs and ballads, forms associated with speaking with and for the people. He suggests that the terms under which these men and women wrote changed so considerably after the war that the poems were of a completely different order.

At the turn of the century, poets no longer had a sense that they might work as representatives of a social whole, and the available forms of circulation no longer supported the kind of broad network of poetic response to events that we have seen in the previous chapters. And yet the idea of participating in an important common cause maintained an appeal after the war years passed. A sense of loss—the loss of a national circulation system and a national audience—influenced poets at the turn of the century. I will suggest some of the ways the poetic practices of the Civil War may have continued to shape the work of later poets by taking as a case study the poetry of Stephen Crane. The few critics who have analyzed Crane's poetry have located it on the experimental edge of literary production, poised for a leap into modernism.[5] Arguing against this trend, Elissa Zellinger sees Crane looking backward, toward "a nineteenth-century tradition of longing for heroic selfhood" and a time when cliché and convention could summon common feeling.[6] Building on Zellinger's insight, I suggest that Crane mourns the loss of popular poetic practices that circulate among a broad readership, helping to shape affective responses to events. His poems express a desire to be useful in an important common cause. The world of poetic circulation for which Crane longs assumed its ideal form during the Civil War, when events and media systems converged to make a central place for poetic expression. Crane shares with his predecessors a desire to write about war as a representative of the social whole; his speakers are impersonal not only because Crane is interested in the plight of the alienated individual; he is also searching for ways to speak representatively in a time when the social whole is no longer a powerful organizing principle. At the same time, Crane dramatizes the strains on fantasies of national unity at the end of the century. While he attends to the heritage of popular poetry as a means of speaking for the nation, he also brings out the impossibility of doing so.[7] Rather than understanding Crane as making a break with the past, I look to the ways that he brings the past into his present moment as a means of articulating the shifting role of poetry in the late nineteenth century.[8]

A second, related legacy registers in Crane's style. Crane absorbed Civil War poets' tendency to conflate writing with fighting in a way that collapses the relation between metaphoric terms. What once circulated as a common coinage or convention, however, now has become an aspect of individual style, indicating the turn to poetic singularity and the rise of the page's importance as the location of the poet's words, as the movement through broader circulatory systems diminishes by the turn of the century.[9] Critics have repeatedly drawn attention to Crane's interest in stylistic effects as a way of affirming his distance from experience in the material world. For Michael Fried, Crane's writings about war are actually about his war with writing. Crane's repeated representation of violent acts against bodies in *Red Badge of Courage* and elsewhere covers for his unconscious preoccupation with putting words on a page.[10] Jerome McGann pays homage to Crane's self-reflexivity by titling his book on the subject *Black Riders*—a phrase take from the title of Crane's first book of poetry—noting that Crane's writings show full consciousness that "the poetic field is self-signifying."[11] Locating Crane in relation to late-nineteenth-century ideas about American realism and naturalism, Michael Davitt Bell notes the exceptional way that "Crane cultivates a style that deliberately calls attention to itself as a style." If "one of the deepest of appeals of American naturalism" for late nineteenth-century readers was a sense of the "direct transmission of real life in a transparent style," Crane "worked out his own literary practice in deliberate opposition" to this approach. Instead he ironically deployed a multitude of styles in order to reveal "the scarcity and fragility of authentic experience in a world dominated by established styles." Crane's style serves as an instrument of irony in which he critiques the idea that one's relation to the real is unmediated; the "self-conscious deployment of style as style" exposes the gap between "the rhetoric of preconception" and the "truth of experience."[12]

But while Crane's interest in style is indeed conspicuous, it needn't conflict with his interest in apprehending experience via nonmimetic means. In his war journalism, he expresses an interest in capturing "the real." "War Memories" opens with the declaration "but to get the real thing! It seems impossible!"[13] It may then follow that writing with a journalistic eye and hand requires Crane to admit writing as a challenge to mimesis, to acknowledge that one must recognize the difference between words and soldiers in battle while trying to formulate a relation between them. He is interested less in exposing the limitations of the belief in a transparent style that Bell identifies than in identifying stylistic strategies that might articulate the relation between writing and war. Crane is particularly interested in the simultaneously transitive and intransigent relation between war and writing. Counterintuitively, what is transitive is the ways that watching war from a distance—as Crane often did as a reporter—reduces events to abstractions that resemble print: at the Battle of San Juan, he describes "a thin line of black figures moving across a field," for example; the black figures resemble writing as much as they do soldiers. The resemblance to writing comes from a desire to read and interpret the scene. The intransigence comes with not knowing what the observations mean, what the soldiers are experiencing. On that point Crane says that "one cannot speak of it—the spectacle of the common man serenely doing his work. . . . One pays them the tribute of the toast of silence."[14] Sacred, untellable, unknowable, the men's experience is distinct from Crane's experience as a writer. They inhabit different spheres of action, yet he watches them with reverence and refers the reader to them.

Without the charge of mimetic representation that fiction and journalism carry, poetry offers a space to explore the problems of writing's abstraction from social events and of the author's role as the mediator of the gap. Even before he became a war correspondent, Crane wrote about war, famously in *Red Badge of Courage*, but also in *Black Riders and Other Lines*, his book of poems published in the same year. The first poem in *Black Riders* takes as its subject writing's wars, played out on the page:

Black riders came from the sea.
There was clang and clang of spear and shield,
And clash and clash of hoof and heel,
Wild shouts and the wave of hair
In the rush upon the wind:
Thus the ride of sin.[15]

Saturated with alliteration and assonance, perfect and partial rhymes, the words' sonic presence is so insistent that the black riders announce themselves as the writer's words, jostling to make their way onto the page. Michael Fried might say that the clang of spear and shield enact a primal scene of contact between pen and page, from which the words take their animating force. Metamorphism figures centrally in the poem. Traces of men and horses—hoof and heel—blend together, and they suggest other transmutations and crossings as well, between men's worldly wars and Crane's war of words. For if the poem is restricted to self-signification it nevertheless exhibits a strain against this containment. Crane acts out a battle in miniature that foregrounds its claustrophobic limits. The page is too small to wage a full war, so the riders/writers appear briefly and fight with few and repetitive words. Recognizing the limitations of his representation, the spectatorial narrator curtails the scene with a brief moral that seems premature, because the scene isn't developed enough to justify the conclusion. Crane's black riders draw attention to their dislodgement from worldly events: they come from nowhere and fight for no reason; their print-like contours recall the "thin black figures" that fight in the Battle of San Juan, but they conspicuously lack a location. Crane stresses their incompleteness, drawing attention to the wars they do not refer to. And yet Crane's odd form of metaphor, where the black riders signify at once warriors and letters, brings conflict to the page in a way that intensifies the transitive forms of Civil War metaphors.

If the surface of the page serves as the field for Crane's war, the Civil War writers see the war as the field for their writing: In a poem by A. J. H. Duganne entitled "Bethel," published in the *Atlantic Monthly* in September 1862, a sword and pen doubly inscribe a soldier's heroism when he falls in battle:

> Where he fell shall be sunshine as bright as his name,
> And the grass where he slept shall be green as his fame;
> For the gold of the Pen and the steel of the Sword
> Write his deeds—in his blood—on the land he adored,—
>   "Column! Forward!"[16]

In contradistinction from Crane's dislocation from event, in "Bethel" both the battle and the soldier "WINTHROP" (Theodore Winthrop, one of the first officers killed in the war) are specified. While Crane's verbal figures double as soldiers fighting on the page, here writing and fighting are unified in the figure

of the sword and pen writing Winthrop's deeds together in blood: the battlefield serves as the page. The column charging forward doubles the poem's
column, which circulates in memory of the fallen soldier and the Battle of
Big Bethel on the Virginia Peninsula in June 1861. The parallels between Civil
War–era poems and Crane's suggests that Crane inherits a legacy of conflating
page with battlefield, sword with pen, but his battles distinctly lack reference
to specific events or a readership that is called upon to cheer on the troops and
preserve the memory of the dead.

If Civil War poems such as "Bethel" seek to weave violent events into a
larger social fabric, Crane's poems register the atomization of relations between
poetry, war, and media in his stylized engagements. Rather than publishing
in broadly disseminated magazines and newspapers alongside the news, Crane
circulated his poems among a small, elite group of readers. The *Philistine;
A Periodical of Protest*, where a number of his poems appeared, was one of
the most successful "little magazines" of the 1890s–1910s, which published
controversial, progressive essays and poetry.[17] Nancy Glazener identifies the
little magazines as one of three challenges to the *Atlantic Monthly*'s dwindling
cultural centrality, a centrality that anchored the Civil War literary publishing
world in the North decades before.[18] In spite of its elite status, which hadn't
yet consolidated in the ways Glazener discusses in the postbellum period, the
Atlantic Monthly Civil War poems—by John Greenleaf Whittier, Elizabeth
Akers Allen, Julia Ward Howe, Ralph Waldo Emerson, Henry Wadsworth
Longfellow, Lucy Larcom, and others—were often reprinted across the publishing scene. With *Harper's Illustrated Weekly, Frank Leslie's Illustrated News*,
and other nationally distributed newspapers and magazines, the *Atlantic*
was one of the most central literary publications of the war on the Union
side. While Crane addressed a small, elite group of readers with his poetry,
he reached a mass audience with his journalistic coverage of the Greco-
Turkish and Spanish-American wars in the New York yellow newspapers that
famously promoted war as much as covered it.[19] As a celebrity reporter whose
very name sold papers, Crane aided that dual endeavor. A shorter war fought
outside U.S. borders, the Spanish-American war didn't focus people's atten-
tions and emotions in the way the Civil War did. And while poetry appeared
in newspapers and magazines during the Spanish-American War—much of it
collected in a nine hundred–page volume in which Crane's "Blue Battalions"
appears—poetry, news, and the reading public had diversified in significant
ways by the end of the century.[20] The sense of joining a collective of writers
who experienced a sense of social totality was lost, at least for Crane.

If poetry no longer held a significant place in war's networks, helping to forge a social whole, Crane nevertheless envisioned war as a place of idealized collective experience, which he usually observed rather than joined. Amy Kaplan notes that if "Crane decontextualizes war as an object for the storyteller, he recontextualizes it as an object to by viewed as a spectator."[21] In his journalism, Crane works from this removed position to convey the perception of soldiers' cooperation as a harmonious collectivity. He also offers other conflicting observations on the randomness of death, the indifference of officers to their soldiers' welfare, and the absurdity of individual events in the chaos of battle: at one point in "War Memories" he proclaims that war is "a bunch of bananas."[22] While admiring the cooperative sociality of military service among enlisted men, he also notes the governmental, political, and perhaps even divine forces that promote needless killing; and he stresses that the ultimate condition of this more localized social unity is death. The basis for Crane's admiration of war is the common soldier's willingness to work with and sacrifice himself for others, but he notes the extreme cost of this comradeship.

What stands out in Crane's journalism is a powerful combination of heterogeneous viewpoints that lack an overarching principle or object. While covering the Greco-Turkish War and particularly the Spanish-American War in Cuba, he unironically celebrated what he called the "splendid gallantry of the private soldier." In "Stephen Crane's Vivid Story of the Battle of San Juan," published in the *New York World* on July 14, 1898, he describes the charge of the American soldiers: "Yes, they were going up the hill, up the hill. It was the best moment of anybody's life."[23] At the same time Crane showed an awareness that this perspective could not only be contradicted but rendered absurd by other ways of looking at the same event. He describes at length his ecstasy at witnessing his first big battle in the Greco-Turkish War of 1897: "The roll of musketry was tremendous . . . it was the most beautiful sound of my experience." But he followed up this impression with an abrupt corrective: "This is one point of view. Another might be taken from the men who died there," an impression he could not access.[24] Rather than incorporating these points of view into a meaningful system, he allows the impressions to remain incommensurate. He does not condemn his own pleasure in the beautiful sound of musketry even as he acknowledges the possibility of another's tremendous suffering. The perspectives float free without any broader social whole holding them together.

This interest in multiple, incommensurate perspectives registers in three of Crane's uncollected poems, often with attention to the war dead. The poems set cynicism alongside a sentimental celebration of soldiers' solidarity and sacrifice. For those accustomed to reading Crane as an ironist, these poems are remarkable in their readability as sincere expressions of conventional sentiments that would not be out of place during the Civil War, combined with a range of irreconcilable perspectives that mark the loss of a discursive community. Crane discusses commemoration in what he calls "a Decoration Day thing" that he wrote for the press, which would have appeared in May 1894 if it had not been rejected.[25] In this piece, which was accompanied by a poem, Crane expresses a utopian certainty that after the last veterans are dead, people will properly memorialize all the common soldiers of the Civil War: "We can expect that when the last veteran has vanished there will come a time of great monuments, eulogies, tears. Then the boy in blue will have grown to heroic size, and painters, sculptors, and writers will have been finally impressed, and strive to celebrate the deeds of the brave, simple quiet men who crowded upon the opposing bayonets of their country's enemies. In the tremendous roll of events the pages and paragraphs of future histories are nothing."[26] Like Walt Whitman, Crane singles out "the boy in blue," the common soldier, for recognition. The men crowding upon bayonets evoke pathos over a futile sacrifice: massive, mindless, even suicidal. Crane does not believe in dying for one's country, yet he seeks to honor it. Though he projects into the future a nostalgic desire to see the monuments, eulogies, and tears for the common soldier, a despair emerges in the logic that they must all be dead before their sacrifice can be valued. The dreamy evocation of the scene, moreoever, suggests that he does not actually think this event will come to pass, but rather that it should. While improbable monuments might be desirable, moreover, "the pages and paragraphs of future histories are nothing." The combination of cynicism and longing is striking; the sense of futility is enhanced by the genuine desire to be a part of a meaningful commemoration. They sit uneasily side by side, not ironically—a trait almost always bestowed on Crane—but in simple, poignant juxtaposition.

Crane goes on to insist that writers must not wait for all the veterans to die and urges them to pay homage in the present, calling them to a common occasion that, again, he suggests is highly unlikely to happen. He follows his advice in the poem that prefaces the article, also never published, which celebrates the bravery of the young men who fought in the Civil War. In Crane's elegiac poem, the poet is remarkably useless, describing rather than consoling and exhorting the way his Civil War predecessors worked to do. The last stanza from William Ross Wallace's 1863 "Burial Hymn for the Union Soldiers" offers a counterpoint:

> Soldier of the Union, rest!
> Lo! a Nation guards thy breast!
> With a larger, grand desire,
> Freedom sweeps her mighty lyre
> Lo! the Immortal in her bloom
> Writes upon thy sacred tomb,
> "Honor, Glory, UNION, wave
> Wreaths eternal o'er thy grave!"[27]

The speaker leaves no room for doubt that the soldier will be remembered forever for his sacrifice to freedom, honor, glory, and union. The multiplication of causes guarantees immortality and eternal remembrance, not just by individuals but by a "Nation." The soldier's death is firmly embedded in a broader network that justifies, sanctifies, but also renders his sacrifice secondary to a larger cause.

Whereas the Union speaker, vested with the voice of the nation, marshals patriotic forces to "guard" the soldier's tomb, the speaker in Crane's tribute to the Civil War soldiers stands apart. Lacking a ceremony and a nation to address, Crane observes from a distance war's evacuation of a young man's vitality. He is a curiously flat-toned storyteller:

> A soldier, young in years, young in ambitions
> Alive as no grey-beard is alive
> Laid his heart and his hope before duty
> And went staunchly into the tempest of war.
> There did the bitter red winds of battle
> Swirl 'gainst his youth, beat upon his ambitions,
> Drink his cool clear blood of manhood
> Until at coming forth time
> He was alive merely as the grey-beard is alive.[28]

The vampiric red winds drink the soldier's blood so that he comes away drained of life—either prematurely aged or dead. Though the scenario is stark, Crane offers compassion via cliché. The poem is a collage of conventional expressions: the soldier "laid his heart and hope before duty"; he went "staunchly" into the "tempest of war." The clichés summon an earlier, collective language of commemoration even as they render its effectiveness questionable, if nevertheless desirable, in the present circumstances.

Unsettling the clichés is the figure of the blood-filled wind, not a meta-phor, exactly, but a creation derived from fusing two natural substances into an unnatural combination that gains an animating, sinister force. Crane refrains from Wallace's embrace of the soldier's martyrdom to a fallen cause and ren-ders it both an object of scrutiny and of pathos. Nevertheless, the sentiments expressed would not be out of place in 1866, when the same story was told in myriad ways: young men gave their lives in battle, sacrificing "heart and hope before duty." Missing is the sense of social wholeness that would link the man's death to a larger purpose: "Honor, Glory, UNION." Crane seeks a way to mourn the dead after losing faith in the national ideology that structures war.

He finds the solution in women's grief. A reconfigured nation—albeit fantastical—does appear as the poem continues. Its response to the man's sac-rifice at first seems dubious, but Crane goes on to reassure the reader that it is genuine:

And for this—
The nation rendered him a flower.
A little thing—a flower
Aye, but yet not so little
For this flower grew in the nation's heart
A wet soft blossom
From tears of her who loved her son
Even when the black battle rages

If nothing else, the nation's heart is the women's suffering. Their tears come together to water a single flower that grows large enough to represent the com-mon loss. Again, the sentiments closely resemble those expressed in commem-oration of the Civil War soldiers during and directly after the war: elegies, grieving women, and graveside flowers are key aspects of wartime commem-orative occasions. Crane's poem stages a stylized ritual of collective mourn-ing suited to the page more than the graveyard: the single, surreal flower substitutes for a cemetery scene of bestowing flowers on the grave. Missing still is the idea that the men died for a just political cause. Here the cause is sacrifice itself, unjustified, but valued by the women who lost their loved ones through no choice of their own. The occasion of public memorialization provides Crane an occasion to participate in the long nineteenth-century tra-dition of Decoration Day poems and to offer an unironized celebration of Civil War sacrifice. Still, his tribute was rejected by the press and never reached a readership, perhaps because he stands at a remove from the commemoration he stages, unfolding it for his readers, eliding his own presence, refusing national celebration. Though he provides a space for mourning that explicitly acknowledges the soldiers' sacrifice and women's suffering, he does so in a way that nevertheless denies patriotic ideals.

Crane's Decoration Day poem blends conflicting perspectives of distanced, stylized observation with sentimental mourning over the dead, responding to Civil War commemorative practices with a more isolated, yet sympathetic poetic practice. Crane again offers a consecration of the dead—especially the common soldier—in a poem entitled "Blue Battalions," published in the *Philistine* in 1898, which also bears a strong resemblance to Civil War–era poems of mourning and memorialization. Indeed, the figure "Blue Battalions" is vague enough to suggest both the soldiers of the Civil War and of the Spanish-American War, who both wore blue uniforms. For readers who have arrived at an understandably cynical interpretation of Crane's better-known poem "War Is Kind," which was published two years earlier, "Blue Battalions" may appear remarkable in its readability as an expression of conventional sentiments, adapted to a later time. In his essay "Stephen Crane's Refrain," for example, Max Cavitch finds that the refrain in "War Is Kind"—"Do not weep. / War is kind."—functions "not only as part of a refrain against mourning, but also as an obscene Orwellian slogan tending to overwrite and override . . . General Sherman's legendary dictum 'war is hell.'"[29] But for Crane mourning is still an obligation and a necessity, at least as one of an amalgam of perspectives. While overwriting William Tecumseh Sherman, he also pays powerful tribute to the mourner—the "Mother whose heart hung humble as a button"—whose love is not demolished no matter how perverse war becomes.[30]

The power of mourning, however futile, is the subject of "Blue Battalions." Here is the last stanza:

The clang of swords is thy wisdom
The wounded make gestures like Thy Son's
The feet of mad horses is one part,
—Aye, another is the hand of a mother on the brow of a son.
Then swift as they charge through a shadow,
The men of the new battalions
—Blue battalions—
God lead them high. God lead them far
Lead them far, lead them high

These new battalions
—The blue battalions—.[31]

Heaven is essential for Crane, just as it was for Civil War poets, as a place to reconstitute the lost men in the figure of Christ. "Blue Battalions" expresses a hope that the men will rise en masse to heaven as God's angels, rewarded for their fidelity in a war he sanctified. Complete arbitrariness drives the war the men fight in: "A church and a thief shall fall together," the "eyeless" command the swords. The men's suffering is also purposeless—the mad horses charge with no stipulated goal. But mothers suffer sincerely from losing their sons, and that sincerity is marked by clichéd language: "the hand of a mother on the brow of her son" is "a part" of war. Crane resolves the loss into a larger unseen whole, a harmony of new, blue battalions. Whether they die in battle or as veterans, or perhaps even as grieving mothers (the abstract image is so vague, it accommodates everyone), Crane calls the battalions to rise together into the afterlife with God as their leader. The blue battalions themselves offer comfort internally in their homogeneous collectivity; the soldiers' comradeship is consolidated into a single blue cloud. The neat, rhyming refrain the "new battalions, / —The blue battalions—" underscores the certainty of transfiguration from American soldiers to God's army of souls. The scenario is repeated in countless Civil War poems; in "The Old Sergeant," by Forceythe Willson, for example, a soldier dying on Shiloh's battlefield suddenly sees a red, white, and blue tower with "a winding stair of light" for the dead to ascend to heaven, another pathway plotted out by God.[32]

And yet, the forms of expression trouble this reading. As in all his poems, Crane has distilled into shorthand certain truisms in such a way that they are recognizable, but need to be expanded upon with the cooperation of the reader. But in doing so Crane's word choice—again, highly clichéd—causes problems. God's swords are righteous, but "clang" suggests an unruly racket. The wounded make gestures like Christ's, but does God heed their call as he did his son's? As the men charge through the shadow and emerge on the other side, God is no longer addressed directly, but in the third person: does that mean he disappeared? In spite of all these questions, the final lines offer an unironic hope that the battalions will rise. It may be simply a hope, insisted upon by Stephen Crane, whose pen's blue battalions make a new battalion, one that mimics the soldiers' in its multitude of letters, then words, then stanzas, then a poem. Through his power of insistence Crane elevates the soldiers, eulogizes them, and urges God to take them; whether he will is another matter.

Crane does what he can to bring the men into his poem and transport them to a higher plane. Without a sense of a social whole and without the benefit of a broad circulation network, Crane's singular force is the solitary impetus.

Crane's unpublished "Battle-Hymn," found in his saddlebags upon return from Cuba (according to a typed note on the manuscript), offers a far more doubt-filled and polyvalent play of perspectives that nevertheless stays focused on speaking for the people. Though the poem contains allusions to the war in Cuba, these are combined with ambiguous allusions to the Civil War—the title, for example, recalls Julia Ward Howe's famous "Battle Hymn of the Republic." A prayer, the poem suspends a range of possibilities without resolving them, including the suggestion that God is a warlord; that he is merely manipulating humans for his own amusement; or that he is playing out a larger, benevolent plan. The suspensions, juxtapositions, and unfinished postulations generate a terror not only of war's atrocities and God's complicity in or indifference to human suffering, but of uncertainty itself. Through this chaos, one thing remains stable, and that is Crane's advocacy for the people who are subject to and complicitous with larger, destructive powers.

Speaking for his nation, the poem's supplicant calls upon God to hear his people and see the war they are waging, however tiny it is from his immense distance:

> All-feeling God, hear in the war-night
> The rolling voices of a nation;
> Through dusky billows of darkness
> See the flash, the under-light of bared swords—
> —Whirling gleams like wee shells
> Deep in the streams of the universe[33]

"The rolling voices of a nation" summon a vision of a strongly united social totality, identifiable in Civil War poetry. Here, however, God is remote and potentially unresponsive. The supplicant imagines war from God's perspective as a miniatiure light display, a beautiful but inconsequential fact.

Though the supplicant speaks for the nation, it becomes clear in the following lines that his nation has fractured; he distinguishes some components as hostile and insidious:

> Bend and see a people, O, God,
> A people rebuked, accursed,

> By him of the many lungs
> And by him of the bruised, weary war drum
> (The chanting disintegrate and the two-faced eagle).

The speaker calls on God to save the nation's people from jingoism—"him of the many lungs" that promotes and perpetuates war for dubious reasons; the ambiguous singular-plural metonymy suggests the yellow journalism of William Randolph Hearst and Joseph Pulitzer among other corrupting forces. "Him of the bruised, weary war drum" encompasses the mechanisms that perpetuate war so that it continues via an unidentifiable initiative. The refrain, with its two unfinished images tied together with a conjunction, surrounded by parentheses, is even more ambiguous. Perhaps the sound of chanting disintegrates, or a disintegrating entity chants, in choral accompaniment to the tragic scene. In any case, disintegration suggests a loss of support for the war effort, or for the prayer to God carried on "the rolling voices of the nation" that opens the poem. The disintegrated whole is loosely related to the figure of the two-faced eagle, which suggests national hypocrisy and internal division.

The possibilities continue to multiply in a disorienting way throughout the poem: God leads and perhaps misleads the people in "Never-Ending Circles," on a "new path," perhaps "awry," perhaps "straight." The army may have a righteous mission liberating an enslaved people, as in the Civil War: it is "applauded, acclaimed / By him of the red raw shoulders, / The manacle marked, the thin victim." While it may be motivated by a just purpose, "the lunge of a long blue corps" may simply end in death, encouraged by God. The final lines maintain the ambiguity about the goals of God and men:

> We shall sweep and swarm through jungle and pool,
> Then let the savage one bend his high chin
> To see on his breast, the sullen glow of the death medals
> For we know and we say our gift.
> His prize is death, deep doom.
> (He shall be white amid the smoking cane.)

"The savage one" may be a general, or anyone in high command, including God, to whom the bravery of common soldiers accrues in trivialized form as medals on his chest. The parentheses, the brevity, and the solitary figure of the incinerated man imply neglect and ignorance on the part of the public of what is happening in the distant, Cuban landscape. "He shall be white" alone offers hope that the dead man could be transfigured from a charred body to an angel through God's will. "The Battle Hymn" offsets the slight possibility of a caring God with an extreme suspicion that the "lunge of a long blue corps" will arrive at nothing but death.

Either way, the supplicant has taken on the Whitmanian role of speaking at first on behalf of the nation, and later in the poem, more narrowly, on behalf of the soldiers, elucidating their sacrifices and suffering. Rather than address the nation as Whitman did, however, the supplicant addresses a quizzical god, perhaps because it makes more sense than appealing to distracted civilians, the warmongering press, or the uncaring government. Addressing God individually and in isolation implies a despair that there is no social network that would be responsive to the poet's call. The problem is not only that "God is cold," but that the soldiers' countrymen, the poet's readers, aren't paying attention, or even that the poem has no readers ("Battle Hymn" was never published).[34]

This reading complicates the idea, developed by Cavitch, that Crane's "irregular forms" are a "projection of the illusion of individual consciousness," something that makes the poem "modern" and "untraditional."[35] Whether Crane's subject is the illusion of individual consciousness or the adaptation of consciousness with the aim of addressing a fragmenting social whole is a difficult question to consider. Always an observer, Crane the poet sets himself outside his creations, just as Crane the journalist underscores his distant yet attentive engagement with war. And it is Crane's pen and paper that constitute the black riders and the blue battalions. His commemorations of the dead, in terms that bear the traces of Civil War patriotic rhetoric combined with an ambiguous and ambivalent language of figural abstraction, suggest that he finds potential power in earlier nineteenth-century forms of impersonal, representative engagements with the social whole, even while marking their increasing inaccessibility. Through Crane's emphasis on the scene of writing, he registers both the distance and the connection between his pages and the wars he inscribes.[36] If we broadened our study of Crane's poems, very few of which have been interpreted, we would have to revise our understanding of Crane as a despairing commentator on the futility of modern life and the emptiness of the universe. We would need to attend to the way that Crane looks backward while scrutinizing the present. Crane marks the loss of a time when writing poetry bore a more direct relation to important events unfolding and poets possessed the ability to mediate events affectively for a broad range of readers via poetry that circulated beyond a small, specialized readership.

This awareness in turn would encourage us to seek continuities rather than disjunctions between poetry of the nineteenth and twentieth centuries. The case of Crane suggests that the Civil War legacy of writing for the social whole was an important force for realist and modernist writers, who sought ways to adapt to a time when poetry was no longer a central cohering force for national community.

Notes

INTRODUCTION

Note to epigraph: Emily Dickinson, Poem #1379A, in *The Poems of Emily Dickinson: Variorum Edition*, ed. R. W. Franklin. 3 vols. (Cambridge, MA: Belknap Press of Harvard Univ. Press, 1998). I discussed this poem in Eliza Richards, "'How News Must Feel When Traveling': Dickinson and Civil War Media," *A Companion to Emily Dickinson*, ed. Martha Nell Smith and Mary Loeffelholz (Oxford: Blackwell: 2008), 157–179.

1. After a long period of neglect, the literature of the Civil War has been a "flood subject," to borrow Dickinson's language, in recent years. While I will be referencing much of this work in the pages that follow, work has continued to emerge after I submitted the manuscript to the Press, and I haven't always been able to cite the newest scholarship. I'd like to note three book-length essay collections here, as some of the most recent publications in the field. See *A History of American Civil War Literature*, ed. Coleman Hutchison (New York: Cambridge Univ. Press, 2015); Colleen Boggs, ed., *Teaching the Literature of the Civil War* (New York: Modern Language Association of America, 2015); and Timothy Sweet, ed., *Literary Cultures of the Civil War* (Athens: Univ. of Georgia Press, 2016). Early, highly influential works on the literature of the Civil War include Daniel Aaron's still very helpful and capacious *The Unwritten War: American Writers and the Civil War* (New York: Knopf, 1973); and Edmund Wilson's *Patriotic Gore: Studies in the Literature of the American Civil War* (1962; New York: W. W. Norton Co., 1994).

2. Oliver Wendell Holmes Sr., "Bread and the Newspaper," *Atlantic Monthly*, September 1861, 348.

3. Ibid.

4. Ibid., 347.

5. "All this change in our manner of existence implies that we have experienced some very profound impression, which will sooner or later betray itself in permanent effects on the minds and bodies of many among us." Ibid., 346.

6. Lorman Ratner and Dwight Teeter, *Fanatics and Fire-eaters: Newspapers and the Coming of the Civil War* (Chicago: Univ. of Illinois Press, 2003), 8. Scholars have repeatedly remarked upon the inestimable impact of these lines of communication on the military conflict. Ratner and Teeter assign to newspaper polemicism the primary responsibility for shattering American national unity in the middle decades of the nineteenth century (119). Brayton Harris asserts that the rapid and vast news networks made the Civil War the "first truly public war": *Blue and Gray in Black and White: Newspapers in the Civil War* (Washington, DC: Brassey's, 1999), 2. On specific aspects of this information network see also Menahem Blondheim, *News over the Wires: The Telegraph and the Flow of Public Information in America, 1844 to 1897* (Cambridge,

MA: Harvard Univ. Press, 1994); Joshua Brown, *Beyond the Lines: Pictorial Reporting, Everyday Life, and the Crisis of Gilded Age America* (Berkeley: Univ. of California Press, 2002); William Fletcher Thompson, *The Image of War: The Pictorial Reporting of the American Civil War* (New York: T. Yoseloff, 1960.

7. Harris, *Blue and Gray*, 14.

8. According to Blondheim, by standardizing the transmission and reception of the news, the Associated Press (AP) consolidated the "first mass communication medium of national scope," starting about 1850. During the Civil War the Associated Press played a crucial role in addressing a national readership; the Lincoln administration considered the AP central to their strategies for information management. Blondheim, *News over the Wires*, 133.

9. W. Fletcher Thompson argues that "the single most significant factor in establishing new images of war was the development of journalism in the U.S." *Image of War*, 19. War generated a demand for newspapers to publish original reports on events as they unfolded, in place of delayed and often secondhand accounts of local and national events. Harris, *Blue and Gray*, 319. The reports were as much visual as they were verbal; British engraver Henry Carter ("Frank Leslie") pioneered a process—dependent on an assembly-line-like division of labor—to produce woodcuts from correspondents' sketches within hours, rather than days, so that they could be included alongside printed columns about depicted events. Brown, *Beyond the Lines*, 39. It was the coverage of the Civil War in *Frank Leslie's Illustrated Newspaper* that "finally secured a public for the pictorial press" (30). Along with many other scholars, Brown recognizes the visualization of the conflict as a crucial and unique aspect of the coverage; the "new informational forms" of photography and journalistic engraving shaped the public understanding of the war (48). See also Alice Fahs, *The Imagined Civil War: Popular Literature of the North and South, 1861–1865* (Chapel Hill: Univ. of North Carolina Press, 2001); Franny Nudelman, *John Brown's Body: Slavery, Violence, and the Culture of War* (Chapel Hill: Univ. of North Carolina Press, 2004); Shirley Samuels, *Facing America: Iconography and the Civil War* (New York: Oxford Univ. Press, 2004); Timothy Sweet, *Traces of War: Poetry, Photography, and the Crisis of the Union* (Baltimore: Johns Hopkins Univ. Press, 1990); Thompson, *Image of War*.

10. Holmes Sr. "Bread and the Newspaper," 346; Fahs, *Imagined Civil War*, 19–20

11. Anon., "In Time of War," *Harper's Weekly*, August 15, 1863, 513.

12. Walt Whitman, *Memoranda During the War*, ed. Peter Coviello (New York: Oxford Univ. Press, 2004), 108.

13. See, for example, Sweet, *Traces of War*, 1–6; Fahs, *Imagined Civil War*, 93–119; Faith Barrett, *To Fight Aloud Is Very Brave: American Poetry and the Civil War* (Amherst: Univ. of Massachusetts Press, 2012), 50; Drew Gilpin Faust, *This Republic of Suffering: Death and the American Civil War* (New York: Knopf, 2008), 160.

14. Anon., "The Volunteer," *Atlantic Monthly*, May 1862, 640.

15. Anon., "The War," *Harper's Weekly*, July 6, 1861, 418.

16. Dickinson, Poem #1379A, in Franklin, *Poems*.

17. In *The Language of War*, James Dawes explores the impact of violence on language and notes Melville's interest in "the new requirements that war demands of poetry." James Dawes, *The Language of War: Literature and Culture in the U.S. from the Civil War Through World War II* (Cambridge, MA: Harvard Univ. Press, 2002), 13.

18. George Henry Boker, *Poems of the War* (Boston: Ticknor and Fields, 1864), 160.

19. Thomas Wentworth Higginson, "Letter to a Young Contributor," *Atlantic Monthly*, April 1862, 409.

20. Julia Ward Howe, "Our Orders," *Atlantic Monthly*, July 1861, 1.

21. Julia Ward Howe, *Reminiscences, 1819–1899* (Boston: Houghton, Mifflin and Company, 1899), 276.

22. John Greenleaf Whittier, "In Wartime," *Atlantic Monthly*, August 1862, 235–236.

23. [Ralph Waldo Emerson], "The Test, Musa Loquitur," *Atlantic Monthly*, January 1861, 85.

24. This insight is central to Barrett's study. She charts a tension between individual utterance and a new, or at least newly all encompassing, call to speak for the nation. Barrett, *To Fight Aloud*.

25. Certainly the Crimean War offered lessons in forging relations between poetry and violence via media circulation, though the relation between these two literary engagements is beyond the scope of this study. See Mary Favret, *War at a Distance: Romanticism and the Making of Modern Wartime* (Princeton, NJ: Princeton Univ. Press, 2010); and Stefanie Markovits, *The Crimean War in the British Imagination* (New York: Cambridge Univ. Press, 2009).

26. Though critics like Barrett, Fahs, and Coleman Hutchison have written about the popular literature of the period, Dickinson, Whitman, and Melville continue to dominate studies of Civil War poetry. Barrett, *To Fight Aloud*; Fahs, *Imagined Civil War*; Coleman Hutchison, *Apples and Ashes: Literature, Nationalism, and the Confederate States of America* (Athens: Univ. of Georgia Press, 2012).

27. Ratner and Teeter, *Fanatics and Fire-eaters*, 9.

CHAPTER 1. "STRANGE ANALOGIES"

1. Walt Whitman, *Complete Prose Works* (Philadelphia: David McKay, 1892), 65.

2. M. Wynn Thomas, "Weathering the Storm: Whitman and the Civil War," *Walt Whitman Quarterly* 15, no.2 (1997): 96.

3. Mary Favret, *War at a Distance: Romanticism and the Making of Modern Wartime* (Princeton, NJ: Princeton Univ. Press, 2010).

4. Cody Marrs argues that Dickinson construes war, via the weather, as an end to history in *Nineteenth-Century American Literature and the Long Civil War* (New York: Cambridge Univ. Press, 2015), 122–152.

5. Anon., "Weather in War," *Atlantic Monthly*, May 1862, 593.

6. For more on this topic see Harold Winters, *Battling the Elements: Weather and Terrain in the Conduct of War* (Baltimore: Johns Hopkins Univ. Press, 1998), 5, 34.

7. George Frederickson, "Uncle Tom and the Anglo-Saxons: Romantic Racialism in the North," in *Uncle Tom's Cabin: A Norton Critical Edition*, ed. Elizabeth Ammons, 2nd ed. (New York: Norton, 2010), 464–473.

8. Anon., "The Snow at Fredericksburg," *Harper's Weekly*, January 31, 1863, 74.

9. James M. McPherson, *Battle Cry of Freedom: The Civil War Era* (New York: Ballantine Books, 1988), 571–574.

10. Favret, *War at a Distance*, 119–137.

11. James Thomson, "Winter," *The Seasons* (Boston: Manning and Loring, 1808), 114,

12. Ibid., 115.

13. William Cowper, "The Winter Evening," in *The Task* (Philadelphia: Johnson, 1806), 101. Favret discusses this section of the poem brilliantly and extensively in the context of war; *War at a Distance*, 54–90.

14. Cowper, "The Winter Evening," 101.

15. Ibid., 102.

16. Ibid., 102.

17. Ibid., 105.

18. Ibid., 105.

19. Ibid., 113.

20. Ralph Waldo Emerson, "The Snow-Storm," in *Collected Poems and Translations* (New York: Library of America, 1994), 34.

21. Elizabeth Akers Allen, "Snow," *Atlantic Monthly*, February 1864, 200–201.

22. Jennifer Putzi, "'Some Queer Freak of Taste': Gender, Authorship, and the 'Rock me to Sleep' Controversy," *American Literature* 84, no.4 (2012): 769–795.

23. Mrs. Paul Akers [Elizabeth Akers Allen], "Spring at the Capital," *Atlantic Monthly*, June 1863, 766–767.

24. Drew Gilpin Faust, *This Republic of Suffering: Death and the American Civil War* (New York: Knopf, 2008), 61–101.

25. Edward Gibbons, *The History of the Decline and Fall of the Roman Empire*, vols. 1–4 (London: Electric Book Company, 1776–1789).

26. Emily Dickinson, Poem #291B, in *The Poems of Emily Dickinson: Variorum Edition*, ed. R. W. Franklin (Cambridge, MA: The Belknap Press of Harvard Univ. Press, 1998). After a long period during which Dickinson's poems were thought to have nothing to do with the war, there has been an outpouring of work on the subject. For an orientation to recent work on Dickinson and war, beginning with the groundbreaking work of Barton St. Armand, Karen Dandurand, and especially Shira Wolosky, see Faith Barrett's review essay, "Public Selves and Private Spheres: Studies of Emily Dickinson and the Civil War," *Emily Dickinson Journal* 16 no.1 (2007): 92–104. Substantial treatments since Barrett's essay include: Faith Barrett, *To Fight Aloud Is Very Brave: American Poetry and the Civil War* (Amherst: Univ. of Massachusetts Press, 2012), 130–186; Marrs, *Nineteenth-Century American Literature* 122–152; Dominick Mastroianni, *Politics and Skepticism in Antebellum American Literature* (New York: Cambridge Univ. Press, 2014), 119–168; Cristanne Miller, *Reading in Time: Emily Dickinson in the Nineteenth Century* (Amherst: Univ. of Massachusetts Press, 2012), 147–175; Shira Wolosky, "War and the Art of Writing: Emily Dickinson's Relational Aesthetics," in *A History of American Civil War Literature*, ed. Coleman Hutchison (New York: Cambridge Univ. Press, 2015), 195–210.

27. Faust, *This Republic of Suffering*, 82–98.

28. Cowper, "The Winter Evening," 176.

29. Faust, *This Republic of Suffering*, 70–74.

30. Pope's *Homer* and Cowper's *Poems* were in Dickinson's father's library; Capps lists Thomson's *The Seasons* in appendix A, his annotated bibliography of Emily Dickinson's reading. Jack Capps, *Emily Dickinson's Reading, 1836 to 1886*. (Cambridge, MA: Harvard Univ. Press, 1966), 12, 187.

31. *The Iliad of Homer*, trans. Alexander Pope, book 12 (London: G. Bell and Sons, 1889), 220.

32. *Oxford English Dictionary* online, s.v. "alabaster," http://www.oed.com/view/Entry/4488?redirectedFrom=alabaster (accessed March 31, 2018).

33. Timothy Sweet offers the most sustained critique of pastoral rhetoric in Civil War literary and photographic representations: "Where Whitman and the photographers draw a pastoral or picturesque frame around the war, and thereby enlist nature in the service of legitimating its violence, Melville's battle pieces reflect critically on any such attempt to naturalize the war or its ideological implications." Timothy Sweet, *Traces of War: Poetry, Photography, and the Crisis of the Union* (Baltimore: Johns Hopkins Univ. Press, 1990), 7.

34. "If we choose to read Dickinson's 'This Is My Letter to the World' as a commentary on the difficulties of being a woman writer during a time of war, then the speaker's insistence that her work conveys nothing but 'the simple news that nature told' takes on a particular irony in light of some of Dickinson's Civil War poems." Faith Barrett, "Addresses to a Divided Nation: Images of War in Emily Dickinson and Walt Whitman," *Arizona Quarterly* 61, no.4 (2005): 79.

35. Henry Timrod, *The Collected Poems of Henry Timrod: A Variorum Edition*, ed. Winfield Parks and Aileen Wells Parks (Athens: Univ. of Georgia Press, 2007), 92.

36. Ibid., 180n55.

37. Henry Timrod, *Poems* (Boston: Ticknor and Fields, 1860).

38. Timrod, "Ethnogenesis," in Parks and Parks, *Collected Poems*, 92–93.

39. In his reading of "Ethnogenesis," Coleman Hutchison stresses the poem's "*agro-literary appeals*," identifying them as characteristic of Confederate nationalist poetry. Coleman Hutchison, *Apples and Ashes: Literature, Nationalism, and the Confederate States of America* (Athens: Univ. of Georgia Press, 2012), 9. For Hutchison's reading of "Ethnogenesis," see 4–14.

40. Timrod, "Ethnogenesis," 95.

41. Timrod, "The Cotton Boll," in Parks and Parks, *Collected Poems*, 96.

42. Ibid., 95.

43. Ibid., 96.

44. Ibid., 95.

45. Timrod, "Spring," in Park and Park, *Collected Poems*, 122.

46. Ibid., 123.

47. Ibid., 124.

48. Quoted in McPherson, *Battle Cry of Freedom*, 241.

49. Hershel Parker, *Melville: The Making of a Poet* (Evanston, IL: Northwestern Univ. Press, 2009), 189.

50. Herman Melville, "Donelson," from *Battle-Pieces*, in Herman Melville, *The Writings of Herman Melville, Published Poems: Battle-Pieces; John Marr; Timoleon*, ed. Robert C. Ryan et al., historical note by Hershel Parker (Evanston: Northwestern University Press; Chicago: Newberry Library, 2009), vol. 11, 28. Italics are in the original.

51. In her extended reading of the poem, Faith Barrett emphasizes these disruptions and inaccuracies as well as the "temporal gap that divides readers and listeners from soldiers on the battlefield." Barrett, *To Fight Aloud*, 261–263.

52. "Nowhere else in *Battle-Pieces* does Melville make such extensive use of the accounts of a particular battle as he does in 'Donelson.'" Frank Day, *Melville's Use of "The Rebellion Record" in His Poetry* (Clemson, SC: Clemson Univ. Digital Press, 2002), 26.

53. Melville, "Donelson," 23.

54. Ibid., 24.

55. "New York 'Times' Account," in *Rebellion Record: A Diary of American Events*, ed. Frank Moore (New York: David Van Nostrand, 1865), vol. 4, 170.

56. See discussion and endnote 76, below.

57. Melville, "Donelson," 24.

58. Ibid., 25.

59. "New York 'Times'" account, 170.

60. On the Battle of Fort Donelson, see McPherson, *Battle Cry of Freedom*, 397–404; see also Timothy Smith, *Grant Invades Tennessee: The 1862 Battles for Forts Henry and Donelson* (Lawrence: Univ. Press of Kansas, 2016); James R. Knight, *The Battle of Fort Donelson: No Terms*

but Unconditional Surrender (Charleston, SC: The History Press, 2011); Jack Hurst, *Men of Fire: Grant, Forrest, and the Campaign That Decided the Civil War* (New York: Basic Books, 2007).

61. Melville, "Donelson," 27.

62. Ibid., 27.

63. Ibid., 29.

64. Helen Vendler makes a related point, stating that in "Donelson" "the fallibility and interruptedness of the daily newspaper bulletin becomes, in Melville's hands, a symbol of the unknowability of war; modern battles are always too complex to be fully grasped. The successive headlines become a symbol of modern epic discontinuity." Helen Vendler, "Melville and the Lyric of History," in Herman Melville, *Battle-Pieces and Aspects of the War*, ed. James McPherson (Amherst, NY: Prometheus Books, 2001), 263.

65. Sweet, *Traces of War*, 181–182. Hsuan Hsu also discusses how Melville disrupts the pastoral in order to resist the aestheticization of the war in "War, Ekphrasis, and Elliptical Form in Melville's *Battle-Pieces*," *Nineteenth-Century Studies* 16 (2002): 51–71.

66. Melville, "Donelson," 30.

67. Ibid., 30.

68. Ibid., 32.

69. Ibid., 35.

70. Herman Melville, *The Battle-Pieces of Herman Melville*, ed. Hennig Cohen (New York: Thomas Yoseloff, 1963), 22; Stanton Garner, *The Civil War World of Herman Melville* (Lawrence: Univ. Press of Kansas, 1993), 139.

71. Melville, *Battle-Pieces*, ed. Cohen: for Cohen, Melville emphasizes "the universal prevalence of suffering. The weather afflicts the soldiers, both North and South, and the watchers at the bulletin board" (220). Garner, *Civil War World of Herman Melville*, 138–140; Franny Nudelman, *John Brown's Body: Slavery, Violence, and the Culture of War* (Chapel Hill: Univ. of North Carolina Press, 2004), 97; Barrett, *To Fight Aloud*, 261.

72. Melville, "Donelson," 27.

73. Milette Shamir, "Herman Melville and the Civilian Author," in *A History of American Civil War Literature*, ed. Coleman Hutchison (Cambridge: Cambridge Univ. Press, 2015), 222–223.

74. Oliver Wendell Holmes Sr., "Bread and the Newspaper," *Atlantic Monthly*, September 1861, 348.

75. Melville, "Donelson," 31.

76. Ibid., 27.

77. Ibid., 35.

CHAPTER 2. THE "GHASTLY HARVEST"

1. George Smalley, "The Battle of Antietam," *New York Tribune*, September 19, 1862, reprinted as "*New York Tribune* Narrative," *Rebellion Record: A Diary of American Events*, ed. Frank Moore, 11 vols. (New York: David Van Nostrand, 1865), 5:471.

2. Timothy Sweet, *Traces of War: Poetry, Photography, and the Crisis of the Union* (Baltimore: Johns Hopkins Univ. Press, 1990), 7.

3. Dickinson, Poem #465A, in *The Poems of Emily Dickinson: Variorum Edition*, ed. R. W. Franklin. 3 vols. (Cambridge, MA: Belknap Press of Harvard University Press, 1998). "Dickinson's quotation of the word "autumn" in her poem . . . represents her attempt to trope the

linguistic contours of the name 'Antietam,'" in Tyler Hoffman, "Emily Dickinson and the Limit of War," *Emily Dickinson Journal* 3, no. 2 (1994): 4. "Ultimately the 'Blood' that the poem offers as a metaphor can only be read as literal blood"; Faith Barrett, *To Fight Aloud Is Very Brave: American Poetry and the Civil War* (Amherst: Univ. of Massachusetts Press, 2012), 147. See also David Cody, "Blood in the Basin: The Civil War in Emily Dickinson's 'The name – of it – is 'Autumn,' – '" *Emily Dickinson Journal* 12, no.1 (2003): 25–52. Michelle Kohler discusses a collection of six wartime poems about autumn in relation to John Keats's "To Autumn," most centrally "The name – of it – is 'Autumn' – ." "The Ode Unfamiliar: Dickinson, Keats, and the (Battle) fields of Autumn," *Emily Dickinson Journal* vol. 22, no.1 (2013): 30–54.

4. Barrett, *To Fight Aloud*, 148

5. James M. McPherson, *Battle Cry of Freedom: The Civil War Era* (New York: Ballantine Books, 1988), 544.

6. George Smalley, "The Battle of Antietam," 471. The report was reprinted widely and is still considered one of the best pieces of journalism to emerge from the Civil War.

7. Edwin Forbes, *Thirty Years After: An Artist's Memoir of the Civil War* (Baton Rouge: Louisiana State Univ. Press, 1993), 258. On Forbes's coverage, see William Fletcher Thompson, *The Image of War: The Pictorial Reporting of the American Civil War* (New York: T. Yoseloff, 1960), 56. Thompson identifies the battle as an artistic opportunity: "During a day of the hardest fighting of the war, the artists had a superb opportunity to show their skill" (56).

8. Smalley, "Battle of Antietam," 471.

9. A report from a *World* correspondent (in the issue where Waud's pictures and texts appear), records a similar scene at the end of the day, when the strategic positions of the fight have resulted in countless dead amassed along the road: "Passing after night from Sharpsburg to Hagerstown upon the turnpike, it required the greatest care to keep my horse from trampling upon the dead, so thickly were they strewn around. Along the line for not more than a mile at least one thousand five hundred lay unburied." Reprinted in "The Battle of Antietam," *Harper's Weekly*, October 11, 1862, 655.

10. Major General Joseph Hooker (Commander I Corps Army of the Potomac), quoted in James McPherson, *Antietam: The Battle That Changed the Course of the War* (New York: Oxford Univ. Press, 2002), 118.

11. Anon., "After the Battle of Antietam," *Harper's Weekly*, July 4, 1863, 423.

12. Alice Fahs, *The Imagined Civil War: Popular Literature of the North and South, 1861–1865* (Chapel Hill: Univ. of North Carolina Press, 2001), 96. See also Drew Gilpin Faust, *This Republic of Suffering: Death and the American Civil War* (New York: Knopf, 2008), 189–190. Faust explores a range of religious responses to the war in chapter 6, "Believing and Doubting," but she agrees with Fahs that "the predominant response to the unexpected carnage was in fact a resolute sentimentality that verged at times on pathos" (194). While that may be true—it would be hard to quantify the enormous number of literary responses to the war—there is a tremendously wide range of modes outside of that sentimental register.

13. Faust, *This Republic of Suffering*, 174.

14. John Keats, "To Autumn," in *John Keats: Complete Poems*, ed. Jack Sillinger (Cambridge, MA: Belknap Press of Harvard Univ. Press, 1978), 360–361. Kohler offers a fascinating extended reading of Keats's poem in relation to Dickinson's wartime autumn poems; she most centrally claims that Dickinson's poems "insist on intensifying autumn rather than settling it down, and on including the presence of death and decay rather than subduing or obscuring it," as Keats does. Kohler, "Ode Unfamiliar," 43. Kohler ties these differences to national ideology, claiming that Dickinson disrupts American pastoral ideals as a way of critiquing Civil War rhetorics.

15. Cody, "Blood in the Basin," 32. As Faith Barrett notes, New England writers in particular pick up the figure, "redraw[ing] the boundaries between the personal and the public by layering a local autumnal New England landscape . . . onto the contested national landscape of Southern battlefields." Barrett, *To Fight Aloud*, 148.

16. Cody, "Blood in the Basin," 32.

17. Lydia Sigourney, "Vision of a Birthplace," in *Pocahontas, and Other Poems* (London: R. Tyas, 1841), 92.

18. Lydia Sigourney, "The Indian Summer," in *Illustrated Poems* (Philadelphia: Carey and Hart, 1849), 141–142.

19. John Greenleaf Whittier, "Battle Summer of August 1862," *Atlantic Monthly*, October 1862, 510–511.

20. Charles Morris, "Antietam," *Saturday Evening Post*, February 7, 1863, 4.

21. Ibid., 4.

22. Oliver Wendell Holmes Sr., "Doings of the Sunbeam," *Atlantic Monthly*, July 1863, 12.

23. McPherson, *Antietam*, 117–118.

24. Lucy Larcom, "Re-enlisted," *Atlantic Monthly*, May 1864, 629.

25. Elizabeth Akers Allen, *Poems* (Boston: Ticknor and Fields, 1866), 201. Like many other poems by Allen, this topical poem was probably published in a journal of the time.

26. Anon., "At Gettysburg," *Harper's Weekly*, May 21, 1864, 322.

27. N. G. Shepherd, "Roll Call," *Harper's New Monthly Magazine*, December 1862, 49.

28. Ibid., 50.

29. John James Piatt and Sarah Morgan Bryan Piatt, *The Nests at Washington, and Other Poems* (New York: W. Low, 1864).

30. John James Piatt, "First Fire," in Piatt and Piatt, *Nests at Washington*, 27. A different version appears in the *Saturday Evening Post*, December 13, 1862, 5.

31. Ibid.

32. The *Oxford English Dictionary* lists the first use of "shell" in its meaning of bombard (rather than the shelling of a nut, for example) as 1856. *Oxford English Dictionary* online, v. "shell," http://www.oed.com/view/Entry/177874?rskey=bIOzCZ&result=2 (accessed March 31, 2018).

33. Piatt, "First Fire," 27.

34. "Sorrow seems more general than it did, and not the estate of a few persons, since the war began"; Letter #298, in *The Letters of Emily Dickinson*, ed. Thomas Johnson (Cambridge, MA: Belknap Press of Harvard Univ. Press, 1958), 436.

35. Piatt, "First Fire," 30.

36. Ibid., 30.

37. Herman Melville, "The March into Virginia Ending in the First Manassas," from *Battle-Pieces*, in Herman Melville, *The Writings of Herman Melville, Published Poems: Battle-Pieces; John Marr; Timoleon*, ed. Robert C. Ryan et al., historical note by Hershel Parker (Evanston: Northwestern University Press; Chicago: Newberry Library, 2009), vol. II, 14–15.

38. I work from the text of the first edition. The only reprint, superbly edited and introduced by F. DeWolfe Miller, is no longer in print. *Walt Whitman's Drum-Taps and Sequel to Drum-Taps*, ed. F. DeWolfe Miller (Gainesville, FL: Scholars' Facsimiles and Reprints, 1959), 37, 41, 46.

39. Ibid. Cody Marrs offers another reading, claiming that the short poems like "A farm picture" are "brief stunning scenes": "What makes these scenes so beautiful and so moving has

less to do with their particular contents than with their timing: these are pauses before and after loss, moments that either precede or follow death." (Marrs, *Nineteenth-Century American Literature and the Long Civil War* (New York: Cambridge Univ. Press, 2015), 33.

40. Whitman, *Drum-Taps*, 46.

41. Ibid., 71.

42. Ibid., 17.

43. Walt Whitman, *Leaves of Grass* (Brooklyn, NY: n.p., 1855), 29, in *The Walt Whitman Archive*, gen. ed. Ed Folsom and Kenneth M. Price, http://www.whitmanarchive.org.

44. Whitman, *Drum-Taps*, 71.

45. Ibid., 47

46. Sweet, *Traces of War*, 61.

47. Ibid., 77.

48. M. Jimmie Killingsworth, *Walt Whitman and the Earth: A Study in Ecopoetics* (Iowa City: Univ. of Iowa Press, 2004), 36.

49. Whitman, *Leaves of Grass*, 32.

50. Whitman, *Drum-Taps*, 47.

51. See endnote 3 of this chapter.

52. Hoffman, "Emily Dickinson and the Limit of War," 1–18.

53. Ibid., 14, 16.

54. Barrett makes a related point when she says that New England writers, including Dickinson, "redraw the boundaries between the personal and the public by layering a local autumnal New England landscape . . . onto the contested national landscapes of Southern battlefields." *To Fight Aloud*, 148. Kohler stresses the importance of Dickinson's engagements with the rhetorics of war in addition to the landscapes of war. "Ode Unfamiliar."

55. Adam Frank, among others, has posited Dickinson's poetic interest in photography; he cites several suggestive occasions of verbal and imagistic wordplay in support of the assertion. Adam Frank, "Emily Dickinson and Photography," *Emily Dickinson Journal* 10, no. 2 (2001): 1–21. See also Marta Werner, "'The Soul's Distinct Connection – ': Emily Dickinson, Photography, and Nineteenth-Century American Culture," The Classroom Electric: Dickinson, Whitman and American Culture, http://www.classroomelectric.org/volume3/werner/; Marta Werner, "'For Flash and Click and Suddenness – ': Emily Dickinson and the Photography-Effect," in *A Companion to Emily Dickinson*, ed. Martha Nell Smith and Mary Loeffelholz (Oxford: Blackwell, 2008), 477. Renee Bergland, "The Eagle's Eye: Dickinson's View of Battle," in Smith and Loeffelholz, *Companion to Emily Dickinson*, 133–156.

56. Roland Barthes, *Camera Lucida: Reflections on Photography*, trans. Richard Howard (New York: Hill and Wang, 1981), 92, 96.

57. Jay Ruby explores the persistent tendency in the United States to use photography as a tool for mourning in *Secure the Shadow: Death and Photography in America* (Cambridge, MA: MIT Press, 1995). See also Stanley Burns's chronology of death in America, especially the entry for 1841: "Daguerreotypes of deceased people are made; over the next 19 years an estimated 30 million daguerreotypes of all types are taken in America." Stanley Burns, ed. *Sleeping Beauty: Memorial Photography in America* (Altadena, CA: Twelvetrees Press, 1990), appendix. Burns's *Sleeping Beauty* is an anthology of posthumous photography in America from its beginnings until the 1920s. For an insightful reading of posthumous photography of children in the nineteenth century and the relation of mourning to the commercial sphere, see Karen Sanchez-Eppler, *Dependent States: The Child's Part in Nineteenth-Century American Culture* (Chicago: Univ. of Chicago Press, 2005), 101–148.

58. On the difficulty of capturing Civil War images see Robert Taft, *Photography and the American Scene: A Social History, 1839–1889* (1938; reprint New York: Dover, 1964), 233–235. See also Keith Davis, *The Origins of America Photography: From Daguerreotype to Dry-Plate, 1839–1885* (London: Hall Family Foundation, 2007); Jeff Rosenheim, *Photography and the Civil War* (New York: Metropolitan Museum of Art, 2013).

59. On the reception of the photographs see Bob Zeller, *The Blue and Gray in Black and White: A History of Civil War Photography* (Westport, CT: Praeger, 2005), 74–80. See also *On Alexander Gardner's Sketch Book of the Civil War*, ed. Anthony W. Lee and Elizabeth Young (Berkeley: Univ. of California Press, 2007).

60. William A. Frassanito, *Antietam: The Photographic Legacy of America's Bloodiest Day* (New York: Charles Scribner's Sons, 1978), 26. See Frassanito for a description of the Antietam photographs and a study of where they were taken on the battlefield. Unlike daguerreotypes, which were unique artifacts, wet-plate photographs could be reproduced.

61. Alan Trachtenberg, "Albums of War," in *Reading American Photographs: Images as History, Mathew Brady to Walker Evans* (New York: Hill and Wang, 1989), 83. See also Alan Trachtenberg, "Photography: The Emergence of a Key Word," in *Photography in Nineteenth-Century America*, ed. Martha A. Sandweiss (New York: Abrams, 1990), 16–47.

62. Barthes expresses certainty that photography bears a historical relation to "the crisis of death" that emerges in the second half of the nineteenth century. He attributes the phrase "crisis of death" to Edgar Morin. Barthes, *Camera Lucida*, 92.

63. Ibid., 76–77.

64. Oliver Wendell Holmes Sr., "The Stereoscope and the Stereograph," *Atlantic Monthly*, June 1859, 748. Holmes is frequently cited by historians and cultural critics as one of the most significant analysts of early photographic forms in the United States. See, for example, Frassanito, *Antietam*, 56; Sweet, *Traces of War*, 83; Taft, *Photography and the American Scene*, 136; Trachtenberg, *Reading American Photographs*, 17–20, 90–92.

65. Oliver Wendell Holmes Sr., "My Hunt After 'The Captain,'" *Atlantic Monthly*, December 1862, 749.

66. Holmes, "Doings of the Sunbeam," 11.

67. Unlike many of the reports that described the scene, Holmes saw the corn still standing in that part of the field: "It surprised me to notice, that, though there was every mark of hard fighting having taken place here, the Indian-corn was not generally trodden down." Holmes, "My Hunt After the Captain," 748.

68. Dickinson, Poem #355A, in *Poems*. In this essay I build on the insights of a number of critics who have argued forcefully for Dickinson's engagements with historical events, especially with the Civil War. Critics since Shira Wolosky's groundbreaking book have sought to bring Dickinson out of the lyric isolation that previous critics enclosed her within. On the history of this process see Virginia Jackson, *Dickinson's Misery: A Theory of Lyric Reading.* (Princeton, NJ: Princeton Univ. Press, 2005); Shira Wolosky, *Emily Dickinson: A Voice of War* (New Haven, CT: Yale Univ. Press, 1984). These critics nevertheless continue to interpret Dickinson's war poems as statements of personal feeling. See, for example, Paul Cappucci, "Depicting the Oblique: Emily Dickinson's Poetic Response to the American Civil War," *War, Literature, and the Arts: An International Journal of the Humanities* 10, no. 1 (1998): 260–273; Thomas Ford, "Emily Dickinson and the Civil War," *University Review—Kansas City* 31 (1965): 199–203; Hoffman, "Emily Dickinson and the Limit of War"; Daneen Wardrop, "The Poetics of Political Involvement and Non-Involvement," *Emily Dickinson Journal.* 10, no. 2 (2001): 52–67. Faith Barrett claims that Dickinson "addresses a divided nation," by rejecting "sentimental models for identification with

the suffering other." "Addresses to a Divided Nation: Images of War in Emily Dickinson and Walt Whitman," *Arizona Quarterly* 61, no. 4 (2005): 91

69. Franklin's dating raises a conjectural challenge to this possibility. He estimates that Dickinson's poem was composed in summer 1862, and Holmes's article was not published until the following summer. But the dating of the poems is highly speculative, as Franklin himself stresses: "It should be clear that dating is a judgment, albeit an informed one, subject to imprecision that increases across time" (Dickinson, *Poems*, 39).

70. Holmes, "Doings of the Sunbeam," 12.

71. Ibid., 12.

72. Holmes, "Stereoscope and the Stereograph," 739.

73. Dickinson, Poem #355A, in *Poems*.

74. Werner, "'For Flash and Click and Suddenness,'" 477.

75. Holmes, "Doings of the Sunbeam," 12. According to Jay Ruby, daguerreotypes were almost always stored in specially designed cases. *Secure the Shadow*, 191.

76. The reference to autumn offers internal evidence that the poem may have been written slightly later than Franklin suggests; he places the composition time at "about summer 1862" (Dickinson, *Poems*, 379).

77. Holmes, "Stereoscope and the Stereograph," 747.

78. Dickinson, Poem #465A, in *Poems*. According to Franklin, this poem was composed "about late 1862" (Dickinson, *Poems*, 483). Poem #465A has been interpreted a number of times as a Civil War poem; see endnote 3 for this chapter.

79. For a suggestive reading of the ways "The Name – of it – is 'Autumn' – " may respond to periodicals' often absurd mixture of materials and responses to the war, see Kohler, "Ode Unfamiliar," especially 49–50.

80. A number of recent scholars have asked to what extent Civil War photography served as an ideological tool of warfare, or, to the contrary, exposed the ideological apparatus of war by revealing its physical carnage. For Alan Trachtenberg, though photographs show war as a series of quotidian events, their achievement comes with a "loss of clarity" about the big picture, what Trachtenberg calls the "*form*" of war. Understanding the political and social meaning of events depicted in photographs requires a broader, historically informed mode of inquiry: the photographs alone are not enough. Trachtenberg, *Reading American Photographs*, 74–75. Countering these claims, Timothy Sweet puts the mediated, and—to him—manipulative aspects of Civil War photography at the center of his analysis: Civil War photography "naturaliz[ed] the body of the soldier as a pastoral feature of that landscape. In this way [photographers] justified the use of violence as a means to maintain a political structure." *Traces of War*, 106. Franny Nudelman claims that photographs expose their own "artificiality" in their fragmented partiality. She contrasts photography with the newspaper: "Photographs of the battlefield dead confronted civilians not only with their inability to adequately mourn the war dead, but also with the partial and inadequate nature of the information they received from the battlefront." Franny Nudelman, *John Brown's Body: Slavery, Violence, and the Culture of War* (Chapel Hill: Univ. of North Carolina Press, 2004), 121. On the ideology of the visual iconography of war, including photographs, see also Shirley Samuels, *Facing America: Iconography and the Civil War* (New York: Oxford Univ. Press, 2004).

81. Cody Marrs, *Nineteenth-Century American Literature*, 125.

82. On this topic, see Shira Wolosky, "War and the Art of Writing: Emily Dickinson's Relational Aesthetics," in *A History of American Civil War Literature*, ed. Coleman Hutchison (New York: Cambridge Univ. Press, 2015), 195–210.

83. Kenneth Price and Ed Folsom, "Dickinson, Whitman and the San Domingo Moment," in *The Walt Whitman Archive*, http://whitmanarchive.org/resources/teaching/dickinson/intro.html.

84. Marrs, *Nineteenth-Century American Literature*, 127.

85. Ibid., 125.

86. Dickinson, Poem #1419A, in *Poems*. Franklin assigns "about 1877" as the date.

87. I provide the variants, as listed in Franklin, for the first stanza only.

88. Barrett makes a related point: "the lyric self and the collective voice of nationalism are not diametrically opposed in Civil War–era poetry: rather they are related positions on a continuous spectrum of potential stances." *To Fight Aloud*, 2.

CHAPTER 3. "TO SIGNALIZE THE HOUR"

1. Frederick Douglass, "Why Should a Colored Man Enlist," in *Freedom's Journey: African American Voices of the Civil War*, ed. Donald Yacovone (Chicago: Lawrence Hill Books, 2004), 107. Originally published in *Douglass' Monthly*, April 1863.

2. W. E. B. Du Bois offered a more cynical formulation, declaring that only by killing white men could the slave become a man, because "only murder makes men." W. E. B. Du Bois, *Black Reconstruction* (New York: Harcourt, Brace, and Co., 1935), 29.

3. On the Battle of Fort Wagner, see Luis Emilio, *A Brave Black Regiment: The History of the Fifty-Fourth Regiment of Massachusetts Volunteer Infantry, 1863–1865* (1894; reprint, New York: Da Capo Press, 1995), 91–92; Luis Emilio, *The Assault on Fort Wagner, July 18, 1863: The Memorable Charge of the Fifty-Fourth Regiment of Massachusetts Volunteers, Written for "The Springfield Republican"* (Boston: Rand Avery Co., 1887); Robert Gould Shaw, *Blue-Eyed Child of Fortune: The Civil War Letters of Robert Gould Shaw*, ed. Russell Duncan (Athens: Univ. of Georgia Press, 1992), 51–55; Stephen R. Wise, *Gate of Hell: Campaign for Charleston Harbor, 1863* (Charleston: Univ. of South Carolina Press, 1994), 100–110.

4. Charles Ives, "The 'St. Gaudens' in Boston Common (Col. Shaw and His Colored Regiment)," the first movement of *Three Places in New England: Orchestral Set No. 1*, ed. James B. Sinclair (score) (Bryn Mawr, PA: Mercury Music/Theodore Presser, 2008).

5. Dana Luciano, *Arranging Grief: Sacred Time and the Body in Nineteenth-Century America* (New York: New York Univ. Press, 2007), 171.

6. Faith Barrett, *To Fight Aloud Is Very Brave: American Poetry and the Civil War* (Amherst: Univ. of Massachusetts Press, 2012), 3. See also Barrett, "Imitation and Resistance in Civil War Poetry and Song," in *A History of American Civil War Literature*, ed. Coleman Hutchison (New York: Cambridge Univ. Press, 2015), 96–118. Christian McWhirter explores song's deep significance during the Civil War in *Battle Hymns: The Power and Popularity of Music in the Civil War* (Chapel Hill: Univ. of North Carolina Press, 2012). Michael Cohen treats Civil War "contraband songs," arguing that they must be understood in terms of their social relations, in *The Social Lives of Poems in Nineteenth-Century America* (Philadelphia: Univ. of Pennsylvania Press, 2015), 102, see also Cohen's introduction

7. The author imagines the men as thunderbolts "ready to strike and signalize the hour." W. M. F., "On Seeing the 54th and 55th Massachusetts (Black) Regiments," *Anglo-African*, August 22, 1863, 4. In Elizabeth Lorang and R. J. Weir, eds., "'Will Not These Days Be by Thy Poets Sung': Poems of the *Anglo-African* and *National Anti-Slavery Standard*, 1863–64, *Scholarly Editing* 34 (2013), http://scholarlyediting.org/2013/editions/intro.cwnewspaperpoetry.html. All

poems from the *Anglo-African* and the *National Anti-Slavery Standard* are cited from this edition (hereafter cited as "Will Not These Days").

8. Douglass, "Why Should a Colored Man Enlist," 106.

9. Ibid., 104–106.

10. Fanny Jackson, "The Black Volunteers," *Anglo-African*, May 2, 1863, 4.

11. William Wells Brown, *The Negro in the American Rebellion: His Heroism and His Fidelity* (Boston: Lee and Shepherd, 1867), 147.

12. Joshua 9:23; Jackson, "Black Volunteers," "Will Not These Days," note 1.

13. Barrett, *To Fight Aloud*, 26.

14. George Stephens, *Voice of Thunder: A Black Soldier's Civil War*, ed. Donald Yacovone (Chicago: Univ. of Illinois Press, 1998), 47.

15. Noah Webster, *An American Dictionary of the English Language* (New York: Harper & Brothers, 1844).

16. McWhirter, *Battle Hymns*, 162.

17. [Frank Myers], "A Negro-Volunteer Song," *Anglo-African*, June 20, 1863, 1. There is also a manuscript copy at the Massachusetts Historical Society, box 1, folder 13, July 1863, Luis F. Emilio Personal Correspondence. A sign of its widespread popularity, the song was published in the *Liberator*, June 19, 1863, 4; it was cited by William Wells Brown in *The Negro in the American Rebellion*, 157; and it was collected in Frank Moore's *Songs of the Soldiers* (New York: G. P. Putnam, 1864), 234. Versions of the song also carry the title "The Colored Volunteers"; see Cohen, *Social Lives of Poems*, on broadside versions, 122–124.

18. [Myers], "Negro-Volunteer Song."

19. In verse 3, "A Negro-Volunteer Song" also remobilizes Stephen Foster's "That's What's the Matter," a song associated with minstrel depictions of contrabands. "Negro-Volunteer Song," "Will Not These Days," note 6.

20. McWhirter notes the critical relation between the two songs, *Battle Hymns*, 162–163.

21. Billy Holmes and Septimus Winner, *Hoist up the Flag*, notated music (Philadelphia: Winner and Co., 1863), at the Library of Congress website, http://www.loc.gov/item/ihas.2000 02314/#about-this-item.

22. Myers played a prominent role at Fort Wagner. Captain Luis Emilio, who wrote the official history of the regiment, relates that "Frank Myers, of Company K, whose arm was shattered, states that he stood under the uplifted arm of Colonel Shaw, while that officer was on the parapet, waving his sword, and crying, 'Forward Fifty-fourth!'" Emilio, *Brave Black Regiment*, 91–92. The scenario was also recorded in the *New York Evening Post*'s account, prefaced by Myers's own words: "I went in to live or die, as he please." Frank Myers [misspelled as Myres], "The Colored Volunteer," *Anglo-African*, February 20, 1864, 4, "Will Not These Days," note 6.

23. Myers, "Colored Volunteer."

24. [Myers], "Negro-Volunteer Song."

25. First quotation [Myers], "Negro Volunteer Song"; second quotation Myers, "Colored Volunteers."

26. Barrett, *To Fight Aloud*, 39.

27. Corporal Jos. A. Hall and Geo. Parker, "The Fifty-Fourth Mass.," box 9, folder 17, Luis Emilio Papers, Massachusetts Historical Society.

28. "54th Regiment!," Massachusetts Historical Society website, http://www.masshist.org/online/54thregiment/essay.php?entry_id=528.

29. Frances Ellen Watkins Harper, "The Massachusetts Fifty-Fourth," *Anglo-African*, October 10, 1863, 1.

30. In addition to the song-poems already cited, see James Madison Bell, "The Black Brigade," *Anglo-African*, February 6, 1864, 4; George William Curtis, "The American Flag," *Liberator*, March 3, 1864, 48; George William Curtis, "Fort Wagner 1863—Who Shall Vote?" (1865), in *The Flower of Liberty*, ed. Julia A. M. Furbish (Cincinnati: White, Corbin, Bouve & Co., 1869), 11; Joshua McCarter Simpson, "Let the Banner Proudly Wave," in *The Emancipation Car* (Zanesville, OH: Sullivan and Brown, *1874), 143–146. There are certainly more poems than I have been able to identify.*

31. E. Murray, "Col. Robert G. Shaw," *Anglo-African*, August 29, 1863, 2; E. S., "Colonel Shaw," *Liberator*, August 14, 1863, 132; E. S., "Together," *Living Age*, August 27, 1863, 386; L. H., "To Robert Gould Shaw," *Anglo-African*, October 31, 1863, 4; Elizabeth Sedgwick, "'Buried with His Niggers'" *National Anti-Slavery Standard*, October 31, 1863, 4; L. Holbrook, "To Robert Gould Shaw," in *The Rebellion Record: A Diary of American Events*, ed. Frank Moore, 11 vols. (New York: David Van Nostrand, 1865), 7: 92; [Henry Howard Brownell], "Bury Them," *Anglo-African*, February 6, 1864, 1; Marian Bigelow, "The Martyr of Freedom, Col Robert G Shaw," *Anglo-African*, April 30, 1864, 4.

32. William James, "Robert Gould Shaw," *Memories and Studies* (New York: Longman, Green, and Co., 1911), 29.

33. Shaw, *Blue-Eyed Child of Fortune.*

34. Stephens, *Voice of Thunder*, 246.

35. A. H. Hoyt, "The Storming of Fort Wagner," August 8, 1863, 4.

36. Oliver Wendell Holmes Sr. named him "Our Battle Laureate" in an essay by that title, *Atlantic Monthly*, May, 1865, 589–591.

37. On the circumstances of Shaw's burial, see Shaw, *Blue-Eyed Child of Fortune*, "Introduction," 53–54. Shaw's parents asked that Shaw's body not be recovered: "We would not have his body removed from where it lies surrounded by his brave and devoted soldiers." Letter dated August 3, 1863, *Blue-Eyed Child of Fortune*, 54.

38. [Brownell], "Bury Them."

39. Pierre Grimal, *The Penguin Dictionary of Classical Mythology*, ed. Stephen Kershaw, trans. A. R. Maxwell (New York: Penguin, 1992), 79.

40. Elizabeth Sedgwick, "Buried with His Niggers."

41. Shaw, *Blue-Eyed Child of Fortune*, 309. The description appears in a letter from Shaw to his mother, dated March 17, 1863.

42. E. S., "Colonel Shaw."

43. L. H., "To Robert Gould Shaw." Allen Flint notes the consistency of the tributes: "Black Americans are not likely to appreciate the imputation to them of inferiority nor of them being 'saved' by Robert Gould Shaw. The former is one of the essential ingredients in the characterizations of slaves in the earliest poems written about Shaw and the 54th, and the latter is also a predominant theme in much of the same poetry." "Black Response to Colonel Shaw," *Phylon* 45, no. 3 (Fall 1984): 218.

44. Holbrook, "To Robert Gould Shaw."

45. Quoted in Stephen Axelrod, "'For the Union Dead' and Its Precursors," *American Quarterly* 24, no. 4 (October 1972): 527. In relation to "Memoriae Positum" and the commemoration ode, Martin Griffin remarks that Lowell shows an acute awareness of "the inadequacy of the poetic act as it seeks to represent the moral sublime of unselfish sacrifice." Martin Griffin, *Ashes of the Mind: War and Memory in Northern Literature, 1865–1900* (Amherst: Univ. of Massachusetts Press, 2009), 54.

46. Stephen Whitfield notes this absence: "But the black soldiers who died with him are, incredibly, not mentioned in the entire poem." "'Sacred in History and Art': The Shaw Memorial," *New England Quarterly* 60, no.1 (March 1987): 7–8.

47. James Russell Lowell, "Memoriae Positum," *Atlantic Monthly*, January 1864, 88–90.

48. Whitfield, "'Sacred in History and Art,'" 18.

49. Ralph Waldo Emerson's poem "Voluntaries" is another example of extremely vague commemoration: "So nigh is grandeur to our dust, / So near is God to man, / When Duty whispers low, *Thou Must*, / The youth replies, *I can*." *Atlantic Monthly*, October 1863, 504. The main reason why scholars assign the identity of Shaw to "the youth" is because Emerson identified the figure as such. Whitfield, "'Sacred in History and Art,'" 19.

50. James Smethurst offers a related formulation: "Representations of the 54th and the African American soldier clearly demonstrate how black and white authors interacted and influenced one another while maintaining distinct sensibilities and traditions." "'Those Noble Songs of Ham': Poetry, Soldiers, and Citizens at the End of Reconstruction," in *Hope and Glory: Essays on the Legacy of the Fifty-Fourth Massachusetts Regiment*, ed. Martin H. Blatt, Thomas J. Brown, and Donald Yacovone (Amherst: Univ. of Massachusetts Press, 2001), 187.

51. Whitfield, "'Sacred in History and Art,'" 7–8.

52. Marilyn Richardson, "Taken from Life: Edward M. Bannister, Edmonia Lewis, and the Memorialization of the Massachusetts 54th," in Blatt, Brown, and Yacovone, *Hope and Glory*, 107. See Richardson for an extended discussion of Bannister and Lewis.

53. Richardson, "Taken from Life," 107

54. Martha Lowe, "The Picture of Colonel Shaw in Boston," *Liberator*, November 25, 1864, 192. Also quoted in Richardson, "Taken from Life," 100–101.

55. [Anna Quincy Waterston], "Edmonia Lewis," *Liberator*, December 16, 1864, 204. Also quoted in Richardson, "Taken from Life," 107.

56. Richardson, "Taken from Life," 107.

57. "The Shaw Memorial," Saint-Gaudens National Historic Site website, National Park Service, http://www.nps.gov/saga/learn/historyculture/the-shaw-memorial.htm.

58. Richardson makes this point, "Taken from Life," 109. "Shaw Memorial," Saint-Gaudens National Historic Site website.

59. Brown, *Negro in the American Rebellion*, 155.

60. Augustus Saint-Gaudens, *Reminiscences of Augustus Saint-Gaudens*, ed. Homer Saint-Gaudens (New York: Century, 1913), 2:83.

61. David Blight discusses the monument and describes the unveiling and the speeches in *Race and Reunion: The Civil War in American Memory* (Cambridge, MA: Belknap Press of Harvard Univ. Press, 2001), 338–344. See also David Blight, "The Shaw Memorial in the Landscape of Civil War Memory," in Blatt, Brown, and Yacoveone, *Hope and Glory*, 79–93.

62. James, "Robert Gould Shaw," 29.

63. See essays in Blatt, Brown, and Yacovone, *Hope and Glory*, especially by Blight, Richardson, and Kirk Savage, "Uncommon Soldiers: Race, Art, and the Shaw Memorial," 156–167. Also Flint, "Black Response to Col. Shaw"; Albert Boime, ed., *Art of Exclusion: Representing Blacks in the Nineteenth Century* (Washington DC: Smithsonian Institute Press, 1990); Gary Scharnhorst, "From Soldier to Saint: Robert Gould Shaw and the Rhetoric of Racial Justice," *Civil War History* 34, no.4 (1988): 308–322.

64. Saint-Gaudens, "Reminiscences," 2:468.

65. James, "Robert Gould Shaw," 29.

66. Thomas Wentworth Higginson, "The Shaw Memorial and the Sculptor St. Gaudens," *Century Magazine*, June 1897.

67. Whitfield, "'Sacred in History and Art,'" 9.

68. Savage, "Uncommon Soldiers," 156.

69. Saint-Gaudens, "Reminiscences," 2:333.

70. Sarah Greenough and Nancy K. Anderson, *Tell It With Pride: The 54th Regiment and Augustus Saint-Gaudens' Shaw Memorial* (New Haven, CT: Yale Univ. Press, 2014).

71. Higginson, "The Shaw Memorial," 196.

72. Notably Axelrod, Flint, Griffin, and Blight treat the sonnet and not the song-poem. Smethurst is an exception; he considers "The Colored Soldiers" as a part of a tradition that stressed "black sacrifice and bravery and promoted African American citizenship." "'Those Noble Songs of Ham,'" 168).

73. Paul Laurence Dunbar, "The Colored Soldiers," in *The Collected Poetry of Paul Laurence Dunbar*, ed. Joanna Braxton (Charlottesville: Univ. of Virginia Press, 1993), 50.

74. Quoted in Yacovone, "Introduction," *Freedom's Journey*, xxxi.

75. Paul Laurence Dunbar, "Robert Gould Shaw," *Atlantic Monthly*, October 1900, 488.

76. In his brilliant, extended reading of the sonnet, Griffin makes a related point: "the less obvious but more important question this poem is asking is not whether the sacrifice of the 54th Massachusetts was a pointless gesture but whether, if they had known that their struggle and their death would not bring equality and an end to racism, Shaw and his men would have made the same decision, would have taken the same path that they took at Fort Wagner. The answer the poem offers is that to commemorate their actions on that day is to offer at least prima facie evidence that they indeed would have so chosen." *Ashes of the Mind*, 195.

77. For another treatment of the standard English poems of Dunbar see Margaret Ronda, "'Work and Wait Unwearying': Dunbar's Georgics," *PMLA* 127, no. 4 (2012): 863–878.

78. Elegiac traditions, as Max Cavitch says, help "constitute the 'work' of mourning." *American Elegy: The Poetry of Mourning from the Puritans to Whitman* (Minneapolis: Univ. of Minnesota Press, 2007). Particularly relevant to the current chapter is Cavitch's mapping out of a black elegiac tradition, 180–232.

79. Jon W. Finson, *The Voices That Are Gone: Themes in Nineteenth-Century American Popular Song* (New York: Oxford Univ. Press, 1997).

80. Virginia Jackson makes this case in *Dickinson's Misery: A Theory of Lyric Reading* (Princeton, NJ: Princeton Univ. Press, 2005).

81. Luciano, *Arranging Grief*, 171.

CHAPTER 4. POETRY UNDER SIEGE

1. James Dawes, *The Language of War: Literature and Culture in the U.S. from the Civil War Through World War II* (Cambridge, MA: Harvard Univ. Press, 2002), 15.

2. Anon., "The Gun," *Harper's Weekly*, July 4, 1863, 426. Faith Barrett identifies Emily Dickinson's "My Life had stood – a Loaded Gun" (F767) as a poem in this genre and compares it to "The Gun." Faith Barrett, *To Fight Aloud Is Very Brave: American Poetry and the Civil War* (Amherst: Univ. of Massachusetts Press, 2012), 173–180.

3. Carl von Clausewitz, *On War*, ed. Michael Howard and Peter Paret (Princeton, NJ: Princeton Univ. Press, 1976), 605.

4. Craig Symonds asserts that the siege of Charleston "stands to this day as the longest siege in American military history." Craig Symonds, *The Civil War at Sea* (Santa Barbara, CA: Praeger, 2009), 120.

5. *New York Tribune*, June 1862, quoted in Symonds, *Civil War at Sea*, 120. Information on the siege is drawn both from Symonds and Stephen Wise, *Gate of Hell: Campaign for Charleston Harbor, 1863* (Columbia: Univ. of South Carolina Press, 1994), 172. See also E. Milby Burton, *The Siege of Charleston, 1861–1865* (Columbia, SC: Univ. of South Carolina Press, 1970); Douglas Bostick, *Charleston Under Siege: The Impregnable City* (Charleston, SC: The History Press, 2010). Wise is the most respected source for information on the siege.

6. Henry Timrod, "Charleston," *The Collected Poems of Henry Timrod, A Variorum Edition*, ed. Winfield Parks and Aileen Wells Parks (Athens: Univ. of Georgia Press, 1965), 115, published in the *Charleston Mercury*, December 3, 1862. I will cite the Parks edition for Timrod's poems as well as giving their original publication information when available.

7. Paul Hamilton Hayne, "Charleston!" *Charleston Mercury*, May 8, 1862, 1.

8. Symonds, *Civil War at Sea*, 131; Margaret E. Wagner, Gary W. Gallagher, and Paul Finkelman, eds., *The Library of Congress Civil War Desk Reference* (New York: Simon and Schuster, 2002), 27.

9. [Frank Vizetelly], "The Civil War in America: Federal Attack on the Harbour Defences of Charleston," *Illustrated London News*, May 16, 1863, 542.

10. Ibid. The same illustration was published on the Union side as "Charleston Harbor from the Battery," *Frank Leslie's Illustrated Newspaper*, June 20, 1863, 196. Vizetelly's sketches were sometimes intercepted in transit by Union blockade forces, which may explain their double publication. Douglas Bostick, *The Confederacy's Secret Weapon: The Civil War Illustrations of Frank Vizetelly* (Columbia, SC: The History Press, 2009), 102–103.

11. William Gilmore Simms, *War Poetry of the South* (New York: Richardson, 1866), 255.

12. Walter Brian Cisco, *Henry Timrod: A Biography* (Madison, NJ: Fairleigh Dickinson Univ. Press, 2004), 89.

13. Henry Timrod, "Carmen Triumphale," in Parks and Parks, *Collected Poems*, 128, published in *Southern Illustrated News*, June 7, 1863.

14. Amanda Jones, "June," *Frank Leslie's Illustrated Newspaper*, May 30, 1863, 154.

15. Letter from Beauregard to Gillmore dated August 22, 1863. Quoted in Burton, *Siege of Charleston*, 252.

16. Symonds, *Civil War at Sea*, 136. Also Wise, *Gate of Hell*, 148. Symonds says that "the shells fired by the 'swamp angel' foreshadowed the bombing of European Cities by the US Army Corps in World War II." *Civil War at Sea*, 136).

17. Wise, *Gate of Hell*, 172.

18. Bostick, *Charleston Under Siege*, 86.

19. Symonds, *Civil War at Sea*, 135.

20. Anon., "The Swamp Angel," *Harper's Weekly*, December 12, 1863, 796–797.

21. T. N. J., "The Swamp Angel," *Rebellion Record: A Diary of American Events*, ed. Frank Moore (New York: David Van Nostrand, 1865), 8:3.

22. J. Warren Newcomb, "The Song of the Shell," *Frank Leslie's Illustrated Newspaper*, October 10, 1863, 37. Byline is New York, September 10, 1863.

23. Paul Hamilton Hayne, "Invocation from the Besieged," *Southern Illustrated News*, November 14, 1863, 146.

24. William Gilmore Simms, "Ode—'Shell the Old City! Shell!,'" in Simms, *War Poetry of the South*, 295. Simms notes in the preface that the poems were collected from newspapers and

magazines around the South; this poem was certainly published in a Southern paper, though I haven't been able to identify it—probably the *Charleston Mercury* or the *Charleston Courier*. These papers remain undigitized and are difficult to read on microfilm; some of the issues are missing.

25. William Gilmore Simms, "The Angel of the Church," in Simms, *War Poetry of the South*, 291. This poem was published in December 1863 in the *Charleston Mercury*, according to Robert Rosen, *Confederate Charleston: An Illustrated History of the City and the People During the Civil War* (Columbia: Univ. of South Carolina Press, 1994), 122.

26. Herman Melville, "The Swamp Angel," from *Battle-Pieces*, in Herman Melville, *The Writings of Herman Melville, Published Poems: Battle-Pieces; John Marr; Timoleon*, ed. Robert C. Ryan et al., historical note by Hershel Parker (Evanston: Northwestern University Press; Chicago: Newberry Library, 2009), vol. 11, 78.

27. Henry Timrod, "Hymn," in Timrod, *Collected Poems*, 129. Published in the *Daily South Carolinian*, November 6, 1864.

28. Henry Timrod, "Christmas," in Timrod, *Collected Poems*, 118.

29. Henry Timrod, "1866," in Timrod, *Collected Poems*, 136.

30. Henry Timrod, "Storm and Calm," in Timrod *Collected Poems*, 139–140.

31. Simms, *War Poetry of the South*, v.

32. David Blight, *Race and Reunion: The Civil War in American Memory* (Cambridge, MA: Belknap Press of Harvard Univ. Press, 2001).

33. Simms, *War Poetry of the South*, vi.

34. Henry Timrod, *The Last Years of Henry Timrod, 1864–67*, ed. J. B. Hubbell (New York: AMS Press, 1966), 47.

35. Stoddard named Timrod "the best Southern poet"; Timrod, *Last Years*, 99. Whittier expressed pride that he "was one of the very first to recognize the rare gifts of the Carolinian poet Timrod"; Timrod, *Last Years*, 111.

36. Henry Timrod, *Poems of Henry Timrod* (Boston: Houghton, Mifflin, and Co., 1899).

CHAPTER 5. POETRY AT SEA

1. For an in-depth study of the ballad in the nineteenth-century United States, see Michael Cohen, *The Social Lives of Poems in Nineteenth-Century America* (Philadelphia: Univ. of Pennsylvania Press, 2015). The ballad has received a great deal of recent attention. See, for example, two special issues: "The Ballad: A Special Issue on Historical Poetics and Genre Convened by Michael Cohen," *Nineteenth-Century Literature* 71, no. 2 (2016); and "Ballads," ed. Letitia Henville, special issue, *Victorian Poetry*, 54 no. 4 (2016).

2. David Hackett Fisher, *Paul Revere's Ride* (New York: Oxford Univ. Press, 1994), 331. Paul Revere was one of several men who participated in the ride, but he did not finish the journey: he was captured by British troops.

3. Henry Wadsworth Longfellow, "Paul Revere's Ride," *Atlantic Monthly*, April 1861, 27–30.

4. James Sloan Gibbons, "Three Hundred Thousand More," in *Words for the Hour: A New Anthology of American Civil War Poetry*," ed. Cristanne Miller and Faith Barrett (Amherst: Univ. of Massachusetts Press, 2005), 92–93. Gibbons wrote the poem in response for Abraham Lincoln's call for more recruits. First published in the *Evening Post* on July 16, 1862, the poem was immensely popular.

5. Though oral ballads have long—or perhaps always—circulated alongside printed ballads, scholars continue to make the distinction between "traditional" ballads, which bear significant

traces of orality, and the "journalistic" or "broadside" ballad, which developed with popular commercial printing and recounted specific current events. For a summary description of the difference, see D. Dugaw, "Ballad," *The Princeton Encyclopedia of Poetry and Poetics* (Princeton, NJ: Princeton Univ. Press, 2012), 114–118.

6. Craig Symonds, *The Civil War at Sea* (Denver: Praeger, 2009), 7–8.

7. Frank Day, *Melville's Use of "The Rebellion Record" in His Poetry* (Clemson, SC: Clemson Univ. Digital Press, 2002), 27.

8. Henry Wadsworth Longfellow, "The Cumberland," *Atlantic Monthly*, December 1, 1862, 669–670.

9. Henry Wadsworth Longfellow, "The Wreck of the Hesperus," in *The Poetical Works of Longfellow* (Boston: Houghton Mifflin, 1975), 13. First published in the *New World*, January 10, 1840.

10. Charles Calhoun, *Longfellow: A Rediscovered Life* (Boston: Beacon Press, 2004), 138–139. Meredith McGill calls this poem a "mash-up of Felicia Hemans's popular 1826 recitation piece 'Casabianca' . . . with the traditional ballad 'Sir Patrick Spens.'" "What Is a Ballad? Reading for Genre, Format, and Medium," *Victorian Poetry* 71, no. 2 (September 2016): 169. McGill reads this ballad as an experiment in bringing "poetry into rapport with the terms of an emergent mass culture" (168). That mass culture, combined with modern warfare, is the subject of Longfellow's later ballad "The Cumberland."

11. George Henry Boker, "On Board the Cumberland," *Littell's Living Age*, April 19, 1862, 140.

12. Henry Howard Brownell, "Hearts of Oak—An Epitaph," *Boatswain's Whistle*, November 19, 1864, 73.

13. David Garrick, "Heart of Oak," in *Our National Songs: A Collection of One Hundred and Eighty Songs of England, Ireland, Scotland and Wales*, ed. Alfred H. Miles (London: Hutchinson & Co., 1890), n.p.

14. Herman Melville, "The Cumberland," from *Battle-Pieces*, in Herman Melville, *The Writings of Herman Melville, Published Poems: Battle-Pieces; John Marr; Timoleon*, ed. Robert C. Ryan et al., historical note by Hershel Parker (Evanston: Northwestern University Press; Chicago: Newberry Library, 2009), vol. II, 37–38.

15. This incident is recounted in a report of the event, on which Melville draws. Day, *Melville's Use of "The Rebellion Record,"* 27.

16. After the clash between the *Cumberland* and the *Virginia* on March 8, the Battle of the Ironclads the following day resulted in a standoff, concluding the Battle of Hampton Roads. Symonds, *Civil War at Sea*, 12–24.

17. Henry Howard Brownell, introduction to *Lines of Battle and Other Poems*, ed. M. A. DeWolfe (Boston: Houghton Mifflin Company, 1912), 15–16.

18. Lloyal Farragut, *The Life of David Glasgow Farragut, First Admiral of the United States Navy, Embodying His Journal and Letters* (New York: Appleton and Company, 1879), 221–222.

19. Brownell, *Lines*, 99. Brownell's rendition of the orders was later embedded in the poem "The River Fight," and I quote from that poem.

20. Farragut, *Life of David Glasgow Farragut*, 436.

21. Brownell, introduction, *Lines*, 19.

22. Henry Howard Brownell, *Lyrics of a Day: or News-Paper Poetry. By a Volunteer in the United States Service* (New York: Carleton, 1864).

23. Richard Burton, "A Battle Laureate," in *Literary Likings* (Boston: Copeland and Day, 1898), 288–289.

24. Oliver Wendell Holmes Sr., "Our Battle Laureate," *Atlantic Monthly*, May 1865, 590.

25. Ibid., 590.

26. Ibid., 589.

27. On theories of experience and literature, see Theo Davis, *Formalism, Experience, and the Making of Nineteenth-Century American Literature* (New York: Cambridge Univ. Press, 2007.

28. Holmes, "Our Battle Laureate," 590.

29. Brownell, preface in *Lyrics of a Day*, iii.

30. Anon., *New Englander*, January 1866, 175.

31. Farragut, *Life of David Glasgow Farragut*, 458. Admiral Farragut replied in a letter written from the Brooklyn Navy Yard, on September 22, 1866.

32. Holmes, "Our Battle Laureate," 591.

33. Julia Ward Howe, "Battle Hymn of the Republic," *Atlantic Monthly*, February 1862, 10.

34. Burton, "Battle Laureate," 32.

35. Holmes, "Our Battle Laureate," 590.

36. Burton, "Battle Laureate," 290.

37. Henry Howard Brownell, "The Bay Fight," *Harper's New Monthly Magazine*, December 1864, 97.

38. *Oxford English Dictionary* online, s.v. "gobbet," www.oed.com/view/Entry/79590 (accessed March 30, 2018).

39. Holmes, "Our Battle Laureate," 590.

40. William Ellery Channing, "Lashed to the Mast," in *The Collected Poems of William Ellery Channing, the Younger*, ed. Walter Roy Channing (Gainesville, FL: Scholars' Facsimile reprints, 1967), 910.

41. Civil War lore has it that, upon the sinking of the *Tecumseh*, Farragut cried "Damn the torpedoes! Full speed ahead!" The precise phrasing is unlikely, though he probably said something to that effect. Symonds, *Civil War at Sea*, 154.

42. On nineteenth-century writers' engagements with the idea of chance, see Maurice Lee, *Uncertain Chances: Science, Skepticism, and Belief in Nineteenth-Century American Literature* (New York: Oxford Univ. Press, 2012).

43. Channing, "Lashed to the Mast"; Isaac McLellan, "We'll Fight It Out," *Wilkes' Spirit of the Times*, October 8, 1864, 86; John Hay, "After You, Pilot," in *The Complete Poetical Works* (Boston: Houghton Mifflin, 1916), 228–231.

44. Hershel Parker's study of Melville's poetic influences doesn't attend to popular writers of the period; it focuses most intensively on English literary tradition and canonical American predecessors and contemporaries. See his "Historical Note," in Melville, *Published Poems*, 464–517. Parker goes so far as to say that "Melville seems not to have been influenced by any of the war poems which peppered collections like the *Rebellion Record* and appeared in newspapers and magazines" (509). Parker says specifically that there is no evidence that Melville read Brownell (509). While it is not essential to my argument that Melville read Brownell, I believe the internal evidence supports a direct engagement with Brownell's work. Frank Day has identified some of Melville's sources as popular poems published in *The Rebellion Record*.

45. Henry Howard Brownell, *War-Lyrics and Other Poems* (Boston: Ticknor and Fields, 1866).

46. Day, *Melville's Use of "The Rebellion Record,"* 54–58.

47. *Philadelphia Inquirer*, September 3, 1866; *Boston Commercial Bulletin*, September 8, 1866; *Round Table*, September 15, 1866; in *Herman Melville: The Contemporary Reviews*, ed. Brian Higgins and Hershel Parker (Cambridge: Cambridge Univ. Press, 1995), 514–517.

48. Melville, "The Battle for the Bay," in Melville, *Battle-Pieces*, 80.

49. Ibid., 81.

50. Ibid., 82.

51. Ibid., 81.

52. Ibid., 83.

53. Through an analysis of some of Melville's battleship poems, Cody Marrs has traced Melville's theory that the Civil War is not unique, but part of a larger historical process that is characterized by cyclical returns and violent ruptures. Cody Marrs, "A Wayward Art: Battle-Pieces and Melville's Poetic Turn," *American Literature* 82 no. 1 (March 2010): 107.

54. Naomi Schor, *Reading in Detail: Aesthetics and the Feminine* (New York: Routledge, 2007).

55. See Marrs on Melville and temporality in "Wayward Art" and *Nineteenth-Century American Literature and the Long Civil War* (New York: Cambridge Univ. Press, 2015). Peter Coviello offers a reading of fate or destiny in *Battle-Pieces* that also addresses Melville's dissatisfaction with industrialization, signified by the ironclad. Peter Coviello, "Battle Music: Melville and the Forms of War," in *Melville and Aesthetics*, ed. Samuel Otter and Geoffrey Sanborn (New York: Palgrave Macmillan, 2011), 193–212.

56. James Dawes explores this idea in *The Language of War: Literature and Culture in the U.S. from the Civil War Through World War II* (Cambridge, MA: Harvard Univ. Press, 2002).

EPILOGUE

1. Kerry Larson, *Imagining Equality in Nineteenth-Century American Literature* (Cambridge: Cambridge Univ. Press, 2008), 5, 7.

2. Oliver Wendell Holmes Sr., "Bread and the Newspaper," *Atlantic Monthly*, September 1861, 348.

3. Edmund Clarence Stedman, *An American Anthology, 1787–1900* (Boston: Houghton Mifflin, 1900), xv, xix.

4. Ibid., xxix.

5. Daniel Hoffman identifies Crane's "anticipation in verse and prose of symbolist, imagist, stream-of-consciousness, and naturalist techniques." *The Poetry of Stephen Crane* (New York: Columbia Univ. Press, 1956), 4. For Judith Saunders, Crane follows in an experimental tradition that goes back to Walt Whitman and looks forward to Wallace Stevens. Judith P. Saunders, "Stephen Crane: American Poetry at a Crossroads," in *Teaching Nineteenth-Century American Poetry*, ed. Paula Bernat Bennett, Karen L. Kilcup, and Philipp Schweighauser (New York: Modern Language of America, 2007), 185. Keith Gandal finds that Crane "anticipates two very different twentieth-century movements in American letters and the tension between them—'expressionist' writers and the modernists." Keith Gandal, "A Spiritual Autopsy of Stephen Crane," *Nineteenth-Century Literature* 51, no. 4 (March 1997): 501.

6. Elissa Zellinger, "Stephen Crane and the Poetics of Nostalgia," *Texas Studies in Literature and Language* 57, no. 3 (Fall 2015): 305. Zellinger notes: "As one who faced the nostalgic fantasies of his age, Crane found within them . . . a human fellowship based on a shared belief in the heroic self" (319).

7. The argument I am making is consistent with Virginia Jackson's claim that twentieth-century critics "lyricized" nineteenth-century poetry. The poetry of the Civil War is unrecognizable in terms of "the lyric," and Crane's rearticulations of an earlier field are foreign to the lyric

model as well. Virginia Jackson, *Dickinson's Misery: A Theory of Lyric Reading* (Princeton, NJ: Princeton Univ. Press, 2005).

8. The dilemma makes Crane a turn-of-the-century writer who indicates that the "Victorian/Modern Divide" was largely invented by critics, as Sarah Ehlers and Elizabeth Renker, among others, have asserted. According to Ehlers, "those who have attempted to restore to critical view the poetry produced during the 'interval of twilight' [Edmund Clarence Stedman's formulation] have read (or misread) this supposed interregnum as a sign of progress toward modernism," "Making It Old: The Victorian/Modern Divide in Twentieth-Century American Poetry," *Modern Language Quarterly* 73, no. 1 (March 2012): 39–40. Influential turn-of-the-century critic Stedman posited that ninteenth-century poets had fallen into a "twilight" and that poetry was on the verge of a new, revolutionary practice that would displace the poets of the past. Edmund Clarence Stedman, "The Twilight of the Poets," *Century Magazine*, September 1885, 787–799. Renker stresses the difference between this influential formulation and "actual poetic practices that Stedman and his [elite] literary sphere did not and could not recognize as poetry." Elizabeth Renker, "The 'Twilight of the Poets' in the Era of American Realism, 1875–1900," in *The Cambridge Companion to Nineteenth-Century American Poetry*, ed. Kerry Larson (New York: Cambridge Univ. Press, 2011), 135. Ehlers on the other hand suggests that "rather than simply dispute narratives about poetry's twilight . . . one might understand them as strategic fictions that idealize, preserve, and recirculate the poetry of an earlier period" (39).

9. See Michael Cohen for accounts of the vibrancy of that system and tracings of various social lives that poetry of the period conducted. Michael Cohen, *The Social Lives of Poems in Nineteenth-Century America* (Philadelphia: Univ. of Pennsylvania Press, 2015).

10. Michael Fried, *Realism, Writing, Disfiguration: On Thomas Eakins and Stephen Crane* (Chicago: Univ. of Chicago Press, 1987), 119.

11. Jerome McGann, *Black Riders: The Visible Language of Modernism* (Princeton, NJ: Princeton Univ. Press, 1993), 93.

12. Michael Davitt Bell, *The Problem of American Realism: Studies in the Cultural History of a Literary Idea* (Chicago: Univ. of Chicago Press, 1993), 133, 145–146.

13. Stephen Crane, "War Memories," in *Wounds in the Rain; War Stories* (New York: F. A. Stokes, 1900), 229. Quoted in Michael Robertson, *Stephen Crane, Journalism, and the Making of Modern American Literature* (New York: Columbia Univ. Press, 1997), 170.

14. Ibid., 172.

15. Stephen Crane, poem #1, *Black Riders*, in *The Works of Stephen Crane*. vol. 10, *Poems and Literary Remains*, ed. Fredson Bowers (Charlottesville: Univ. Virginia Press, 1975), 3.

16. A. J. H. Duganne, "Bethel," *Atlantic Monthly*, September 1862, 346.

17. Bruce A. White, *Eliot Hubbard's "The Philistine, a Periodical of Protest" (1895–1915)* (Lanham, MD: Univ. Press of America, 1989).

18. Nancy Glazener, *Reading for Realism: The History of a U.S. Literary Institution, 1850–1910* (Durham, NC: Duke Univ. Press, 1997), 236–237.

19. Robertson, *Stephen Crane*, 150.

20. Sidney A. Witherbee, *Spanish-American War Songs; A Complete Collection of Newspaper Verse During the Recent War with Spain* (Detroit, MI: S. A. Witherbee, 1898).

21. Amy Kaplan, *The Social Construction of American Realism* (Chicago: Univ. of Chicago Press, 1988), 285.

22. Crane, "War Memories," 229.

23. Robertson, *Stephen Crane*, 160

24. Robertson notes this multiperspectival awareness. Ibid., 146.

25. Letter from Crane to Hamlin Garland, May, 1894. Quoted in Hoffman, *Poetry of Stephen Crane*, 149.

26. Ibid., 149–150.

27. William Ross Wallace, "Burial Hymn for the Union Soldiers," in *Poetical Pen-Pictures of the War: Selected from Our Union Poets*, ed. J. Henry Hayward (New York: J. Henry Hayward, 1863), 174.

28. Crane, poem #113, *Works*, 10:77.

29. Max Cavitch, "Stephen Crane's Refrain," *ESQ* 54, nos. 1–4 (2008): 44; Stephen Crane, "War Is Kind," in *War Is Kind* (New York: F. A. Stokes Co., 1899), 1.

30. Crane, "War Is Kind," 1.

31. Crane, poem #125, *Works*, 10:82.

32. Forceythe Willson, "The Old Sargeant," in *The Old Sargeant and Other Poems* (Boston: Ticknor and Fields, 1867), 131. First published as "The Carrier's New Year Address" in the *Louisville Journal*, January 1, 1863.

33. Crane, "The Battle Hymn," poem #130, *Works* 10:86.

34. Crane, poem #126, *Works*, 10:83.

35. Cavitch, "Stephen Crane's Refrain," 38, 48.

36. In his discussion of Crane's *Red Badge of Courage*, John Limon asserts that "Crane's method does more than make of its own art a metaphor of war: tenor and vehicle trade places, exchange qualities. Symbols are wounded." John Limon, *Writing After War: American War Fiction from Realism to Postmodernism* (New York: Oxford Univ. Press, 1994), 58.

Bibliography

Aaron, Daniel. *The Unwritten War: American Writers and the Civil War*. New York: Knopf, 1973.

Allen, Elizabeth Akers. *Poems*. Boston: Ticknor and Fields, 1866.

———— [Mrs. Paul Akers]. "Spring at the Capital." *Atlantic Monthly*, June 1863, 766–767.

————. "Snow." *Atlantic Monthly*, February 1864, 200–201.

Ammons, Elizabeth, ed. *Uncle Tom's Cabin: A Norton Critical Edition*. 2nd ed. New York: Norton, 2010.

Anon. *New Englander*, January 1866, 175–177.

————. "After the Battle of Antietam." *Harper's Weekly*, July 4, 1863, 423.

————. "At Gettysburg." *Harper's Weekly*, May 21, 1864, 322.

————. "The Battle of Antietam," *Harper's Weekly*, October 11, 1862, 654–655.

————. "Charleston Harbor from the Battery," *Frank Leslie's Illustrated Newspaper*, June 20, 1863, 196.

————. "The Gun." *Harper's Weekly*, July 4, 1863, 426.

————. *New Englander*, January 1866, 175.

————. "In Time of War." *Harper's Weekly*, August 15, 1863, 513.

————. "The Snow at Fredericksburg." *Harper's Weekly*, January 31, 1863, 74.

————. "The Swamp Angel." *Harper's Weekly*, December 12, 1863, 796–797.

————. "The Volunteer." *Atlantic Monthly*, May 1862, 640.

————. "The War." *Harper's Weekly*, July 6, 1861, 418.

————. "Weather in War." *Atlantic Monthly*, May 1862, 593–606.

Axelrod, Stephen. "'For the Union Dead' and Its Precursors." *American Quarterly* 24, no. 4 (October 1972): 523–537.

Barrett, Faith. "Addresses to a Divided Nation: Images of War in Emily Dickinson and Walt Whitman." *Arizona Quarterly* 61, no. 4 (2005): 67–99.

————. "Imitation and Resistance in Civil War Poetry and Song." In Hutchison, *History of American Civil War Literature*, 96–118.

————. *To Fight Aloud Is Very Brave: American Poetry and the Civil War*. Amherst: Univ. of Massachusetts Press, 2012.

————. "Public Selves and Private Spheres: Studies of Emily Dickinson and the Civil War." *Emily Dickinson Journal* 16, no. 1 (2007): 92–104.

Barthes, Roland. *Camera Lucida: Reflections on Photography*. Translated by Richard Howard. New York: Hill and Wang, 1981.

Bell, James Madison. "The Black Brigade." *Anglo-African*, February 6, 1864, 4.

Bell, Michael Davitt. *The Problem of American Realism: Studies in the Cultural History of a Literary Idea*. Chicago: Univ. of Chicago Press, 1993.

Bennett, Paula Bernat, Karen L. Kilcup, and Philipp Schweighauser, eds. *Teaching Nineteenth-Century American Poetry.* New York: Modern Language of America, 2007.

Bergland, Renee. "The Eagle's Eye: Dickinson's View of Battle." In Smith and Loeffelholz, *Companion to Emily Dickinson*, 133–156.

Bigelow, Marian. "The Martyr of Freedom, Col. Robert G. Shaw." *Anglo-African*, April 30, 1864, 4.

Blatt, Martin, Thomas J. Brown, and Donald Yacavone, eds. *Hope and Glory: Essays on the Legacy of the Fifty-Fourth Massachusetts Regiment.* Amherst: Univ. of Massachusetts Press, 2001.

Blight, David. *Race and Reunion: The Civil War in American Memory.* Cambridge, MA: Belknap Press of Harvard Univ. Press, 2001.

———. "The Shaw Memorial in the Landscape of Civil War Memory." In Blatt, Brown, and Yacovone, *Hope and Glory*, 79–93.

Blondheim, Menahem. *News over the Wires: The Telegraph and the Flow of Public Information in America, 1844 to 1897.* Cambridge, MA: Harvard Univ. Press, 1994.

Boggs, Colleen, ed. *Teaching the Literature of the Civil War.* New York: Modern Language Association of America, 2015.

Boime, Albert, ed. *Art of Exclusion: Representing Blacks in the Nineteenth Century.* Washington, DC: Smithsonian Institution Press, 1990.

Boker, George Henry. "On Board the Cumberland." *Littell's Living Age*, April 19, 1862, 140.

———. *Poems of the War.* Boston: Ticknor and Fields, 1864.

Bostick, Douglas. *Charleston Under Siege: The Impregnable City.* Charleston: The History Press, 2010.

———. *The Confederacy's Secret Weapon: The Civil War Illustrations of Frank Vizetelly.* Columbia, SC: The History Press, 2009.

Brownell, Henry Howard. "The Bay Fight." *Harper's New Monthly Magazine*, December 1864, 97.

——— [Anon.]. "Bury Them." *Anglo-African*, February 6, 1864, 1.

———. "Hearts of Oak—An Epitaph." *Boatswain's Whistle*, November 19, 1864, 73.

———. *Lines of Battle and Other Poems.* Edited by M. A. DeWolfe. Boston: Houghton Mifflin Co., 1912.

———. *Lyrics of a Day: or News-Paper Poetry. By a Volunteer in the United States Service.* New York: Carleton, 1864.

———. *War-Lyrics and Other Poems.* Boston: Ticknor and Fields, 1866.

Brown, Joshua. *Beyond the Lines: Pictorial Reporting, Everyday Life, and the Crisis of Gilded Age America.* Berkeley: Univ. of California Press, 2002.

Brown, William Wells. *The Negro in the American Rebellion: His Heroism and His Fidelity.* Boston: Lee and Shepherd, 1867.

Burns, Stanley, ed. *Sleeping Beauty: Memorial Photography in America.* Altadena, CA: Twelvetrees Press, 1990.

Burton, E. Milby. *The Siege of Charleston, 1861–1865.* Columbia: Univ. of South Carolina Press, 1970.

Burton, Richard. *Literary Likings.* Boston: Copeland and Day, 1898.

Calhoun, Charles. *Longfellow: A Rediscovered Life.* Boston: Beacon Press, 2004.

Capps, Jack. *Emily Dickinson's Reading, 1836 to 1886.* Cambridge, MA: Harvard Univ. Press, 1966.

Cappucci, Paul. "Depicting the Oblique: Emily Dickinson's Poetic Response to the American Civil War." *War, Literature, and the Arts: An International Journal of the Humanities* 10, no. 1 (1998): 260–273.

Cavitch, Max. *American Elegy: The Poetry of Mourning from the Puritans to Whitman*. Minneapolis: Univ. of Minnesota Press, 2007.

———. "Stephen Crane's Refrain." *ESQ* 54, nos. 1–4 (2008): 33–53.

Channing, William Ellery. *The Collected Poems of William Ellery Channing, the Younger*. Edited by Walter Roy Channing. Gainesville, FL: Scholars' Facsimile reprints, 1967.

———. "Lashed to the Mast." In Channing, *Collected Poems of William Ellery Channing*, 910.

Cisco, Walter Brian. *Henry Timrod: A Biography*. Madison, NJ: Fairleigh Dickinson Univ. Press, 2004.

Clausewitz, Carl von. *On War*. Edited by Michael Howard and Peter Paret. Princeton, NJ: Princeton Univ. Press, 1976.

Cody, David. "Blood in the Basin: The Civil War in Emily Dickinson's 'The Name – of it – is "Autumn – ."'" *Emily Dickinson Journal* 12, no.1 (2003): 25–52.

Cohen, Michael, ed. "The Ballad: A Special Issue on Historical Poetics and Genre Convened by Michael Cohen." Special issue, *Nineteenth-Century Literature* 71 no. 2 (September 2016).

———. *The Social Lives of Poems in Nineteenth-Century America*. Philadelphia: Univ. of Pennsylvania Press, 2015.

Coviello, Peter. "Battle Music: Melville and the Forms of War." In Otter and Sandborn, *Melville and Aesthetics*.

Cowper, William. *The Task*. Philadelphia: Johnson, 1806.

Crane, Stephen. *War Is Kind*. New York: F. A. Stokes Co., 1899.

———. *The Works of Stephen Crane*. Vol. 10, *Poems and Literary Remains*. Edited by Fredson Bowers. Charlottesville: Univ. of Virginia Press, 1975.

———. *Wounds in the Rain; War Stories*. New York: F. A. Stokes, 1900.

Curtis, George William. "The American Flag." *Liberator*, March 3, 1864, 48.

———. "Fort Wagner 1863—Who Shall Vote?" In Furbish, *Flower of Liberty*, 11.

Davis, Keith. *The Origins of America Photography: From Daguerreotype to Dry-Plate, 1839–1885*. London: Hall Family Foundation, 2007.

Davis, Theo. *Formalism, Experience, and the Making of Nineteenth-Century American Literature*. New York: Cambridge Univ. Press, 2007.

Dawes, James. *The Language of War: Literature and Culture in the U.S. from the Civil War Through World War II*. Cambridge, MA: Harvard Univ. Press, 2002.

Day, Frank. *Melville's Use of "The Rebellion Record" in His Poetry*. Clemson, SC: Clemson Univ. Digital Press, 2002.

Dickinson, Emily. *The Letters of Emily Dickinson*. Edited by Thomas Johnson. Cambridge, MA: Belknap Press of Harvard Univ. Press, 1958.

———. *The Poems of Emily Dickinson: Variorum Edition*. Edited by R. W. Franklin. 3 vols. Cambridge, MA: Belknap Press of Harvard Univ. Press, 1998.

Douglass, Frederick. "Why Should a Colored Man Enlist." In Yacovone, *Freedom's Journey*, 107.

Du Bois, W. E. B. *Black Reconstruction*. New York: Harcourt, Brace, and Co., 1935.

Duganne, A. J. H. "Bethel." *Atlantic Monthly*, September 1862, 345–346.

Dunbar, Paul Laurence. *The Collected Poetry of Paul Laurence Dunbar*. Edited by Joanna Braxton. Charlottesville: Univ. of Virginia Press, 1993.

———. "Robert Gould Shaw." *Atlantic Monthly*, October 1900, 488.

Ehlers, Sarah. "Making It Old: The Victorian/Modern Divide in Twentieth-Century American Poetry." *Modern Language Quarterly* 73, no.1 (March 2012): 37–67.

Emerson, Ralph Waldo. *Collected Poems and Translations*. New York: Library of America, 1994.

—— [Anon.]. "The Test, Musa Loquitur." *Atlantic Monthly*, January 1861, 85.

——. "Voluntaries." *Atlantic Monthly*, October 1863, 504–506.

Emilio, Luis. *The Assault on Fort Wagner, July 18, 1863: The Memorable Charge of the Fifty-Fourth Regiment of Massachusetts Volunteers, Written for "The Springfield Republican."* Boston: Rand Avery Co., 1887.

——. *A Brave Black Regiment: The History of the Fifty-Fourth Regiment of Massachusetts Volunteer Infantry, 1863–1865.* 1894. Reprint, New York: Da Capo Press, 1995.

——. Papers. Massachusetts Historical Society, Boston, MA.

E. S. "Colonel Shaw." *Liberator*, August 14, 1863, 132.

——. "Together." *Living Age*, August 27, 1863, 386.

Fahs, Alice. *The Imagined Civil War: Popular Literature of the North and South, 1861–1865.* Chapel Hill: Univ. of North Carolina Press, 2001.

Farragut, Lloyal. *The Life of David Glasgow Farragut, First Admiral of the United States Navy, Embodying His Journal and Letters.* New York: Appleton and Company, 1879.

Faust, Drew Gilpin. *This Republic of Suffering: Death and the American Civil War.* New York: Knopf, 2008.

Favret, Mary. *War at a Distance: Romanticism and the Making of Modern Wartime.* Princeton, NJ: Princeton Univ. Press, 2010.

"Fifty-Fourth Regiment!" Massachusetts Historical Society website. http://www.masshist.org/online/54thregiment/essay.php?entry_id=528.

Finson, Jon W. *The Voices That Are Gone: Themes in Nineteenth-Century American Popular Song.* New York: Oxford Univ. Press, 1997.

Fisher, David Hackett. *Paul Revere's Ride.* New York: Oxford Univ. Press, 1994.

Flint, Allen. "Black Response to Colonel Shaw." *Phylon* 45, no. 3 (Fall 1984): 210–219.

Forbes, Edwin. *Thirty Years After: An Artist's Memoir of the Civil War.* Baton Rouge: Louisiana State Univ. Press, 1993.

Ford, Thomas. "Emily Dickinson and the Civil War." *University Review—Kansas City* 31 (1965): 199–203.

Frank, Adam. "Emily Dickinson and Photography." *Emily Dickinson Journal* 10 no. 2 (2001): 1–21.

Frassanito, William A. *Antietam: The Photographic Legacy of America's Bloodiest Day.* New York: Charles Scribner's Sons, 1978.

Frederickson, George. "Uncle Tom and the Anglo-Saxons: Romantic Racialism in the North." In Ammons, *Uncle Tom's Cabin*, 464–473.

Fried, Michael. *Realism, Writing, Disfiguration: On Thomas Eakins and Stephen Crane.* Chicago: Univ. of Chicago Press, 1987.

Furbish, Julia A. M., ed. *The Flower of Liberty.* Cincinnati: White, Corbin, Bouve & Co. 1869.

Gandal, Keith. "A Spiritual Autopsy of Stephen Crane." *Nineteenth-Century Literature* 51, no. 4 (March 1997): 500–530.

Garner, Stanton. *The Civil War World of Herman Melville.* Lawrence: Univ. Press of Kansas, 1993.

Garrick, David. "Heart of Oak." In Miles, *Our National Songs*, 23–25.

Gibbons, Edward. *The History of the Decline and Fall of the Roman Empire.* London: Electric Book Company, 1776–1789.

Gibbons, James Sloan. "Three Hundred Thousand More." In Miller and Barrett, *Words for the Hour*, 92–93.

Glazener, Nancy. *Reading for Realism: The History of a U.S. Literary Institution, 1850–1910.* Durham, NC: Duke Univ. Press, 1997.

Greenough, Sarah, and Nancy K. Anderson. *Tell It with Pride: The 54th Regiment and Augustus Saint-Gaudens' Shaw Memorial.* New Haven, CT: Yale Univ. Press, 2014.

Griffin, Martin. *Ashes of the Mind: War and Memory in Northern Literature, 1865–1900.* Amherst: Univ. of Massachusetts Press, 2009.

Grimal, Pierre. *The Penguin Dictionary of Classical Mythology.* Edited by Stephen Kershaw. Translated by A. R. Maxwell. New York: Penguin, 1992.

Harper, Frances Ellen Watkins. "The Massachusetts Fifty-Fourth." *Anglo-African,* October 10, 1863, 1.

Harris, Brayton. *Blue and Gray in Black and White: Newspapers in the Civil War.* Washington, DC: Brassey's, 1999.

Hay, John. *The Complete Poetical Works.* Boston: Houghton Mifflin, 1916.

Hayne, Paul Hamilton. "Charleston!" *Charleston Mercury,* May 8, 1862, 1.

———. "Invocation from the Besieged." *Southern Illustrated News,* November 14, 1863, 146.

Hayward, J. Henry, ed. *Poetical Pen-Pictures of the War: Selected from Our Union Poets.* New York: J. Henry Hayward, 1863.

Henville, Letitia, ed. "Ballads." Special issue, *Victorian Poetry,* 54 no. 4 (2016).

Higgins, Brian, and Hershel Parker, eds. *Herman Melville: The Contemporary Reviews.* Cambridge: Cambridge Univ. Press, 1995.

Higginson, Thomas Wentworth. "Letter to a Young Contributor." *Atlantic Monthly,* April 1862, 401–411.

———. "The Shaw Memorial and the Sculptor St. Gaudens." *Century Magazine,* June 1897, 194–200.

Hoffman, Daniel. *The Poetry of Stephen Crane.* New York: Columbia Univ. Press, 1956.

Hoffman, Tyler. "Emily Dickinson and the Limit of War." *Emily Dickinson Journal* 3, no. 2 (1994): 1–18.

Holbrook, L. "To Robert Gould Shaw." In Moore, *Rebellion Record,* 7:92.

Holmes, Billy, and Septimus Winner. *Hoist up the Flag,* notated music. Philadelphia: Winner and Co., 1863. At the Library of Congress website, http://www.loc.gov/item/ihas.200002314/#about-this-item.

Holmes Sr., Oliver Wendell. "Bread and the Newspaper." *Atlantic Monthly,* September 1861, 346–352.

———. "Doings of the Sunbeam." *Atlantic Monthly,* July 1863, 1–15.

———. "My Hunt After 'The Captain.'" *Atlantic Monthly,* December 1862, 738–764.

———. "Our Battle Laureate." *Atlantic Monthly,* May 1865, 589–591.

———. "The Stereoscope and the Stereograph." *Atlantic Monthly,* June 1859, 738–748.

Homer. *The Iliad of Homer.* Translated by Alexander Pope. London: G. Bell and Sons, 1889.

Howe, Julia Ward. "Battle Hymn of the Republic." *Atlantic Monthly,* February 1862, 10.

———. "Our Orders." *Atlantic Monthly,* July 1861, 1.

———. *Reminiscences, 1819–1899.* Boston: Houghton, Mifflin and Company, 1899.

Hoyt, A. H. "The Storming of Fort Wagner." *Anglo-African,* August 8, 1863, 4.

Hsu, Hsuan. "War, Ekphrasis, and Elliptical Form in Melville's *Battle-Pieces.*" *Nineteenth-Century Studies* 16 (2002): 51–71.

Hurst, Jack. *Men of Fire: Grant, Forrest, and the Campaign That Decided the Civil War.* New York: Basic Books, 2007.

Hutchison, Coleman. *Apples and Ashes: Literature, Nationalism, and the Confederate States of America.* Athens: Univ. of Georgia Press, 2012.

———, ed. *A History of American Civil War Literature.* New York: Cambridge Univ. Press, 2015.

Ives, Charles. "The 'St. Gaudens' in Boston Common (Col. Shaw and His Colored Regiment),"
    the first movement of *Three Places in New England: Orchestral Set No. 1*. Edited by James B.
    Sinclair (score). Bryn Mawr, PA: Mercury Music/Theodore Presser, 2008.

Jackson, Fanny. "The Black Volunteers." *Anglo-African*, May 2, 1863, 4.

Jackson, Virginia. *Dickinson's Misery: A Theory of Lyric Reading*. Princeton, NJ: Princeton Univ.
    Press, 2005.

James, William. *Memories and Studies*. New York: Longman, Green, and Co., 1911.

Jones, Amanda. "June." *Frank Leslie's Illustrated Newspaper*, May 30, 1863, 154.

Kaplan, Amy. *The Social Construction of American Realism*. Chicago: Univ. of Chicago Press,
    1988.

Keats, John. *John Keats: Complete Poems*. Edited by Jack Sillinger. Cambridge, MA: Belknap
    Press of Harvard Univ. Press, 1978.

Killingsworth, M. Jimmie. *Walt Whitman and the Earth: A Study in Ecopoetics*. Iowa City: Univ.
    of Iowa Press, 2004.

Knight, James R. *The Battle of Fort Donelson: No Terms but Unconditional Surrender*. Charleston,
    SC: The History Press, 2011.

Kohler, Michelle. "The Ode Unfamiliar: Dickinson, Keats, and the (Battle)fields of Autumn."
    Emily Dickinson Journal 22, no.1 (2013): 30–54.

Larcom, Lucy. "Re-enlisted." *Atlantic Monthly*, May 1864, 629–631.

Larson, Kerry, ed. *The Cambridge Companion to Nineteenth-Century American Poetry*. New York:
    Cambridge Univ. Press, 2011.

———. *Imagining Equality in Nineteenth-Century American Literature*. Cambridge: Cambridge
    Univ. Press, 2008.

Lee, Maurice. *Uncertain Chances: Science, Skepticism, and Belief in Nineteenth-Century American
    Literature*. New York: Oxford Univ. Press, 2012.

Lee, Anthony W., and Elizabeth Young, eds. *On Alexander Gardner's Sketch Book of the Civil War*.
    Berkeley: Univ. of California Press, 2007.

L. H. "To Robert Gould Shaw." *Anglo-African*, October 30, 1863, 4.

———. "To Robert Gould Shaw." *Liberator*, October 30, 1863, 176.

Limon, John. *Writing After War: American War Fiction from Realism to Postmodernism*. New York:
    Oxford Univ. Press, 1994.

Longfellow, Henry Wadsworth. "The Cumberland." *Atlantic Monthly*, December 1862, 669–670.

———. "Paul Revere's Ride." *Atlantic Monthly*, April 1861, 27–30.

———. *The Poetical Works of Longfellow*. Boston: Houghton Mifflin, 1975.

Lorang, Elizabeth, and R. J. Weir, eds. "'Will Not These Days Be by Poets Sung': Poems of the
    Anglo-African and *National Anti-Slavery Standard*, 1863–64." *Scholarly Editing* 34 (2013),
    http://scholarlyediting.org/2013/editions/intro.cwnewspaperpoetry.html.

Lowell, James Russell. "Memoriae Positum." *Atlantic Monthly*, January 1864, 88–90.

Lowe, Martha. "The Picture of Colonel Shaw in Boston." *Liberator*, November 25, 1864, 192.

Luciano, Dana. *Arranging Grief: Sacred Time and the Body in Nineteenth-Century America*. New
    York: New York Univ. Press, 2007.

Markovits, Stefanie. *The Crimean War in the British Imagination*. New York: Cambridge Univ.
    Press, 2009.

Marrs, Cody. *Nineteenth-Century American Literature and the Long Civil War*. New York: Cam-
    bridge Univ. Press, 2015.

———. "A Wayward Art: Battle-Pieces and Melville's Poetic Turn." *American Literature* 82, no.
    1 (March 2010): 91–119.

Mastroianni, Dominick. *Politics and Skepticism in Antebellum American Literature*. New York: Cambridge Univ. Press, 2014.

McGann, Jerome. *Black Riders: The Visible Language of Modernism*. Princeton, NJ: Princeton Univ. Press, 1993.

McGill, Meredith L. "What Is a Ballad? Reading for Genre, Format, and Medium." *Nineteenth-Century Literature* 71, no. 2 (September 2016): 156–175.

McLellan, Isaac. "We'll Fight It Out." *Wilkes' Spirit of the Times*, October 8, 1864, 86.

McPherson, James M. *Antietam: The Battle That Changed the Course of the War*. New York: Oxford Univ. Press, 2002.

———. *Battle Cry of Freedom: The Civil War Era*. New York: Ballantine Books, 1988.

McWhirter, Christian. *Battle Hymns: The Power and Popularity of Music in the Civil War*. Chapel Hill: Univ. of North Carolina Press, 2012.

Melville, Herman. *Battle-Pieces and Aspects of the War*. Edited by James McPherson. Amherst, NY: Prometheus Books, 2001.

———. *Battle-Pieces and Aspects of the War*. In Melville, *Writings of Herman Melville*, 11:1–188.

———. *The Battle-Pieces of Herman Melville*. Edited by Hennig Cohen. New York: Thomas Yoseloff, 1963.

———. *The Writings of Herman Melville*. Vol. 11, *Published Poems: Battle-Pieces; John Marr; Timoleon*. Edited by Robert C. Ryan et al. Historical note by Hershel Parker. Evanston: Northwestern Univ. Press; Chicago: Newberry Library, 2009.

Miles, Alfred H., ed. *Our National Songs: A Collection of One Hundred and Eighty Songs of England, Ireland, Scotland and Wales* London: Hutchinson & Co., 1890.

Miller, Cristanne. *Reading in Time: Emily Dickinson in the Nineteenth Century*. Amherst: Univ. of Massachusetts Press, 2012.

———, and Faith Barrett, eds. *Words for the Hour: A New Anthology of American Civil War Poetry*. Amherst: Univ. of Massachusetts Press, 2005.

Moore, Frank, ed. *Rebellion Record: A Diary of American Events*. 11 vols. New York: David Van Nostrand, 1865.

———. *Songs of the Soldiers*. New York: G. P. Putnam, 1864.

Morris, Charles. "Antietam." *Saturday Evening Post*, February 7, 1863, 4.

Murray, E. "Col. Robert G. Shaw." *Anglo-African*, August 29, 1863, 2.

Myers, Frank [*sic* Myres]. "The Colored Volunteer." *Anglo-African*, February 20, 1864, 4.

——— [Anon.]. "A Negro-Volunteer Song." *Anglo-African*, June 20, 1863, 1.

"New York 'Times' Account," in Moore, *Rebellion Record*, 4: 170.

Newcomb, J. Warren. "The Song of the Shell." *Frank Leslie's Illustrated Newspaper*, October 10, 1863, 37.

Nudelman, Franny. *John Brown's Body: Slavery, Violence, and the Culture of War*. Chapel Hill: Univ. of North Carolina Press, 2004.

Otter, Samuel, and Geoffrey Sanborn, eds. *Melville and Aesthetics*. New York: Palgrave Macmillan, 2011.

Parker, Hershel. *Melville: The Making of a Poet*. Evanston, IL: Northwestern Univ. Press, 2009.

Piatt, John James. "First Fire." *Saturday Evening Post*, December 13, 1862, 5.

———, and Sarah Morgan Bryan Piatt. *The Nests at Washington, and Other Poems*. New York: W. Low, 1864.

Price, Kenneth M., and Ed Folsom. "Dickinson, Whitman and the San Domingo Moment." In *Walt Whitman Archive*, http://whitmanarchive.org/resources/teaching/dickinson/intro.html.

————, eds. *The Walt Whitman Archive*. http://whitmanarchive.org/.

The Princeton Encyclopedia of Poetry and Poetics. Princeton, NJ: Princeton Univ. Press, 2012.

Putzi, Jennifer. "'Some Queer Freak of Taste': Gender, Authorship, and the 'Rock me to Sleep' Controversy." *American Literature* 84, no.4 (2012): 769–795.

Ratner, Lorman, and Dwight L. Teeter Jr. *Fanatics and Fire-eaters: Newspapers and the Coming of the Civil War*. Chicago: Univ. of Illinois Press, 2003.

Renker, Elizabeth. "The 'Twilight of the Poets' in the Era of American Realism, 1875–1900." In *Cambridge Companion to Nineteenth-Century American Poetry*, 135–153.

Richards Eliza, "'How News Must Feel When Traveling': Dickinson and Civil War Media." In Smith and Loeffelholz, *Companion to Emily Dickinson*, 157–179.

Richardson Marilyn. "Taken from Life: Edward M. Bannister, Edmonia Lewis, and the Memorialization of the Massachusetts 54th." In Blatt, Brown, and Yacovone, *Hope and Glory*, 94–115.

Robertson, Michael. *Stephen Crane, Journalism, and the Making of Modern American Literature*. New York: Columbia Univ. Press, 1997.

Ronda Margaret. "'Work and Wait Unwearying': Dunbar's Georgics." *PMLA* 127, no. 4 (2012): 863–878.

Rosenheim, Jeff. *Photography and the Civil War*. New York: Metropolitan Museum of Art, 2013.

Rosen, Robert. *Confederate Charleston: An Illustrated History of the City and the People During the Civil War*. Columbia: Univ. of South Carolina Press, 1994.

Ruby, Jay. *Secure the Shadow: Death and Photography in America*. Cambridge, MA: MIT Press, 1995.

Saint-Gaudens, Augustus. *Reminiscences of Augustus Saint-Gaudens*. Edited by Homer Saint-Gaudens. 2 vols. New York: Century, 1913.

Samuels, Shirley. *Facing America: Iconography and the Civil War*. New York: Oxford Univ. Press, 2004.

Sanchez-Eppler, Karen. *Dependent States: The Child's Part in Nineteenth-Century American Culture*. Chicago: Univ. of Chicago Press, 2005.

Sandweiss, Martha A., ed. *Photography in Nineteenth-Century America*. New York: Abrams, 1990.

Saunders, Judith P. "Stephen Crane: American Poetry at a Crossroads." In Bennett, Kilcup, and Schweighauser, *Teaching Nineteenth-Century American Poetry*, 185–199.

Savage, Kirk. "Uncommon Soldiers: Race, Art, and the Shaw Memorial." In Blatt, *Hope and Glory*, 156–167.

Scharnhorst, Gary. "From Soldier to Saint: Robert Gould Shaw and the Rhetoric of Racial Justice." *Civil War History* 34, no.4 (1988): 308–322.

Schor, Naomi. *Reading in Detail: Aesthetics and the Feminine*. New York: Routledge, 2007.

Sedgwick, Elizabeth. "'Buried with His Niggers.'" *National Anti-Slavery Standard*, October 31, 1863, 4.

Shamir, Milette. "Herman Melville and the Civilian Author." In Hutchison, *History of American Civil War Literature*, 211–226.

"Shaw Memorial." Saint-Gaudens National Historic Site website, National Park Service. http://www.nps.gov/saga/learn/historyculture/the-shaw-memorial.htm.

Shaw, Robert Gould. *Blue-Eyed Child of Fortune: The Civil War Letters of Robert Gould Shaw*. Edited by Russell Duncan. Athens: Univ. of Georgia Press, 1992.

Shepherd, N. G. "Roll Call." *Harper's New Monthly Magazine*, December 1862, 49–50.

Sigourney, Lydia. *Illustrated Poems*. Philadelphia: Carey and Hart, 1849.

————. *Pocahontas, and Other Poems*. London: R. Tyas, 1841.

Simms, William Gilmore. *War Poetry of the South*. New York: Richardson, 1866.

Simpson, Joshua McCarter. *The Emancipation Car.* Zanesville, OH: Sullivan and Brown, *1874.*

Smalley, George [anon.], "*New York Tribune* Narrative." In Moore, *Rebellion Record*, 5:471.

Smethurst, James. "'Those Noble Songs of Ham': Poetry, Soldiers, and Citizens at the End of Reconstruction." In Blatt, Brown, and Yacovone, *Hope and Glory*, 168–190.

Smith, Martha Nell, and Mary Loeffelholz, eds. *A Companion to Emily Dickinson*. Oxford: Blackwell, 2008.

Smith, Timothy. *Grant Invades Tennessee: The 1862 Battles for Forts Henry and Donelson.* Lawrence: Univ. Press of Kansas, 2016.

Stedman, Edmund Clarence. *An American Anthology, 1787–1900.* Boston: Houghton Mifflin, 1900.

———. "The Twilight of the Poets." *Century Magazine*, September 1885, 787–799.

Stephens, George. *Voice of Thunder: A Black Soldier's Civil War.* Edited by Donald Yacovone. Chicago: Univ. of Illinois Press, 1998.

Sweet, Timothy, ed. *Literary Cultures of the Civil War.* Athens: Univ. of Georgia Press, 2016.

———. *Traces of War: Poetry, Photography, and the Crisis of the Union.* Baltimore: Johns Hopkins Univ. Press, 1990.

Symonds, Craig. *The Civil War at Sea.* Santa Barbara, CA: Praeger, 2009.

Taft, Robert. *Photography and the American Scene: A Social History, 1839–1889.* 1938. Reprint, New York: Dover, 1964.

Thomas, M. Wynn. "Weathering the Storm: Whitman and the Civil War." *Walt Whitman Quarterly* 15, no.2 (1997): 87–109.

Thompson, William Fletcher. *The Image of War: The Pictorial Reporting of the American Civil War.* New York: T. Yoseloff, 1960.

Thomson, James. *The Seasons.* Boston: Manning and Loring, 1808.

Timrod Henry. *The Collected Poems of Henry Timrod: A Variorum Edition.* Edited by Winfield Parks and Aileen Wells Parks. Athens: Univ. of Georgia Press, 2007.

———. *The Last Years of Henry Timrod, 1864–67.* Edited by J. B. Hubbell. New York: AMS Press, 1966.

———. *Poems.* Boston: Ticknor and Fields, 1860.

———. *Poems of Henry Timrod.* Boston: Houghton, Mifflin, and Co., 1899.

T. N. J. "The Swamp Angel." In Moore, *Rebellion Record*, 8:3.

Trachtenberg, Alan. "Photography: The Emergence of a Key Word." In Sandweiss, *Photography in Nineteenth-Century America*, 16–47.

———. *Reading American Photographs: Images as History, Mathew Brady to Walker Evans.* New York: Hill and Wang, 1989.

Vendler, Helen. "Melville and the Lyric of History." In Melville, *Battle-Pieces and Aspects of the War*, 249–268.

Vizetelly, Frank. "The Civil War in America: Federal Attack on the Harbour Defences of Charleston." *Illustrated London News*, May 16, 1863, 542.

Wagner, Margaret E., Gary W. Gallagher, and Paul Finkelman, eds. *The Library of Congress Civil War Desk Reference.* New York: Simon and Schuster, 2002.

Wallace, William Ross. "Burial Hymn for the Union Soldiers." In Hayward, *Poetical Pen-Pictures of the War*, 174.

Wardrop, Daneen. "The Poetics of Political Involvement and Non-Involvement." *Emily Dickinson Journal* 10, no. 2 (2001): 52–67.

[Waterston, Anna Quincy]. "Edmonia Lewis." *Liberator*, December 16, 1864, 204.

Werner, Marta. "'For Flash and Click and Suddenness –': Emily Dickinson and the Photography-Effect." In Smith and Loeffelholz, *Companion to Emily Dickinson*, 471–489.

―――. "'The Soul's Distinct Connection –': Emily Dickinson, Photography, and Nineteenth-Century American Culture." The Classroom Electric: Dickinson, Whitman and American Culture. http://www.classroomelectric.org/volume3/werner/.

White, Bruce A. *Eliot Hubbard's "The Philistine, a Periodical of Protest" (1895–1915)*. Lanham, MD: Univ. Press of America, 1989.

Whitfield, Stephen. "'Sacred in History and Art': The Shaw Memorial." *New England Quarterly* 60, no.1 (March 1987): 3–27.

Whitman, Walt. *Complete Prose Works*. Philadelphia: David McKay, 1892.

―――. *Leaves of Grass*. Brooklyn, New York: n.p., 1855. In Folsom and Price, *Walt Whitman Archive, http://whitmanarchive.org/published/LG/index.html*.

―――. *Memoranda During the War*. Edited by Peter Coviello. New York: Oxford Univ. Press, 2004.

―――. *Walt Whitman's Drum-Taps and Sequel to Drum-Taps*. Edited by F. DeWolfe Miller. Gainesville, FL: Scholars' Facsimiles and Reprints, 1959.

Whittier, John Greenleaf. "Battle Summer of August 1862." *Atlantic Monthly*, October 1862, 510–511.

―――. "In Wartime." *Atlantic Monthly*, August 1862, 235–236.

Willson, Forceythe. *The Old Sargeant and Other Poems*. Boston: Ticknor and Fields, 1867.

Wilson, Edmund. *Patriotic Gore: Studies in the Literature of the American Civil War*. 1962. Reprint, New York: W. W. Norton Co., 1994.

Winters, Harold. *Battling the Elements: Weather and Terrain in the Conduct of War*. Baltimore: Johns Hopkins Univ. Press, 1998.

Wise Stephen R. *Gate of Hell: Campaign for Charleston Harbor, 1863*. Charleston: Univ. of South Carolina Press, 1994.

Witherbee, Sidney A. *Spanish-American War Songs; A Complete Collection of Newspaper Verse During the Recent War with Spain*. Detroit, MI: S. A. Witherbee, 1898.

W. M. F. "On Seeing the 54th and 55th Massachusetts (Black) Regiments." *Anglo-African*, August 22, 1863, 4.

Wolosky, Shira. *Emily Dickinson: A Voice of War*. New Haven, CT: Yale Univ. Press, 1984.

―――. "War and the Art of Writing: Emily Dickinson's Relational Aesthetics." In Hutchison, *History of American Civil War Literature*, 195–210.

Yacovone, Donald, ed. *Freedom's Journey: African American Voices of the Civil War*. Chicago: Lawrence Hill Books, 2004.

Zeller, Bob. *The Blue and Gray in Black and White: A History of Civil War Photography*. Westport, CT: Praeger, 2005.

Zellinger, Elissa. "Stephen Crane and the Poetics of Nostalgia." *Texas Studies in Literature and Language* 57, no. 3 (Fall 2015): 305–324.

Index

Acknowledgements

I started work on this project at the American Antiquarian Society, with the generous support of a National Endowment for the Humanities fellowship, in 2002. The expertise of the staff and the collegiality of my fellow Fellows, especially Karsten Fitz, Bridget Ford, Jim Sidbury, and Nick Yablon, formed an energizing intellectual environment. From 2010 to 2011, I benefited enormously from my time at the National Humanities Center as the Carl and Lily Pforzheimer Fellow. Thanks to everyone there who worked to make a sustained focus on scholarship possible, especially Brooke Andrade, Marie Brubaker, James Getkin, Kent Mulliken, Eliza Robertson, Don Solomon, Carol Vorhaus, and Lois Whittington. I am especially grateful for the fellowship of Lorraine Aragon, Suzie Clark, and Deborah McGrady. A 2015 UNC Chapman Family Teaching Award provided a term's release from the very teaching the honor recognizes; it allowed me to focus on my writing and return to the classroom refreshed. During my time at UNC's Institute for the Arts and Humanities I worked alongside a cohort of scholars who engaged thoughtfully with my work: special thanks to Michele Berger, our group's facilitator. The English Department at Boston University and the Department of English and Comparative Literature at the University of North Carolina, Chapel Hill provided releases from teaching and other valuable research support. Thanks especially to Chairs James Winn at BU, and Beverly Taylor and Mary Floyd-Wilson at UNC.

I've benefited greatly from presenting work-in-progress to engaged audiences at the University of Houston, the University of Maryland, the University of Buffalo, the University of Michigan, Princeton University, King's College London, UCLA, the University of Georgia at Athens, Armstrong State University, Fudan University in Shanghai, Central China Normal University in Wuhan, Duke University, the Dartmouth Futures of American Studies Symposium, and the Stanford Poetics Workshop. Thanks to everyone involved with those invitations and visits. For many years I learned from conversations with the talented scholars in the Historical Poetics Group: Max Cavitch, Michael Cohen, Virginia Jackson, Tricia Lootens, Meredith McGill, Meredith Martin, Yopie Prins, Jason Rudy, Alexandra Socarides, and Carolyn Williams. The Civil War Caucus, which convenes annually at the Midwest Modern Language Association under the collegial directorship of Kathleen Diffley, has been a wonderful place to share work in progress. I also benefited from advice offered by my UNC summer writing workshop companions Maria Comello, Christian Lentz, and Anna Agbe-Davies.

Colleagues and friends have read portions of the manuscript and offered compelling insights while affirming the sometimes elusive powers of intellectual community. In addition to those already mentioned, thanks to Jana Argersinger, Faith Barrett, Sharon Cameron, Theo Davis, Rebecka Rutledge Fisher, Gregg Flaxman, Janet Floyd, Mary Floyd-Wilson, Philip Gura, Joy Kasson, Michelle Kohler, Josephine McDonagh, Tim Marr, Cody Marrs, Cristanne Miller, Tom Reinert, Elizabeth Renker, Augusta Rohrbach, Susan Rosenbaum, Martha Nell Smith, Matthew Spencer, Matt Taylor, Jane Thrailkill, and Christa Vogelius. Raul Aguilar has asked many clarifying questions about the project over the years of our friendship; it has been a pleasure to share my ideas with him. Kerry Larson read the entire manuscript and has offered incisive commentary on my work and provided steadfast support for more than two decades.

I am deeply grateful for the gift of teaching, which vitalizes my scholarship; my ideas developed in the classroom in discussions with my undergraduate and graduate students, some of whom are now colleagues. Special thanks to Sarah Boyd, Anne Bruder, Emma Calabrese, Angie Calcaterra, Kimmie Farris, Julia Hansen, Katherine Henry, Sarah Kuczyinski, Christina Lee, Leslie McAbee, Eric Meckley, Karah Mitchell, April Pullium, Kylan Rice, Kelly Ross, Aaron Shackelford, Robin Smith, and Elissa Zellinger.

Jerry Singerman supported the project with boundless patience, attentiveness, and good humor as it neared the publication stage. The anonymous readers of the manuscript, revealed to me as Elizabeth Young and Mary Loeffelholz, offered thoughtful, helpful suggestions that I attended to carefully: thank you both for the time and care you took with my work. Thanks to the staff at University of Pennsylvania Press for shepherding the manuscript through the production process. I especially appreciate Lily Palladino's expert attention and responsiveness.

Time with friends in Chapel Hill has provided a welcome counterpoint to the solitude of writing and research. I thank Gregg Flaxman for lively conversations about work over countless dinners, most recently at Mercato. Jane

Thrailkill has been my study partner at various cafés and in our homes, and she and Hawley Truax have often made and shared delicious dinners with me afterwards. Marjorie Hinsdale and Marshall Shouse are the best neighbors ever.

I know they can't read this dedication, but I nevertheless want to express my appreciation for my dogs, Emerson and Cali, and my cat, Annabel Lee. They have provided invaluable companionship, hanging out while I was reading and writing, and reminding me in timely fashion that walking, eating, and playing are also important.

Part of Chapter 1 was previously published as "Weathering the News in US Civil War Poetry," in *The Cambridge Companion to Nineteenth-Century American Poetry*, ed. Kerry Larson (New York: Cambridge Univ. Press, 2011). Reprinted with permission. Portions of the introduction and Chapter 2 appeared in a very different form in "Correspondent Lines: Poetry, Journalism, and the U.S. Civil War," in *ESQ: A Journal of the American Renaissance* 54, nos. 1–4 (2008): 145–170. Reprinted with permission. Parts of Chapter 2 appeared in a different form as "'Death's Surprise, Stamped Visible': Emily Dickinson and Civil War Photography," *Amerikastudien/American Studies* 54, no. 1(2009): 13–33. Also reprinted with permission.

CPSIA information can be obtained
at www.ICGtesting.com
Printed in the USA
LVHW090043190919
631358LV00006BA/39/P